W9-BZY-029

A Court
That Shaped
America

RICHARD CAHAN

WITH A FOREWORD BY JUDGE MARVIN E. ASPEN

NORTHWESTERN UNIVERSITY PRESS | EVANSTON, ILLINOIS

A Court That Shaped America

CHICAGO'S FEDERAL DISTRICT COURT

FROM ABE LINCOLN TO ABBIE HOFFMAN

Northwestern University Press
Evanston, Illinois 60208-4210

Copyright © 2002 by Richard Cahan. Published 2002.
All rights reserved.

Printed in the United States of America
10 9 8 7 6 5 4 3 2 1

ISBN 0-8101-1981-1

Library of Congress Cataloging-in-Publication Data
Cahan, Richard.
  A court that shaped America : Chicago's federal
district court from Abe Lincoln to Abbie Hoffman /
Richard Cahan ; with a foreword by Marvin E. Aspen.
    p. cm.
  Includes bibliographical references and index.
  ISBN 0-8101-1981-1 (pbk. : alk. paper)
  1. United States. District Court (Illinois : Northern
District)—History. 2. District courts—Illinois—
Chicago Metropolitan Area—History. I. Title.
KF8755.I48 C34 2002
347.73'22'0977311—dc21
                                        2002008333

The paper used in this publication meets the minimum
requirements of the American National Standard for
Information Sciences—Permanence of Paper for Printed
Library Materials, ANSI Z39.48-1984.

Contents

Acknowledgments

THE AUTHOR IS GRATEFUL to Daniel J. Lehmann, the court's public information officer, who shepherded this project from its inception to completion. Valuable assistance and advice were provided by the Northern District of Illinois Court Historical Association. Funds for this work came from the District Court's attorney registration fee account, used for the benefit of bench and bar. The author would like to thank the staffs of six research institutions that provided firsthand and historical information to make this book possible. They are the National Archives and Records Administration in Chicago and College Park, Maryland; the William J. Campbell Law Library at the Dirksen Federal Courthouse; the Chicago Historical Society; the *Chicago Sun-Times* library; and the Skokie Public Library. The author also appreciates the help of editors Susan Betz, Mark Jacob, and Cate Cahan, photographers Ronald Olson and Richard A. Chapman, and every member of the District Court family who provided information and support to the project. Also helpful were Adrienne Drell, Kenan Heise, Henry Mueller, William Snyder, Scott Turow, Bernard Judge, Maureen Josh, Trina Cieply, Francis Evan, Charles Staples, Richard Dagdigian, Frank Oliver, Joseph Beeler, Thom Clark, Don Hayner, Bruce Ragsdale, Rayman Solomon, Christopher Rohrbacher, Darren Schmidt, John Lupton, Robert Theel, Richard Napoli, Terence McCarthy, Martin Tuohy, Glenn Longacre, Toby Roberts, and Nina and Stuart Cunningham as well as the staff at Northwestern University Press including Graham Harles, Jonah Horwitz, Karen Keeley, Michelle King, Laura Leichum, Neil Ellis Orts, Amy Schroeder, and Donna Shear.

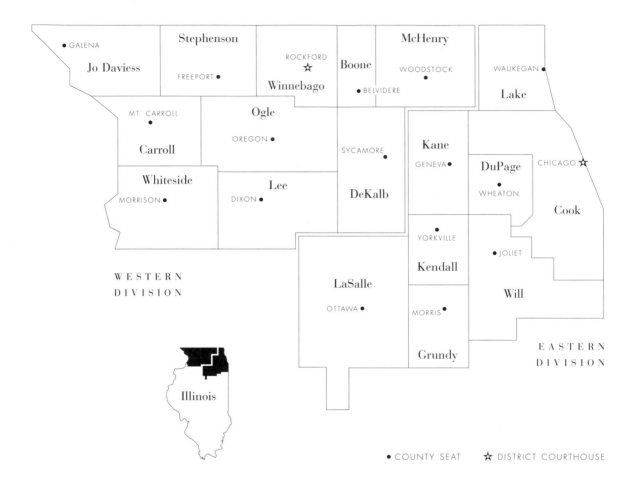

GALENA

Jo Daviess

Stephenson

FREEPORT

ROCKFORD ☆

Winnebago

Boone

BELVIDERE

McHenry

WOODSTOCK

WAUKEGAN

Lake

MT. CARROLL

Carroll

Ogle

OREGON

SYCAMORE

Kane

GENEVA

DuPage

WHEATON

CHICAGO ☆

Whiteside

MORRISON

Lee

DIXON

DeKalb

YORKVILLE

Kendall

JOLIET

Cook

WESTERN

DIVISION

LaSalle

OTTAWA

MORRIS

Will

Grundy

EASTERN

DIVISION

Illinois

● COUNTY SEAT   ☆ DISTRICT COURTHOUSE

Map by Toby Roberts

Foreword

IN THE SPRING OF 2001, it occurred to me that the United States District Court for the Northern District of Illinois had never published a "popular" history, that is, a sweeping account approachable by readers of all backgrounds describing the dramatic role this court has played in the American experience. We decided to remedy this omission and commissioned the services of Richard Cahan, a talented and veteran Chicago writer of excellent journalistic repute.

Our goal was straightforward: to produce a book using both the written word and photographs that captures the spirit of this 183-year-old institution. Cahan's charge was to write a lively biography of the court and its judicial officers, not a turgid tome that only professional researchers would find of interest. Cahan documents our court from its beginnings in 1787, when judges covered the circuit on horseback and the court's proceedings were recorded with quill and ink, to the multi-judge high-tech District Court of the twenty-first century, where computer technology plays a vital role in evidence presentation, legal research, and case documentation. While highlighting the top tier of historically significant events and cases, the book also shows the breadth of the matters routinely handled by the court, from the mundane to the notorious and high profile. It is a fascinating journey of the development of a court that tracks the growth of the country.

Describing the life of a court is by no means a simple task. Where do you begin? Judges? Cases? Courthouses? Cahan has succeeded in putting all the pieces together fairly and intelligently. The result is a chronology of events and the men and women who shaped them. It is a record of a tiny fraction of the cases and the history that has made us who we are today.

Until now, we have not paused to look back. We seek this record so that the court, the product of this nearly two-century record, will better understand itself and so that the community will understand better who we are. We are doing this because we are proud of our institution, aware of its many achievements and even its occasional gaffes.

This book tells us the history of each of our twenty-two District Court judgeships. As to the contemporary sitting judges, each has had many interesting and important cases during his or her career. By necessity, only a small number of these cases are referenced by the author in exemplifying the range of the court's work. For this reason, the section on contemporary judges is simply a sketch, with fuller descriptions left to future accounts when their careers are completed and can be reviewed in proper historical perspective.

The book also notes the development of the magistrate judge system and the Bankruptcy Court. In short, it tells us who we are. It tells about our court traditions and ideals. Our court, like all others, is the result of an amazing interaction among judges, court staff, plaintiffs, defendants, prosecutors, law enforcement agents, and the public. Each has a distinct role in the court's history. Although this book focuses on judges and cases, it should be remembered that the court also includes probation officers, pretrial service officers, federal defenders, secretaries, court reporters, law clerks, clerk's office employees, and other administrative personnel. If our court is judged to have been successful, those dedicated and loyal individuals share fully in such success.

Although the court supported the research of this book and offered guidance, it is not an official history in that neither the author nor the publisher is affiliated with the District Court. This was done so intentionally to give the book needed objectivity and credibility. So while Cahan had the benefit of extensive consultation with individual judges of the court, the book is the author's perspective of our history.

What distinguishes our court? The same things that distinguish the Northern District of Illinois and Chicago as well as the federal judiciary as a whole—our work ethic, our sense of tradition, our acceptance of innovation, and, above all, our respect for the rule of law and the unique position the courts play in protecting basic American liberty and democracy.

As individual judges we feel privileged and are humbled at being afforded the unique opportunity to be a part of this glorious history. We judges are entrusted by the Constitution with the administration of our justice system. We hold this trust for the benefit of the citizens of our nation, who are the users of our courts. We enjoy lifetime tenure and independence and are given extraordinary powers. We can take away freedom, enjoin corporations, find laws unconstitutional, even check presidents. Although criticized on occasion, we receive much respect. But with this considerable authority comes responsibility. By exercising our authority responsibly, we can achieve the ultimate goals of our court—to resolve conflicts fairly and make our democracy even stronger.

—MARVIN E. ASPEN, CHIEF JUDGE, JUNE 2002

Introduction

THE EL RUKNS CASE WAS NASTY.

No modern urban drug gang in America was more notorious than the El Rukns. One judge called the gang members "the most infamous of organized criminals that Chicago has seen since the days of Al Capone." Five El Rukns were convicted in 1987 of conspiring to bomb airplanes and government buildings. Two years later, sixty-five El Rukns were indicted on murder and racketeering charges in connection with a massive South Side heroin, cocaine, and marijuana business. They were officially charged with more than twenty murders, narcotics distribution, terrorism, robbery, extortion, intimidation, fraud, bribery, and kidnapping.

One by one, the El Rukn "generals," "ambassadors," and "soldiers" were brought to court. Eight trials were held in the United States District Court for the Northern District of Illinois in 1991 and 1992, resulting in thirty-seven convictions and twenty-five guilty pleas. The testimony of El Rukn gang members, who agreed to cooperate with the government, formed the basis of the case, but the government also had thirty-five hundred hours of wiretapped conversation and more than one hundred tapes of undercover narcotics purchases. The cooperating witnesses, known as "flippers," explained the coded conversations captured on tape. They told juries that they were former drug dealers who had agreed to testify in exchange for a chance to avoid the death penalty or life in prison. Defense attorneys hammered away at the credibility of the witnesses but were unsuccessful until a rumor—after the trials—surfaced that the flippers had received a series of special privileges while in jail in anticipation of their testimony.

Starting in 1992, three District Court judges held posttrial hearings to determine the relationship between federal law enforcement authorities and their six star witnesses. Defense lawyers at the hearings alleged that the witnesses, held in the nearby federal Metropolitan Correctional Center, were slipped cash, cigarettes, and gifts and offered free phone calls during the years leading up to the trials. Allegations included claims that gang members while in custody had been shown transcripts from ongoing trials and had been allowed to have sex with their wives and girlfriends. Two of the El Rukns even tested positive for drugs while in prison.

Defense lawyers charged the U.S. attorney's office with misconduct. The defenders maintained that they had never received any information during the trials about the alleged privileges and claimed that federal law demanded such release. They also accused the government with knowingly permitting witnesses to testify falsely. Assistant U.S. Attorney William R. Hogan Jr., the lead prosecutor in the case, denied all the charges. Hogan was a rising star, a tireless worker determined to break the iron grip of the El Rukns in one fell swoop. Hogan and the U.S. attorney's office argued that the information about the failed drug tests and the privileges would not have affected the outcome of the trials even if defense attorneys and jurors knew about them in detail.

"I knew we were going to be in for the fight of our lives," Hogan said years later about the massive investigation he inherited in 1988. "I said to everybody from the get-go, we are doing this straight by the numbers, no bad searches, no bad warrants, no kicking in doors."

But then, in the midst of the first posttrial hearing before District Court Judge James F. Holderman, came a prison tape of a sexually explicit telephone conversation between an employee of the U.S. attorney's office and one of the flippers. While not illegal, the conversation indicated that at least one member of the government's staff had crossed the line of professionalism.

Holderman said he was shocked by what was revealed. "Frankly," he said, "this hearing . . . has turned into a scandal. I think it's absolutely outrageous."

It was the telephone tape that turned the tide. "That's what brought the posttrial hearings down," Hogan later said. "That was the coup de grace. Nothing mattered after that."

In June 1993, Holderman determined that three El Rukns found guilty by a jury in his court in 1992 were entitled to a new trial. "Without the jury believing these witnesses . . . the government could not have proven the defendants guilty beyond a reasonable doubt on any of the charges of which they were convicted," he ruled. Holderman, a former assistant U.S. attorney himself, later said that the U.S. attorney's office had built a reputation as one of the toughest and most honorable offices in the nation. "To see it crumble in front of me was difficult."

Ten days later, District Court Judge Suzanne B. Conlon ruled that three El Rukns found guilty in her court were also entitled to a new trial. Then,

three months later, District Court Judge Marvin E. Aspen ruled that six El
Rukn generals and the gang's primary drug supplier should receive new
trials.

"This is the most painful decision that this court has ever been obliged to
render," he wrote, "making the crafting of this opinion a sad and difficult
undertaking. Mindful of the consequences of our ruling, we would have
preferred to have been able to reach a result other than what must be."

Aspen also wrote that it was regrettable to see the reputation of the U.S.
attorney's office tainted. But the decision, he stated, was unavoidable. The
seven defendants, "hardened and antisocial criminals," were entitled to a fair
trial, he wrote. Despite the huge amount of evidence submitted against the
defendants, Aspen believed that the convictions should not stand in the
midst of detailed testimony concerning favors and privileges for star witnesses. "Were the court to condone the abrogation of constitutional protection in this case based on the notoriety of the defendants, injustice would af-
flict not only these defendants but society as a whole."

The El Rukn case was in shambles. Three District Court judges had ordered new trials. A total of fifteen gang members had their convictions reversed. But the American system of justice was affirmed by these rulings,
which declared that every American—even the most reprehensible—was
entitled to the same rights and safeguards guaranteed in the Constitution.

BIG AND SMALL DRAMAS play out every day in the United States District
Court for the Northern District of Illinois. This is where the federal government prosecutes the toughest of criminals, where the powerless assert their
constitutional rights, and where citizens actually do make a federal case out
of it.

"The Northern Illinois District Court defines my concept of what a court
should be," said Scott Turow, who has written best-selling novels based on
his experiences as an assistant U.S. attorney. "As far as I'm concerned, I grew
up as a lawyer in that building. I think of the highest standards of integrity,
the highest quality of lawyering—whether it's on the page or in the courtroom—as being hallmarks of what goes on in the building."

The court, headquartered in Chicago, is one of the busiest federal trial
courts in the nation. Born during the Revolutionary War, the Northern District of Illinois and its predecessors have played a pivotal role in every period
of United States history. It was here where the tide of religious persecution

against the Mormon Church was turned back, signaling that, indeed, there was frontier justice. It was here where one of the most eloquent opponents of slavery spoke out, where the rights of slaves were acknowledged, and where the rights of civilians were upheld during the Civil War.

It was here that the great issues of the twentieth century took center stage: where business monopolies were checked, where big labor was clipped, where Prohibition gangsters and Depression-era schemers were thwarted. John D. Rockefeller, Eugene V. Debs, Al Capone, and Samuel Insull have all had their day in court. And it was here that home-front battles were fought during both world wars and where civil rights issues—from racial segregation to job discrimination—continue to play out.

It was here where Abraham Lincoln changed the course of U.S. history as America expanded west. At a hearing in the court's pre–Civil War home, a place known as the Saloon Building on Lake Street in downtown Chicago, Lincoln argued that railroad companies had the same rights as steamboat companies. Lincoln defended the builders of the first bridge that spanned the Mississippi River. The owners of the Rock Island Bridge Company had received the proper charters to build the bridge and had already defeated an injunction filed in the district to stop construction when the first Chicago Rock Island & Pacific Railroad train creaked over the bridge connecting Rock Island, Illinois, and Davenport, Iowa, on April 23, 1856. In slightly more than two weeks, however, the largest, fastest steamboat on the Mississippi, the *Effie Afton,* slammed into a pier of the bridge, caught fire, and sank, bringing with it a section of the bridge itself. The owner of the steamboat, Captain John Hurd, sued the bridge company for $50,000, the value of the boat and its cargo. Hurd and his attorneys argued that the bridge obstructed navigation and would be a constant peril to the St. Louis–based steamboats. Lincoln declared that the accident was staged, a planned attack against the Chicago-based railroad interests. East-west train traffic was as important and legitimate as north-south water traffic, he declared. "One man has as good a right to cross a river as another had to sail up or down it."

After a two-week trial, the Chicago jury was deadlocked, and the case against the bridge company was finally dismissed. Subsequent lawsuits against the company petered out, and the bridge was rebuilt. The court action determined the destiny of Chicago as a transportation center of America. This is where the West was won.

Fast-forward more than a century. It was here where Abbie Hoffman attempted to put the Establishment on trial. Hoffman, along with seven other defendants, was tried for conspiring to foster the riots that disrupted the 1968 Democratic National Convention in Chicago.

"Dear Abbott," wrote Hoffman's father, John. "On this, the eve of your upcoming trial, I hope and pray that you conduct yourself in a respectable manner. For, after all, the courts of our land are still our way of justice, and when they lose their respect, what have we left? . . . Please stop to realize that your manners and conduct in the court room will both act for and against you."

The parental advice went unheeded. Son Abbie used the trial to goose the justice system, Chicago, and the nation. Just as he had egged on the Chicago police, young Hoffman had a plan to pester the judge. Julius J. Hoffman was symbolic of the court, the federal system, and the older generation. Abbie Hoffman had a vision. He wanted to use the court to take over the six o'clock news. The defendant blew kisses to the jury, testified "I am a cultural revolutionary," and presented his new culture to the American public as if Judge Hoffman's court were a stage. Poet Allen Ginsberg read from *Howl* and singer Judy Collins recited "Where Have All the Flowers Gone?" Arlo Guthrie tried to sing "Alice's Restaurant" but was stopped by Judge Hoffman, who declared, "No singing. No singing, sir."

Abbie Hoffman lost in court. But the court lost, too. In an attempt to save his dignity, Judge Hoffman had lost his legitimacy in the eyes of many. Abbie had upstaged the judge. "It was a low point in judicial history, a goofy time for all of us," said U.S. Court of Appeals Judge William Bauer, who served as the U.S. attorney and as a District Court judge during the early 1970s.

This is the court that fought to open housing in suburban Cicero. Its decision sparked a major race riot in the 1950s. This is the court that gave neo-Nazis the right to march in the predominantly Jewish suburb of Skokie during the 1970s.

This is where two former governors, police captains, dozens of judges, and city aldermen were convicted. Jimmy Hoffa met his fate here. Alexander Graham Bell and Thomas A. Edison persevered here. Heavyweights Jack Johnson and Muhammad Ali, as well as entertainers Charlie Chaplin, Oprah Winfrey, and Michael Jackson, have all been judged in the Northern District.

"I came to this court feeling completely inadequate and humbled by the appointment because I had such respect, really bordering on reverence, for the institution," said Charles P. Kocoras, who became the chief judge of the District Court in 2002. "I thought that if you were a lawyer you couldn't achieve a higher calling than to become a federal district judge, and you know what, I have never changed that opinion. Never. We aren't all brilliant jurists here, I understand. We are just human beings doing the best we can."

The District Court of Northern Illinois, like other district courts, is one of the most significant institutions in America. Historians focus attention on the U.S. Supreme Court, where issues of national importance are finalized. But it is the district courts that wield power on a daily basis.

And it is the District Court that has helped determined Chicago's destiny. "I can't imagine what this city would be like without it," said Ilana Diamond Rovner, former District Court judge now on the Court of Appeals. The District Court sprouted as Chicago sprouted; it was destroyed by the same fire that destroyed Chicago. And it has grown mighty as Chicago has grown large. The court makes Chicago possible—because it provides a place where people can settle disputes and can be judged fairly. This is the conscience of the city, where federal law is defined, applied, and administered. And the city makes the District Court vital—because Chicago generates issues that challenge the court daily.

One of the world's grand engineering feats was the reversal of the Chicago River. But it was the District Court of Northern Illinois that decided how much water would run through it. The district's seventy-six judges, appointed for life, build schools, heel corporations and labor unions, infuriate presidents, and reverse centuries of discrimination. During the 1800s, federal judges shaped Chicago's lakefront by deciding where the Illinois Central Railroad could lay track. A century later, a District Court judge attempted to reshape the Cook County Jail by fining the Cook County Board $1,000 for each day the jail remained crowded. At first, the board merely budgeted $365,000 to pay the first year's fines, but eventually the court's ruling led to construction of a new facility. Almost all of Chicago's historic institutions, from the stockyards to the ball yards, have been affected by the District Court. Almost all the city's disasters have ended up in the federal court in one way or another.

"We are a bread-and-butter, nonideological court," said Judge Holderman. "The culture here among judges is like the culture of the city. We have broad shoulders and work hard. Our court is a reflection of the community."

THE NORTHERN DISTRICT OF ILLINOIS is the third largest of the nation's ninety-four district courts, with twenty-two full-time judges. Only the Southern District of New York in New York City, with twenty-eight judges, and the Central District of California in Los Angeles, with twenty-seven judges, are larger. In Northern Illinois, an additional nine senior judges and ten magistrate judges consider cases. Also, twelve full-time bankruptcy judges on the adjunct Northern Illinois Bankruptcy Court heard 48,435 bankruptcy cases in 2001.

A total of 10,340 civil cases were filed in the District Court that same year. About 98 percent of civil disputes were settled before they went to trial. The court conducted 187 civil trials, including 126 jury trials and 61 bench trials. And 647 criminal cases were filed last year by the U.S. attorney for the Northern District of Illinois. About 90 percent of the criminal charges resulted in a plea-bargain agreement. About 5 percent were dismissed before trial, and another 5 percent went to trial. In 2001, the court held 74 criminal trials, including 60 jury trials and 14 bench trials. About 95 percent of these trials ended in guilty verdicts.

But numbers can't tell the story of the passions that run through the court. On one random day—March 1, 2002—fifty-seven cases were docketed in the clerk of court's office in the Chicago courthouse of the Northern District of Illinois.

Several of the cases involved mortgage foreclosures. Since many mortgage companies are out of state, foreclosure can be filed in federal court as diversity cases, civil disputes that pit residents from different states. The foreclosures take up little of District Court judges' workload. On March 1, a Long Beach, California, company called in the mortgage of a South Side woman who had defaulted on her $77,000 loan. This, like other foreclosures, are processed almost automatically.

Six of the cases concerned the Federal Communications Act. A Florida cable television company charged six Chicago-area restaurant and bar owners with illegally descrambling its broadcast signal and showing a closed-circuit boxing match.

Four cases involved job discrimination. In one, an employee born in Puerto Rico complained that his company did not take proper action against a coworker who made "demeaning, offensive and derogatory comments" about his ethnic characteristics. Three cases turned on other diversity disputes, employee benefits, civil rights complaints, and student loans. The

U.S. government demanded that a Mount Prospect man finish paying the principal and interest on a $1,700 student loan that he took out in 1983 to attend college. Two cases were appeals of federal agency decisions, and two involved trademark infringement and truth-in-lending charges. An Alabama man filed a class-action complaint against a Nevada bank that allegedly sent him a credit card for no reason, opened an account, and started charging him fees with no authorization.

One case involved a patent infringement dispute; another a Civil Rights Act dispute. A former Cook County jail inmate filed a lawsuit in his own handwriting against two Chicago police officers for allegedly falsely arresting him. A suburban Dolton man filed a First Amendment lawsuit after the mayor of his town reportedly ordered him to remove his REELECT JESSE L. JACKSON FOR U.S. CONGRESS sign from his front yard.

Fees are paid; the cases are filed and each is assigned randomly by computer to a judge.

NEARLY NINE MILLION PEOPLE live in the eighteen counties that form the Northern District of Illinois, which extends across the northern tier of the state from Lake Michigan to the Mississippi River. The district is divided into two divisions. Approximately 95 percent of the cases originate and are heard in the Everett McKinley Dirksen United States Courthouse, at 219 South Dearborn Street in the heart of Chicago's Loop. The remainder are heard at the United States Courthouse at 211 South Court Street in Rockford.

Chicago's wood-paneled courtrooms, bathed in fluorescent light, are a time capsule of 1960s elegance. The courtrooms are unlike any other place in the city. Enclosed and windowless, the two-story rooms evoke power through minimalism, not monumentality. Here are simple, austere, geometrically perfect, rectangular rooms, with a grid broken only by one huge, round symbol behind the judge's bench. Here an American eagle rises, holding arrows and olive branches in its talons. It represents, in a sense, the Northern District of Illinois's constant challenge to reach a balance for justice.

BIG AND SMALL DRAMAS play out every day in the Northern District of Illinois.

Fourteen of the fifteen El Rukns who won new trials in 1993 were eventually retried and convicted or pleaded guilty to lesser charges. (One gang member was not retried because he had already been sentenced on other federal charges.) Prosecutor Hogan was fired from the U.S. attorney's office in 1996 for his role in the El Rukn cases. Two years later, however, Hogan was ordered rehired by an administrative law judge following a long hearing with new evidence. The administrative judge determined that the evidence did not establish any personal misconduct on Hogan's part.

The El Rukn case was particularly complex because it inadvertently pitted the District Court judges against the U.S. attorney's office—and both sides came to court with good intentions. The Court of Appeals affirmed Judge Aspen's decision to order new trials in the only El Rukn case that was appealed. The appeals judges ruled that the District Court had properly performed its role as the front line of federal justice.

It is in the District Court where the passions of the El Rukn cases, and thousands of others, are played out. It is here where the government makes its case, where plaintiffs and defendants stand tall, and where the District Court shapes America.

CHAPTER ONE

1778–1871:
"The Freest People
in the Universe"

THE FOURTH OF JULY, that magical day in American history, has special significance for Illinois. It was on that day in 1778, exactly two years after the signing of the Declaration of Independence, that the land that was to become Illinois fell into American hands. George Rogers Clark captured the British outpost at Kaskaskia, near the Mississippi River, and claimed the surrounding western frontier for his native Virginia and America.

Taking Kaskaskia was easy. After a two-month march, Clark and his band of about 150 soldiers reached the town at night, pushed against the gate of the small British encampment, and found it open. Clark's raiders quickly captured the British commandant and the few Redcoats who guarded the village and raced unchallenged through town. Soon after, Clark's small army took the nearby village of Cahokia and smaller British settlements.

Remarkably, not a shot was fired.

Clark then faced his greatest challenge: to convince the two thousand residents of Kaskaskia and Cahokia that his men—notoriously known as Long Knives—were civilized. He knew that to exert authority, he must persuade the French and British residents of the region that he brought with him the prospect of a better life—that he could bring liberty and justice to their frontier outposts. "Embrace whichever side you deem best," Clark told the townspeople, "and enjoy your own religion, for American law respects the believers of every creed and protects them in their rights."

Almost immediately, the residents asked Clark to set up a court that would settle disputes and end the anarchy that plagued the region. Clark, as military commander, took full judicial control. During his first three months in the Illinois area, Clark set himself up as the first American judge in the re-gion. In Kaskaskia, he received civil petitions directly, deciding disputes himself. In Cahokia, he established a court of four judges but personally heard appeals.

By the end of the year, the Virginia legislature had created the County of Illinois, a vast empire stretching northwest of the Ohio River. A public cere-mony, marking the new county, was held on May 12, 1779, in Kaskaskia. Once again, the creation of a judicial system was a priority for Clark, who said:

> You are assembled here, gentlemen, for an affair of the greatest importance, namely, to elect the most capable and illustrious persons to sit in judgment on your differences. I pray you to consider the importance of this choice and to make it without partiality and to elect the persons most worthy of your trust; and I hope that in a short time that you will be convinced that you are the freest people in the universe.

On that very day, Kaskaskia residents elected six justices of the peace. Soon, Cahokia followed suit.

George Rogers Clark crosses the Wabash River through wilderness and flood. The Revolu-tionary War hero first defeated the British in the territory now known as Illinois. EZRA WINTER/ NATIONAL ARCHIVES

Clark, born on the shore of the Rivanna River in the Blue Ridge Mountains of Virginia, is remembered in history for being the only Revolutionary War general who never lost a battle. He also is remembered as a skilled negotiator with Native Americans and as the brother of William Clark, who led the Lewis and Clark expedition of the West. But George Rogers Clark's short judicial career has faded from history.

From Kaskaskia and Cahokia, Clark went on to defeat the British at Vincennes, on the western border of what is present-day Indiana. His claim to the nation's midsection brought wealth to Virginia and to the United States, but the campaign brought calamity to Clark. He had purchased supplies for his soldiers on credit, but the loans were never repaid by Virginia or the United States because the vouchers Clark sent back to Virginia were misplaced. (They were found in the attic of the Virginia capitol in 1913.)

Clark lost most of his land and much of his reputation. Throughout his later life, he was hounded by creditors and became an alcoholic. When the State of Virginia dispatched a messenger to give Clark a sword, a pension, and a message of gratitude for what he had accomplished in Kaskaskia, Clark told the man, "When Virginia needed a sword, I found her one. Now I need bread." Clark died bitter and helpless in 1818, the same year that his beloved Illinois became a state. The court he established in Illinois was a distant ancestor of the United States District Court for the Northern District of Illinois.

George Rogers Clark was the first American to serve as a judge in Illinois. **CHICAGO HISTORICAL SOCIETY**

Virginia's rule of Illinois was short. After the Treaty of Paris ended the Revolutionary War in 1783, the County of Illinois was formally conveyed to the young United States. Under American jurisdiction, the courts at Kaskaskia and Cahokia were reconstituted into local and territorial tribunals. The territorial court, established by Congress, was the forerunner of the trial court that would help determine the future of the nation's heartland.

HALFWAY ACROSS THE CONTINENT, the First Federal Congress met in 1789 to create a national government as envisioned by the recently ratified Constitution. The delegates who gathered at New York's Federal Hall on Wall Street produced an extraordinary record of accomplishment, creating the Bill of Rights and setting rules that governed the new country. One of Congress's first acts was the establishment of the nation's judicial system.

The signers of the Constitution had vaguely sketched out the federal court system. "The judicial power of the United States, shall be vested in one supreme court, and in such inferior courts as the Congress may from time to time ordain and establish," Article III reads. "The judges, both of the supreme and inferior courts, shall hold their offices during good behaviour, and shall, at stated times, receive for their services, a compensation, which shall not be diminished during their continuance in office."

The details, it seemed, needed to be worked out.

The First Congress passed the Judiciary Act of 1789, establishing a three-tier federal court system. The Supreme Court was to serve as the court of ultimate review, over both state and federal courts. The federal circuit and district courts originally both functioned as the nation's trial courts.

The federal circuit courts were given original jurisdiction over major civil and criminal matters and lawsuits filed between residents of different states. Circuit courts also heard some appeals from the lower district courts. Until 1869, when circuit judges were first appointed, each of the circuit courts was presided over by Supreme Court justices and district court judges, who would ride the circuits and decide federal cases as teams.

Over time, the nature of the circuit courts changed. Today, trials are no longer conducted in the federal circuit courts. Only appeals are considered there, and the court is now known as the Circuit Court of Appeals, or simply Court of Appeals. But many of the most noteworthy federal trials in Illinois were held in the early circuit court.

The nation's original thirteen district courts, one for each of the first thirteen states, were given jurisdiction in minor civil and criminal matters, admiralty and maritime cases, bankruptcy cases, and other revenue matters. Each district court had a permanently assigned judge, district attorney, clerk, and marshal. The attorney represented the government. The clerk kept court records, and the marshal protected the court. The cornerstone of the system was the power granted to the district court judges. Like their Supreme Court counterparts, district court judges are nominated by the president, with the advice and consent of the Senate, and are granted lifetime terms. They can be removed from office only if impeached by the House and convicted by the Senate of "treason, bribery, or other high crimes and misdemeanors." Only thirteen federal judges—none from Illinois—have ever been impeached by the House. Seven were convicted by the Senate. Two others resigned before a vote was taken.

The Judiciary Act, signed by President George Washington, was a compromise between those who favored a strong national judiciary and those

who sought strong local judicial control. Federalists won the creation of the
Supreme Court, which could review decisions made in state courts, and secured the rule that federal judges would get lifetime appointments so they
would not have to worry about making unpopular decisions. States' rights
advocates won concessions for independent state and local courts, which
heard the majority of cases.

The judicial system has remained remarkably unchanged from that model
for more than two centuries.

THE FIRST CONGRESS failed to establish law in the wide-open territory
northwest of the Ohio River until the 1790s. The land, called the Northwest
Territory, included what are today the states of Illinois, Indiana, Ohio, Michigan, Wisconsin, and a small section of Minnesota. Congress passed the Ordinance of 1787, which provided for the appointment of a governor, a secretary, and three judges for the territory, but it took years for the frontier
government to take hold. The early judges did not want to travel to what
was considered wilderness.

Territorial judges and governors were given legislative power to adopt
uniform laws best suited to meet the demands of the frontier. These laws
were taken from the civil and criminal laws of the original states. Congress
brought habeas corpus, trial by jury, and English common law to the Northwest Territory.

"All persons shall be bailable, unless for capital offenses, where the proof
shall be evident or the presumption great," stated the 1787 federal ordinance.
"All fines shall be moderate, and no cruel or unusual punishments shall be
inflicted. No man shall be deprived of his liberty or property, but by the
judgment of his peers, or the law of the land."

The territory's first judges—Samuel Holden Parsons, James Mitchell Var-
num, and John Cleves Symmes—were each paid an annual salary of $800.
They met for the first time in the summer of 1788 in the present town of Marietta, Ohio, then the capital of the Northwest Territory.

The territory's first governor, Arthur St. Clair, traveled to Illinois in 1790
to survey the western edge of the region. St. Clair had heard that the local
courts in Kaskaskia were rarely in session and not doing their jobs. He wrote
President Washington in May 1790 that he needed territorial judges to accompany him to craft new law.

"The judges are not yet arrived neither have I the least information about them—their absence has embarrassed me a good deal, as many regulations, suited to the peculiar circumstances of this part of the country are necessary," he wrote, "and cannot, with propriety be established but by law; I have been obliged however, in some instances, to take it upon myself, after waiting for them as long as possible, and direct them by proclamation."

Illinois was far from Marietta, Ohio, and judges resisted the long and dangerous trip. Their absence from Illinois became a serious problem. So serious, in fact, that the first matter handled by a common-law grand jury in Illinois targeted the territorial judges themselves for refusing to travel to Illinois.

To help address the problem, the Northwest Territory was divided by Congress into the Ohio and Indiana territories in 1800. The Indiana Territory encompassed present-day Illinois. The capital of Vincennes, on the Wabash River, was an arduous 180 miles away from Cahokia and Kaskaskia.

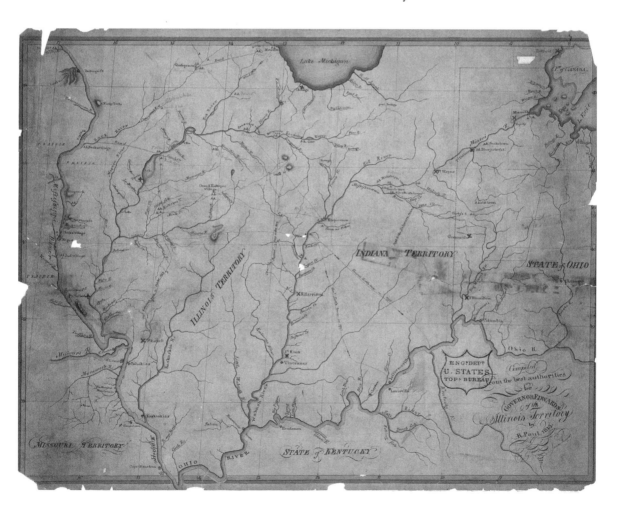

The Indiana Territory's first three judges—William Clark, Henry Vander
Burgh, and John Griffin—were appointed by the president with the advice
and consent of the Senate. In 1801, the territory held its first court session,
most likely in Vincennes. In 1805, about three hundred inhabitants of the
Illinois area petitioned Congress for a further split. They were concerned
about the dangerous journey to the Vincennes court.

Their request was granted in 1809. The western portion of the Indiana
Territory, stretching from Illinois to Wisconsin and parts of Michigan and
Minnesota, was officially designated the Illinois Territory. It was the first for-
mal use of the Illinois name by the federal government.

Ninian Edwards, who had served as a high-ranking judge in Kentucky,
was appointed governor of the Illinois Territory. Nathaniel Pope, who would
go on to be the state's first District Court judge, was appointed territory secretary. The three territorial judges were Jesse B. Thomas, Obadiah Jones,
and Alexander Stuart. Jones was quickly replaced by Stanley Griswold, who
died in 1815. Griswold in turn was succeeded by Thomas Towles. Stuart resigned in 1813 and was replaced by William Sprigg. Richard Graham succeeded him in 1818. Frontier life wore judges down.

Jesse Thomas turned out to be a more important political figure than
judge. A congressman from the Indiana Territory, he had worked to create
the Illinois Territory before moving to the area. Thomas went on to become
president of the first Illinois Constitutional Convention and served as one of
the state's first senators. He also helped write the Missouri Compromise, an
attempt to forge a national policy on slavery.

The judges' first duty was to sit with Governor Edwards to create laws for
the new territory. The governor and judges had complete control of the political life of Illinois until the first territorial legislature was assembled in
1812. The judges composed the state's general court, hearing major civil and
criminal cases in Kaskaskia. Justices of the peace heard minor matters.

"Inasmuch as no prisons or jails had yet been erected, the punishments
provided in their criminal code were decidedly summary," wrote Cook
County Superior Judge George Alexander Dupuy in his 1906 survey of early
Illinois courts. "Death was inflicted for murder, treason and (in some cases)
for arson. Whipping, stocks, and pillory were brought into frequent requisi- *Facing page:* An 1815
tion. For nonpayment of fines the sheriff might bind out the culprit for a map shows the emerg-
term of years." ing Indiana and Illinois

Like the territorial judges before them in Marietta and Vincennes, the territories. NATIONAL

ARCHIVES

Illinois judges were absent for long periods. When the territory's General Assembly finally convened, legislators passed laws defining the federal courts in an attempt to get more work from the judges. The judges declared the laws unconstitutional.

"To the excuse that travel was difficult, the reply was given that federally appointed judges received one hundred dollars a month, which was a good salary," wrote historian Robert P. Howard. "The St. Clair and Randolph county grand juries at one time took official note of the nonattendance of judges, and in 1814 the legislature sought to remedy the situation by creating a system of circuit courts."

Each of the federal judges was assigned two counties and required to hold court at regular intervals. The judges objected. They proclaimed that the state legislators could not pass laws to assign or regulate them because the judges were federal officials. The governor submitted the dispute to Congress, which sided with the legislators. In 1815, however, Congress passed an act regulating and defining the duties of the United States territorial judges. The General Assembly eventually gave up trying to regulate the federal judges.

By 1818, Illinois petitioned Congress for statehood. An act was introduced by Nathaniel Pope, the Illinois Territory's delegate to Congress, that changed the destiny of the area by fixing the northern border of Illinois at a new location. When the Ordinance of 1787 was passed, Congress had foreseen the northern border of the future state as bisecting the southern tip of Lake Michigan. Pope amended the law to move the border to forty-two degrees and thirty minutes north. That added eight thousand square miles to Illinois, including the coast of Lake Michigan and present-day Chicago. "Few if any of the men identified with the early history of Illinois, have exercised so potent an influence upon the destiny of Chicago as Judge Pope," wrote A. T. Andreas in his 1884 *History of Chicago*.

Pope successfully argued that a proposed canal connecting the Illinois River and Lake Michigan would ultimately connect the Mississippi River to the Atlantic Ocean by way of the Great Lakes and the Erie Canal. The Lake Michigan coast would thus help connect the North and the South and aid in preserving the Union by making Illinois a key state.

Illinois was admitted to the Union in 1818. Congress passed an act in 1819 providing for the execution of federal laws within the new state and on March 3, 1819, Illinois was established as a single federal judicial district. On the same day, Pope was nominated by President James Monroe to sit as its

Nathaniel Pope, who is responsible for Chicago being part of Illinois, served as the first judge of the United States District Court of Illinois.
FRANCIS MARION PEBBLES/CHICAGO HISTORICAL SOCIETY

first judge. Pope was confirmed by the Senate, and he conducted the court's first term in December 1819. He was paid $1,000 a year in quarterly payments and was to hold two sessions annually, on the first Mondays in May and December. The judge was directed to appoint a clerk to keep court records. The president also appointed a U.S. attorney and marshal.

The first five decades of the Illinois District Court and the subsequent Northern District of Illinois were shaped by its first two judges, Pope and Thomas Drummond.

Pope defined the court by helping determine the state's boundaries and its power. Drummond, with a firm reputation as one of the most learned, kind, and honest men in the state, created an institution worthy of the lofty ideals of justice.

These men were the court. Their impact is felt more than a century and a half later.

NATHANIEL POPE WAS BORN in Louisville, Kentucky, in 1784, and moved to Kaskaskia after being appointed secretary of the Illinois Territory. He became the leading lawyer of the region and published a compilation of territorial laws in 1815. After his appointment to the federal bench, Pope held court first in Kaskaskia. He moved the court in 1820 when the state capital was transferred from Kaskaskia to Vandalia and again in 1839, when Springfield became the capital.

"In the early days of the court, its business was principally confined to suits brought by citizens of other states against debtors resident in this state," wrote District Court Judge Henry W. Blodgett in his 1896 *History of the United States Courts in Chicago*. "But there was also much litigation in it in those early times between parties claiming lands under old grants made by the French Government in colonial days, and afterward by the State of Virginia and the United States."

The records of all but a few cases filed during the district's early years were destroyed in the Great Chicago Fire of 1871. Many of those cases were disputes over the Military Tract, according to Blodgett. Soldiers who fought in the War of 1812 were often paid for their service by being given property between the Illinois and Mississippi Rivers in western Illinois. The state was sparsely settled during the decades following the war, and these men—most of whom lived in the East—generally ignored their prairie land grants. Much of the acreage was sold for taxes or to speculators at a nominal price. Some of it passed to new owners via forged deeds. As the land increased in value, the former soldiers used the federal court to try to regain the property.

"Judge Pope took a resolute stand against the attempt to deprive the old soldiers or their heirs of their land by these forged deeds," Blodgett wrote, "and also by what he characterized as not less dishonest, the tax deeds." Pope reportedly said he would sit until the seat of his leather breeches wore out before he would rule that a man could acquire 160 acres by paying $1.50 for it at a tax sale.

In March 1837, the Illinois District Court became part of the new Seventh Circuit by combining with courts in Ohio, Indiana, and Michigan. Besides running the District Court in Illinois, Judge Pope now had a role in the U.S. circuit court system, riding a circuit and hearing cases alone or with a Supreme Court justice assigned to the region. John McLean was the first Supreme Court justice to serve the Illinois circuit. He usually sat with Pope during the summer term, while Pope sat alone in the winter.

Chicago attorney Isaac N. Arnold, looking back decades later, described the early federal courts in Springfield: "If we could, in fancy, enter the United States Circuit Court room in this city, in June 1839 we should be impressed with the majestic figure, imposing presence, and dignified bearing of the presiding judge, John McLean, a justice of the Supreme Court of the United States. His person and face were often compared to Washington's—whom he is said to have strikingly resembled.

"Nathaniel Pope, the district judge, was shorter and stouter in person, more blunt and sturdy in manner, and not so familiar with the law-books, the cases, the literature of the law, but of a most clear, vigorous, and logical mind."

Arnold recalled the journeys from Chicago to the U.S. courts in Springfield, comparing those early trips to ones he took during the 1880s in luxurious Pullman cars.

"We made our trips in Frink & Walker's coaches, and I have known the December trip to take five days and nights, dragging drearily through the mud and sleet, and there was an amount of discomfort, vexation, and annoyance about it, sufficient to exhaust the patience of the most amiable. I think I have noticed that some of my impulsive brethren of the Chicago bar have become less profane since the rail-cars have been substituted for stage-coaches.

"But the June journey was as agreeable as the December trip was repulsive. A four-in-hand with splendid horses, the best of Troy coaches, good company, the exhilaration of great speed, over an elastic road, much of it a turf of grass, often crushing under our wheels the most beautiful wild flowers, every grove fragrant with blossoms, framed in the richest green, our roads not fenced in by narrow lanes, but with freedom to choose our route."

The most dramatic case during the court's early years was the 1843 extradition trial of Joseph Smith. The Mormon leader had been arrested in Illinois and charged in connection with an 1842 attempt to kill Lilburn Boggs, a former Missouri governor. Boggs was shot and wounded at his Independence, Missouri, home by an unknown assailant. Boggs accused Smith of planning the murder and charged Smith's bodyguard with the actual shooting. Missouri officials asked that Smith and the bodyguard be extradited.

The Mormon leader had good reason to hate Boggs. When Smith's followers settled in Missouri, the governor issued an order to "expel and exterminate" them. After they moved to the Illinois town of Nauvoo, the Illinois governor approved a warrant for Smith's arrest in connection with the attempt on Boggs's life. Smith was brought before Judge Pope on a writ of habeas corpus, an order by a judge requiring that a person held in custody be taken to the court to determine the legality of his or her detention.

The life of Mormon leader Joseph Smith was likely saved when the District Court of Illinois ruled he could not be extradited to Missouri.
CHICAGO HISTORICAL SOCIETY

"The prophet (so called) was attended by his twelve apostles, and a large number of his followers, and the case attracted great interest," attorney Arnold wrote. "The court-room was thronged with prominent members of the bar, and public men. Judge Pope was a gallant gentleman of the old school, and loved nothing better than to be in the midst of youth and beauty. Seats were crowded on the judge's platform, on both sides, and behind the judge, and an array of brilliant and beautiful ladies almost encircled the court."

Justin Butterfield, one of the first lawyers from Illinois to attain national distinction, advocated that Smith be released. A friend of Daniel Webster, Butterfield modeled his style of argument after the great orator and even dressed like him. At the Smith hearing, Butterfield displayed his sense of humor and intelligence.

"May it please the court, I appear before you today under circumstances most novel and peculiar," Butterfield said. "I am to address the 'Pope' [bowing to the judge], surrounded by angels [bowing still lower to the ladies], in the presence of the holy apostles, in behalf of the prophet of the lord."

Butterfield argued that Smith could not have committed any crime in Missouri.

"On the hearing, it clearly appeared that he had not been in Missouri, nor out of Illinois, within the time in which the crime had been committed, and if he had any connection with the offense, the acts were done in Illinois," wrote attorney Arnold. "Was he, then, a fugitive from justice? It was pretty clear, that if allowed to be taken into Missouri, means would have been found to condemn and execute him."

After a four-day trial, Pope agreed with Butterfield's reasoning.

"It is not averred that Smith was accessory before the fact, in the state of Missouri, nor that he committed a crime in Missouri: therefore, he did not commit the crime in Missouri—did not flee from Missouri to avoid punishment," Pope said.

He discharged Smith from arrest and probable execution. By turning against the popular anti-Mormon sentiment of the time, Pope established

Thomas Drummond was the first judge of the Northern Illinois District Court. Two presidents considered him for the U.S. Supreme Court. ILLINOIS STATE HISTORICAL LIBRARY

the District of Illinois court as a bastion of justice and independence. It was one of the shining moments in early court history.

"The decision excited much comment at the time, but it has borne the test of criticism," wrote attorney Thomas Dent in 1896, "and is now the accepted rule of law in interstate extradition cases."

DURING THE 1840s, Pope traveled to Chicago during the summer to hear a variety of federal cases. Congress passed a law in 1848 authorizing the U.S. District and Circuit Courts of Illinois to hold one session annually in Chicago. Pope sat for his first term at the law office of Morris & Brown, 104 Lake Street. Three years later, Congress approved an additional term to be held in Chicago and provided for the establishment of a clerk's office in the young city.

Pope died in September 1849, soon after the close of the second Chicago summer term. President Zachary Taylor nominated fellow Whig Party member Thomas Drummond to take Pope's place. Drummond, of Galena, had served as an Illinois representative with Whig colleague Abraham Lincoln and as an Illinois Circuit Court judge during the 1840s. He closed his Galena office and took the bench following his Senate confirmation in February 1850. Born in 1809 in Bristol Mills, Maine, Drummond graduated from Bowdoin College at age twenty-one, read the law, and was admitted to the bar in Philadelphia in 1833. He soon moved to Galena, where he became a prominent attorney. The term "reading law" meant serving as an apprentice in the office of an established lawyer, a common method of becoming a lawyer before the widespread establishment of law schools.

During his first years on the federal bench, Drummond held court in Chicago and Springfield. In Chicago, he most often convened sessions at the law office of Manierre & Meeker, 118 Lake Street, and at a nearby vacant store owned by George W. Meeker. Meeker was clerk of the federal court for a short time and served for many years as a U.S. commissioner, an assistant to the District Court judge. Cases that attracted a crowd would be heard in the Cook County Courthouse.

"At that time Chicago was rather an important city, and a very important city in its own estimation, but compared with the Chicago of today it was hardly more than a village," recalled attorney George E. Adams in the 1890s. "The current of city life did not move so rapidly and so confusedly then as it does now, and it was easier then than it would be today for the name of a man like Judge Drummond to be almost a household word in the whole community."

Drummond soon moved to the three-story Salon Building at 123 Lake Street. The Salon, which in true Chicago fashion was known as the "Saloon Building," was one of the most beautiful halls west of Buffalo, New York. The building had a rich history. Built in 1836, it was where Chicago's pioneers met in 1837 to draft the city charter. It was the first home of the Chicago City Council, the site of the city's first formal concert, and the location where the city's first telegram was received. The District and Circuit Courts met on the top floor, which had a raised ceiling. By 1855, however, the building was deteriorating. Judges, lawyers, and grand jurors complained that the building's bare floors and simple furniture made the courtroom "unfit for justice."

On February 13, 1855, the United States District Court of Illinois was divided by a line north of Springfield into Northern and Southern Districts. Chicago was to be the home of the Northern District, Springfield the Southern District. One judge was assigned to each district.

It is remarkable that Chicago was recognized so early as needing a federal court of its own. The midwestern hamlet was surveyed and platted in 1830, organized as a town in 1833, and incorporated as a city in 1837. Until 1833, Chicago and Illinois were considered by European immigrants to be in dan-

The Salon, known as the Saloon, at the southeast corner of Lake and Clark Streets, housed the U.S. District and Circuit Courts during the mid-1800s. **CHICAGO HISTORICAL SOCIETY**

gerous frontier territory. The Treaty of Chicago in 1833, which sent the Potawatomi, Chippewa, and Ottawa Indians across the Mississippi River into the Kansas Territory, opened the state to a mass of East Coast and European immigrants. By 1839, Chicago was in the first stages of establishing itself as the nation's transportation hub—connecting steamboats from the East with stagecoaches to the West. The Illinois & Michigan Canal opened in 1848, linking the city by water to the Mississippi River. That same year, Chicago's first locomotive ran the rails.

The Northern District Court failed to open as scheduled in early 1855. After being officially named as the first judge, Drummond finally opened the new court in mid-February in the Saloon Building. The *Daily Democrat Press* explained that the judge had learned by telegraph about the division of the state into two judicial districts but preferred to wait until he studied the bill that created the new court. Drummond, who moved to Chicago, where he lived the rest of his life, disposed of twenty-five criminal cases during the court's first days.

In 1857, the District and Circuit Courts moved two blocks south to the Larmon Building, at the northeast corner of Clark and Washington, where they remained until the first Federal Building opened in 1860.

Drummond ran the District Court alone and worked with Justice McLean in the Circuit Court until McLean's death in 1861. During that time, the District and Circuit Courts of Northern Illinois developed a fine name. "The reputation of the judges of the court—McLean and Drum-

Two 1858 photos from atop the Cook County Courthouse show the Larmon Building (foreground), a temporary home of the federal courts. The view to the southeast shows the city's first federal courthouse (far right) under construction. The building, visible as roofless walls, opened two years later. ALEXANDER HESLER/ CHICAGO HISTORICAL SOCIETY

mond—for probity and learning and the dispatch of cases caused a rapid increase of the business of the court, lawyers, and suitors preferring the federal tribunals in all cases where jurisdiction could be sustained; and it must be admitted that Judge Drummond was always astute in finding reasons for sustaining the jurisdiction of his court," wrote Henry Blodgett in his account of the early court.

McLean was replaced by Supreme Court Justice David Davis of Illinois, who may have had a more difficult time working with Drummond. After the election of Abraham Lincoln as president, Drummond and Davis were mentioned as likely U.S. Supreme Court candidates. Davis, who had served as Lincoln's campaign manager, received the nod. He worked with his rival on the Northern Illinois Circuit Court.

"Judge Davis, while not what could be called a learned judge in the mere sense of book knowledge, was endowed with quick perceptions, was a man of sound judgment and great natural ability for business, and equipped with a full measure of what is called 'common sense,' which made it easy for him to comprehend business questions," wrote Blodgett.

DRUMMOND'S FIRST LOVE was admiralty law. His father had been a seafarer, and water held Drummond's keenest interest, even in the heartland. In 1845, Congress passed legislation that applied admiralty law to the Great Lakes and to the waters connected to them. District courts had exclusive jurisdiction over admiralty and maritime cases, so when Drummond was later appointed to the bench, he took a passionate interest in admiralty matters. Justice McLean, Drummond, and Andrew G. Miller, a District Court judge in Wisconsin, were instrumental in extending the laws of the oceans to lakes and rivers.

To be a good admiralty judge, one had to be extremely well educated, attorney Robert Rae wrote in his 1896 article "A Sketch of Admiralty Law." As hard as it is to believe today, Rae wrote that an admiralty judge needed:

1. A liberal or a classical education.
2. He should be familiar with the Italian, French, Spanish, and Dutch marine codes, and be able to read the three first in the original.
3. He should be well grounded in the sea laws of maritime countries, and in the general maritime law.
4. He should be a clear and sound expounder of the Constitution of his country.

5. He should be as well accomplished in physics as a patent law judge.

6. He should be a good theoretical seaman, and to a very large extent a practical one.

The best and the brightest lawyers were called to advocate admiralty cases. The hearings in District Court were epic battles of great minds. And nobody was considered more learned than Drummond. None of his admiralty decisions was overruled during his life, according to Rae.

The rewards for attorneys were great.

"From 1855 to 1865 the admiralty docket was quite large and contained cases of much importance," Rae wrote. "The professional compensation to those who practiced there was large. An admiralty lawyer in full practice within that period might safely rely upon an income of $30,000 to $35,000 per annum."

The early Northern District's maritime cases tell of a nautical city long gone.

In 1853, Drummond heard a case in Circuit Court concerning the collision of two steamers on the narrow and crowded Chicago River. The *Rossiter* struck the *St. Louis* in the midst of thick smoke coming from the ruins of the recently destroyed warehouse.

"There can be no doubt that the *Rossiter* was in fault, and liable for the injury done," Drummond wrote. "If those on board of the propeller could not see their way clear, owing to the smoke, it was their duty to proceed with extreme caution, especially as they were approaching a bend in the river. It is a rule of universal application, that a steamer in entering a harbor at night, crowded with craft as the Chicago River was at that time, shall be held to the greatest diligence and circumspection, and if owing to fog, smoke, or other cause, they cannot see their way before them, it is their duty to stop, or at least proceed with such slowness that they can stop at a moment's notice.

". . . They must be more careful and vigilant than they have been, or, clearly understood, they will have to answer in damages for the consequences."

A few years later, Drummond and a jury heard a case of the *S. D. Caldwell*, which tried to make its way through the frozen Chicago River on the last day of 1863. The boat slowly made it down the river, but was stopped at the Madison Street Bridge because the bridge tender could not open the jammed drawbridge.

"The weather was becoming cold and the following day, the first of January 1864, was of unexampled severity; so that some of the persons engaged in

trying to open the bridge on that day had their hands and feet more or less frozen," Drummond wrote. "The bridge tender returned on the second of January, and the next day they succeeded in opening the bridge and the [ship] passed through. But in the meantime the cold had so much increased and strengthened the ice, that after winding and trying with her bow, which was cased in iron, to force her way through, the propeller, after some days of trial, relinquished the attempt to go out in that way."

Eventually, crews were hired to cut the ice and the boat made it to Lake Michigan and Milwaukee in mid-January. The boat was damaged and delayed. Its owners filed a lawsuit against Chicago, arguing that the city was responsible for keeping the river open and was liable for the damage to the boat.

"The Chicago River is a public navigable highway, and vessels have the right to pass up and down, without unnecessary detention; and consequently the propeller *S. D. Caldwell* had the right to go down the river at the time mentioned," Drummond told the jury. "But the right of navigation does not take away the right of crossing the river, and it must be considered settled that the city has the power to construct bridges for the purpose of crossing, provided the bridges are so constructed and maintained as not materially or unnecessarily to obstruct navigation. The two rights coexist, and each one must be construed with reference to the other, precisely as we qualify the right to travel along a street by the right to cross it. The navigator must yield something to the foot passenger, just as the latter must yield something to the navigator."

The jury awarded damages to the ship owners.

Life was dangerous in a city built around the congested Chicago River. In 1865, Drummond heard a case in Circuit Court concerning the death of one John Brady, who was crossing the river at Clark Street with a coworker. The two men stepped on the bridge, which pivoted and swung around for a vessel to pass. "The night was dark, and the gas was not bright and did not shed much light upon that end of the bridge," Drummond wrote. Brady lost his balance and fell, suffering an injury that led to his death. The lawsuit charged the city with negligence, for not providing adequate protection or lighting. The jury agreed.

DRUMMOND ALSO HEARD the district's early patent suits. One of them was filed by Cyrus H. McCormick, famed inventor of the reaper that helped transform the midwestern prairie into farmland. McCormick, who received his first patent for the machine in 1843, appeared in Circuit Court during the 1850s alleging that four men had introduced a machine that infringed on one of his patents. McCormick asked for an injunction. The Circuit Court declined, ruling that the new machine differed from McCormick's in principle as well as in form. The case was appealed to the U.S. Supreme Court, which received an account of the Circuit Court trial that signaled the growing complexity of such cases. It read: "The reporter despairs of giving any intelligible account of the argument in this case. The record was upwards of 1,000 pages of printed matter, of which 750 pages were the depositions of witnesses; and the court room was filled with models and drawings, introduced upon either side, to which constant reference was made by the counsel."

The Supreme Court dismissed McCormick's claim.

No more than one patent case a year was filed in the Northern District through 1871, the year of the Great Chicago Fire. But as Chicago was rebuilt as a manufacturing giant, patent law expanded rapidly. By 1896, Chicago had forty-three patent lawyers.

"All patent suits are necessarily prosecuted in the federal courts," attorney Lester L. Bond wrote, "and the patent bar of this [Seventh] Circuit deservedly has the reputation of conducting suits as thoroughly and exhaustively as the bar of any other circuit, so that it has become a saying that any patent which has passed through a contest in the Chicago district is thereafter safe."

Drummond also had a reputation for never accepting any sort of present.

"On one occasion a great admirer of the judge and of his old federal opinions in politics, hearing him say that he preferred always to write with a quill, presented him with a dozen magnificent feathers from the wings of a swan," recalled Colonel J. K. C. Forrest.

"A few days afterward the gentleman presenting this simple tribute of love and admiration, innocently enough no doubt, was surprised by the clerk handing him back the feathers with the judge's compliments and the statement that he regretted that—seeing that the donor was a member of the bar and had a couple of cases on his docket—he was unable to accept this kindly meant present."

NO ISSUE WAS MORE HEATED in the young State of Illinois than the Fugitive Slave Act, which mandated the U.S. commissioner to issue warrants for the arrests of "fugitives" from Southern plantations. The law, passed in 1850, allowed for "slave catchers" to apprehend and return African Americans to Southern slavery if they did not have papers proving that they were free. Chicago's Common Council, an early city council of antislavery leaders, declared the law null and void and said it was unenforceable in the City of Chicago.

Fugitive slave trials were momentous events. One resident described a case before U.S. Commissioner George W. Meeker in the Saloon Building that resulted in the release of an accused fugitive. "The hall was densely packed when the decision was made, the crowd extending, in solid mass, from the courtroom, in the third story, which was filled through the halls and stairways to the street below," the witness wrote. "The Commissioner's decision was received with the wildest cheers and excitement, and the colored man was passed at once over the heads of the crowd out the courtroom and down the stairways to the street, and in an incredibly short space of time was on his way to Canada, out of reach of process or pursuit by the claimant."

Another case involving slavery became one of the most important early trials in the Northern District of Illinois. This was the 1860 trial of abolitionist John Hossack. The case, *United States v. Hossack,* was analyzed by current Northern District of Illinois Judge William T. Hart and attorney Francis A. Even in a 1999 manuscript.

The case centered around Jim Gray, an African American seized in Southern Illinois during the fall of 1859 by two men determined to transport him back to bondage in Missouri. The slave catchers were noticed by abolitionist Benajah G. Roots, who demanded that Gray be taken before a county judge in downstate Jonesboro. The judge denied the slavers' request to take Gray to Missouri, but decided that he could not let Gray out of custody since the African American man did not possess "freedom papers." Gray was taken to Ottawa for a habeas corpus hearing before John D. Caton, chief justice of the Illinois Supreme Court, who discharged Gray from the custody of the Jonesboro sheriff. He ruled that Gray must be kept in federal custody and taken before the U.S. commissioner in Springfield.

"Hearing the Justice's decision, someone shouted to Gray: 'If you want liberty, run,'" Hart and Even wrote. Sympathizers blocked law officials and summoned Gray through the back door of the courthouse, yelling, "Come along this way!" and "This is the road to freedom." Gray hurdled a fence and scrambled aboard a waiting carriage. "Charles Campbell was in the driver's seat and applied the whip," Hart and Even wrote. "Peter Meyer tried to stop the carriage by grabbing the bridle. John Hossack stepped up with his fists clenched and said, 'Let loose.' Meyer released his hold and the carriage was off at a gallop."

Gray escaped, traveling to Chicago and eventually Canada. A federal grand jury, sitting in Chicago, indicted eight men for violating the Fugitive Slave Act by helping them escape. Hossack and his colleague, Dr. Joseph Stout, were tried in the Larmon Building before Judge Drummond. A jury found them guilty but recommended mercy. Drummond sentenced each to only ten days in the Cook County Jail and fined them $100. Others received even lesser sentences.

Hossack's extemporaneous statement, delivered just before his sentencing, was published throughout the nation by abolitionists. "I have a few words to say why sentence should not be pronounced against me," he told Drummond. "I am found guilty of a violation of the Fugitive Slave law, and it may appear strange to your honor that I have no sense of guilt."

Hossack spoke for a long while and concluded:

A single remark, and I have done. From the testimony, part of which is false, and from your rendering and interpretation of the law, the jury have found me guilty; yes, guilty of carrying out the great principles of the Declaration of Independence; yes, guilty of carrying out the still greater principles of the Son of God. Great God! Can these things be? Can it be possible? What country is this? Can it be that I live in a land boasting of freedom, of morality, of Christianity? How long, O, how long shall the people bow down and worship this great image set up in this nation? Yes, the jury say guilty, but recommend me to the mercy of the Court. Mercy, sir, is kindness to the guilty. I am guilty of no crime, I therefore ask for no mercy; I ask for justice. Mercy is what I ask of my God. Justice in the courts of my adopted country is all I ask. It is the inhuman and infamous law that is wrong, not me.

My feelings are at my home. My wife and my children are dear to my heart. But, sir, I have counted the cost. I am ready to die, if need be, for the oppressed of my race. But slavery must die; and when my country shall have passed through the terrible conflict which the destruction of slavery must cost, and when the history of the great struggle shall be candidly written, the rescuers of Jim Gray will be considered as having done honor to God, to humanity, and to themselves.

I am told there is no appeal from this court; yet I do appeal to the Court of High Heaven, when Judge Drummond and Judge Caton, the rescuer and the rescued, shall all have to stand at the judgment-seat of the Most High.

Drummond worked alone as the District Court judge, but he was assisted by Philip A. Hoyne, who was appointed U.S. commissioner in 1855 and served for nearly forty years. The commissioner took on many roles during that period. At times he served as a federal justice of the peace. At times he provided help to the courts as an examining and committing magistrate. Before the Civil War, the commissioner's most demanding job was being in charge of deporting fugitive slaves to their owners.

"It was a task beset with many difficulties on account of 'the underground railroad,' the ramifications of which were numerous and the agents of which were diligent," wrote Mark A. Foote in 1896. "In other words, the fugitive slave was seldom apprehended, being forewarned and spirited away by his watchful sympathizers.

"The history of the United States courts, and of the colored race, in Chicago, cannot be written well without allusion to Adam Carey, for he was janitor of those courts and prominent amongst that people for many years," wrote Foote.

For most of the decade before the Civil War, Carey worked quietly to warn slaves who made it to Chicago that they were in danger.

"As intimated by Mr. Hoyne, Adam's work as janitor was never so well performed before or after the 'fugitive slave law' was in operation in Chicago. There was no particular time or circumstances when or under which it might not suddenly occur to Adam that the commissioner's office needed dusting; and he was especially industrious in that respect upon the appearance there of any strangers who looked as if they might be from the South, in quest of a warrant to apprehend a fugitive slave. In later years, when spoken to about it, Mr. Hoyne seemed to have forgiven Adam."

THE MOST HISTORICALLY IMPORTANT FIGURE in the early federal court of Northern Illinois was attorney Abraham Lincoln. He tried at least thirteen cases in the District and Circuit Courts, according to the research group Lincoln Legal Papers. He worked almost to the day he was nominated as a Republican candidate for president.

Lincoln had a distinctive courtroom style.

Attorney Abraham Lincoln tried at least thirteen cases in Illinois's District and Circuit Courts. Many of the court's prominent attorneys were his ardent supporters in the Republican Party. **NATIONAL ARCHIVES**

"His law arguments addressed to the judges, were always clear, vigorous and logical: seeking to convince rather by the application of principle, than by the citation of authorities and cases," attorney Isaac Arnold wrote. "On the whole, I always thought him relatively stronger before a jury than with the court. He was a quick and accurate reader of character, and understood, almost intuitively, the jury, witnesses, parties, and judges, and how best to address, convince, and influence them."

One lawyer recalled seeing Lincoln pace in Judge Drummond's courtroom, waiting for his case to be called.

"Robert S. Blackwell was making a most elaborate address to a jury, and was, as it seemed to us, at times rather incoherent, as he talked of many things entirely foreign to the subject, and to illustrate some point in his discourse proceeded to narrate at great length the habits of the storks in Holland."

Lincoln listened, and declared: "That beats me! Blackwell can concentrate more words into the fewest ideas of any man I ever knew. The storks of Holland!"

Drummond agreed that Lincoln was best in front of a jury, partly because he had an "intuitive insight into the human heart." Lincoln could relate to jurors in a plain and homespun manner. His sincerity and earnestness gave him great success.

"With a voice by no means pleasant," Drummond wrote, "and, indeed, when excited, in its shrill tones sometimes almost disagreeable; without any of the personal graces of the orator; without much in the outer man indicating superiority of intellect; without great quickness of perception, still his mind was so vigorous, his comprehension so exact and clear, and his judgment so sure that he easily mastered the intricacies of his profession and became one of the ablest reasoners and most impressive speakers at our bar."

Lincoln joined Drummond, several other lawyers, and Stephen A. Douglas for a memorable dinner in Chicago prior to the presidential election—which pitted Republican Lincoln against Democrats Douglas and John C. Breckinridge.

"There were active and ardent political friends of each at the table," attorney Arnold wrote, "and when the sentiment was proposed, 'May Illinois furnish the next president,' it was, as you may imagine, drank with enthusiasm by the friends of both Lincoln and Douglas."

In 1860, the first federal courthouse ever built in Chicago was opened. The three-story building, at the northwest corner of Dearborn and Monroe Streets, also housed the post office and the custom house, a place where foreign goods were inspected and charged tariffs.

By the outbreak of the Civil War in 1861, Drummond, like Lincoln, had become a Republican. He was an ardent supporter of the Union. "On many occasions during the war he participated in patriotic assemblages in Chicago,

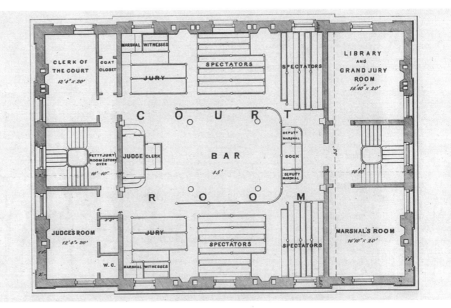

Early floor plan for a proposed federal courtroom in Chicago. Court facilities were a small but important part of federal buildings constructed during the 1800s.

NATIONAL ARCHIVES

either as chairman or one of the speakers; and he supported, with unwavering courage, loyalty and devotion, the efforts of the government to bring the war to a successful conclusion," wrote attorney Stephen Strong Gregory.

Federal court officials were active during the war. Drummond heard cases against men accused of evading the Union's 1863 draft. An injunction was filed against the Chicago and Moline Water Power Company to dismantle a dam built on the Mississippi River that interfered with the Rock Island Arsenal. Rebel-owned property was confiscated; a new income tax was passed to fund the Union effort; and the district attorneys helped prepare against a rumored Confederate raid on Chicago's prisoner of war facility, Camp Douglas.

In 1863, Drummond's loyalty to the Union conflicted with his legal values when Union General Ambrose E. Burnside ordered the *Chicago Times* be closed "on account of the repeated expression of disloyal and incendiary sentiments." The *Times,* run by Democrat Wilbur F. Story, had severely criticized President Lincoln, his cabinet, and his generals in articles that some considered seditious. Publisher Story appealed Burnside's edict to Drummond, who ruled that the paper could continue publishing until the case was decided. The next morning, however, Union troops stopped the presses and destroyed the printed papers.

Drummond was furious.

"These parties have appealed to the court, and the court, so far as it is able

The first federal courthouse built in Chicago. "With a few unimportant exceptions, it is as good as anything we have in Washington," wrote a Treasury Department official about the building, which opened in 1860. It was formerly known as the Post Office, Customs House, and U.S. Court Building. **CHICAGO HISTORICAL SOCIETY**

A double portrait of Ambrose E. Burnside, a Union general who attempted to shut down the *Chicago Times* in 1863 for running articles critical of the Lincoln administration. The general's plan was curtailed by District Court Judge Thomas Drummond.
NATIONAL ARCHIVES

to do so, will determine their rights of property," he said. "I trust nothing will occur in this community which will show a want of confidence in the civil tribunals of the country. It is desirable that we should know whether we live under a government of law or under a government simply of force."

The following day, prominent residents met in the Circuit Courtroom and unanimously voted to ask that Lincoln rescind Burnside's order. "That evening an enormous meeting of, it is said, twenty thousand people was held in the open air at Court House Square, at which resolutions were adopted denouncing Burnside's conduct, insisting on freedom of speech and of the press and that the military must be subordinate to the civil power," Gregory wrote. Two days later, the city was informed that Lincoln had rescinded Burnside's order.

Drummond's stand against the army made a "profound impression" on the nation, Gregory wrote. "He achieved the distinction of true greatness."

1871–1922:
"A Sea of Fire"

EVERYTHING CHANGED IN THE RUBBLE of the Great Chicago Fire. The blaze of 1871 put an end to frontier Chicago. It wiped out the central business district and demolished the splendid three-story building that housed the Northern Illinois District and the Circuit Courts. With it went virtually all of the courts' records.

The fire, however, set the stage for a new city. It set up Chicago, and its federal court, for greatness. During the courts' second half century, federal judges in Chicago flexed their muscles. They stood between the nation's great competing forces: big industry and big labor. Oil giants, beef barons, Wobblies, and Pullman strikers all walked through the gates of the courthouse to be judged. These were heady, brawling times, and federal trial judges in Chicago took their place on the front line to shape America's future. The court was now an agent for change.

In 1869, District Judge Thomas Drummond was appointed by Republican President Ulysses S. Grant to serve as the first full-time circuit judge of the Seventh Circuit. Drummond continued hearing most of his cases in Chicago, but he also traveled around the state and to Indiana and Wisconsin.

The appointment was momentous. Myra Bradwell, editor of the *Chicago Legal News,* wrote that Drummond left the District Court "with a name for honesty and ability second to no district judge in the Union."

She wrote: "The judicial labor that the judge has performed is immense, and can only be fully appreciated by the members of the profession, who were the daily witnesses of his faithfulness. For nearly twenty years, almost without intermission or vacation, Judge Drummond has been constantly engaged in the business of his court, allowing no speculations or outside operations to share his time, or divert his attention from his judicial labors."

But Bradwell was convinced that Henry Blodgett would be an able successor to Drummond as District Court judge.

"The appointment of Judge Blodgett is a good one, and gives satisfaction not only to the bar, but to the whole community," she wrote. "The judge is a close reasoner, an active, practical man, and takes a broad common sense view of all questions upon which he is required to act."

Like Drummond, Blodgett was born in New England. He came to the Chicago area as a boy of nine after his father was smitten by what was called "western fever." Blodgett's father headed in 1830 across the Alleghenies to establish a "Hampshire colony" in the Midwest with New England friends. He made a claim in DuPage County, west of Chicago, then erected a house and waited for the Erie Canal to open so that his family could join him. Young Blodgett and the rest of his family took about two weeks to make the journey along the canal from Albany to Buffalo, Blodgett wrote in his 1906 autobiography. They boarded a schooner on the Great Lakes for the four-day trip to Detroit, and then rode a team of horses for three weeks across Michigan to Chicago.

As a boy, Blodgett helped his father establish a forge in Downers Grove and worked on the construction of the Illinois & Michigan Canal, surviving an illness among workers known as "canal cholera." Only twelve lawyers were working in Chicago in 1844 when Blodgett began studying law. He was one of two law students. In 1845, he started a private practice in nearby Waukegan. Three years later, he appeared in Judge Nathaniel Pope's courtroom in the Manierre & Meeker law office, and wrote: "This was my first experience in a United States court, and I found Judge Pope a very agreeable and able man in the place."

Like most judges of the time, Blodgett was active in politics. He was the first antislavery candidate to win election to the Illinois House, and he helped found the Republican Party. He was a delegate at the 1860 Republican National Convention in Chicago that nominated Abraham Lincoln for president.

Blodgett created a successful law practice representing railroads and quit law for a time to serve as president of the railroad later known as the Chicago and North Western. In 1868, Blodgett campaigned for Grant in his successful bid for president. The following year, when Grant nominated Drummond for the Seventh Circuit, the president offered Blodgett the nomination as district judge. Blodgett served from 1870 to 1892.

Blodgett's biggest challenge was to fill Drummond's shoes in trying admiralty cases. Drummond had established a national reputation as a maritime expert; Blodgett had no experience with the laws of the sea.

"When he first took his seat on the bench he asked the writer to furnish him with some volume on seamanship," attorney and author Robert Rae recounted. "There is a little book on this subject, very thorough and very practical; it is called *The Seamen's Friend*. It is a plain treatise on practical seamanship, embracing general rules of the constitution of vessels, rigging them, working them when built, and a full account of the customs and usages of the merchant service and the laws relating to the practical duties of masters and mariners.

"This book is a friend in need," Rae wrote. "When the name *Seamen's Friend* was pronounced to the judge, he looked up with a humorous smile that all in the bar have seen so often play around his intelligent mouth, and quaintly asked if it was a 'Christian tract,' and said that, as he was profoundly uninformed as to the usages and laws of those who go down to the sea in ships, no doubt, in the course of his judicial voyage he would need providential aid in avoiding shipwrecks and ruins to his suitors."

At first, Blodgett admitted that he "guessed" at the law on collisions, but eventually he became a master in trying admiralty cases, Rae wrote. As Chicago changed from a sea town to a railroad hub, admiralty law diminished in importance. "The business fell off," wrote Rae, "and the profession turned from a practice hitherto so lucrative to other branches of the profession, such as railroad, telegraph, and corporation law."

Here Blodgett excelled. As a former corporate lawyer and railroad president, Blodgett brought broad experience to the bench. His forte, however, was patent law. "He was very familiar with mechanics, could read drawings and specifications, and established a reputation as fine patent judge," wrote attorney Lester Bond. "He did more than any other one man to make Chicago a center for patent litigation and patent matters and to bring to Chicago the splendid and efficient patent bar which it now has."

Less than two years after his appointment, Chicago and the courts were transformed dramatically by the Great Chicago Fire. The fire began at 9 P.M. on October 8, 1871. It burned out seventy thousand homes, sixteen hundred stores, and six hundred factories. About one hundred thousand people were left homeless. Some three hundred died.

"What a sight," wrote lawyer Jonas Hutchinson, "a sea of fire, the heavens all ablaze, the air filled with burning embers, the wind blowing fiercely and tossing fire brands in all directions, thousands upon thousands of people rushing frantically about, burned out of shelter, without food, the rich of yesterday poor today, destruction everywhere—is it not awful?"

The fire swept through downtown. The iron that supported "fireproof" buildings melted until a rain snuffed out the sea of flames three days later. It consumed most every building in the central business district, including the federal courthouse. The building's walls stood, but the interior was gutted.

Christian C. Kohlsaat, a lawyer who would later be appointed as the District Court's fourth judge, was twenty-seven years old when the fire broke out. "Nothing that you have read can possibly exceed the scene," he wrote only days after the fire.

"Our house is safe so far, though we are constantly on the lookout for fires. The city is under strict military and police control. Men have to toe the line close, or get shot. Our office went with all its contents. The library was

Interior of the Post
Office, Customs House,
and U.S. Court Building
after it was demolished
by the Great Chicago
Fire in 1871. The walls
stood, but the building
was gutted, destroying
almost all records.
**CHICAGO HISTORICAL
SOCIETY**

insured for $1,000 in a Chicago company, but of this we shall collect little or nothing. Our safe with our books of account is yet in the ruins. We have been working two days to unearth it. Had to dig down for eight feet."

The fire destroyed records, books, and files of the Northern Illinois District and Circuit Courts, as well as state court records. "It's so strange to have no deeds, no judgment cards, no anything," Kohlsaat wrote. "Nobody owns any land by record title now. Our mortgage is wiped out. Everyone must begin anew. There will be a great deal of law business before things are straightened out."

The file of one District Court case—a dispute between John Currie and Allen Jordan over a farm mortgage in LaSalle County—was found on the street several days after the fire. The court's other records, including those brought to Chicago from Springfield for safekeeping, were destroyed.

But Chicago rose.

"The destruction of the records made it necessary to restore them as far as practicable," Blodgett wrote. "In the cases still pending and undecided new pleadings were filed and the cases again docketed for trial, and cases which had been disposed of, and where judgments and decrees had been entered, were restored whenever the parties deemed such restoration essential to their interest, but the bulk of the old cases were never restored."

The courts moved temporarily to the old Congregational Church, at the corner of Green and Washington. Court officials depended on honesty to piece together real estate and bankruptcy records, Blodgett wrote.

"The destruction of so large an amount of property by the fire necessarily caused much pecuniary embarrassment among the business men of the court; while the foreclosures of mortgages on property where the buildings had been burned, and where default had been made in the payment of principal or interest, caused a great increase in the business of the chancery side of the courts; all of which so increased the labors of the judges as to keep them in what may be termed unceasing drudgery for nearly ten years after the fire," he wrote.

Some of the records, such as the 5,349 bankruptcy petitions filed after the Bankruptcy Law of 1867, were restored following the fire. Mrs. M. G. Lampkins, who published an abstract of these petitions, proudly announced: "In presenting this work to the public, I do so in confidence that it will be of great value to lawyers, merchants, manufacturers, bankers, and the business community in general."

Postfire Chicago offered many opportunities. "The Chicago Fire added immensely to the business of the court, and the growth of the City of Chicago also increased it, so that from the time I went upon the federal bench until my retirement therefrom I was a very busy man," Blodgett wrote. "For the first six years I took no vacation, but worked continuously from the beginning to the end of each year, taking my first vacation in the summer of 1876, when I was away from my court about four weeks."

From 1819 until the fire in 1871, a total of 10,161 cases were filed in the Circuit Court and 3,300 in the District Court. During most of these years, the court included all of Illinois. The pace picked up in postfire Chicago: In the next twenty-four years, a total of 13,734 cases were filed in the Circuit Court and 3,634 in the District Court, plus an additional 2,548 criminal cases.

After the fire, the federal court and custom house moved to Congress Hall, at Michigan and Congress. That building was destroyed by fire in 1874, forcing the federal court to move to the Republic Life Building, on LaSalle Street. Chicago's second Federal Building, an ornate structure with fancy gables on its roof, opened in 1880 on a block bounded by Clark, Adams, Dearborn, and Jackson. "The cornerstone was laid with Masonic ceremonies; the day set apart for the formality was a public holiday in the city; and from that time forward the building attracted a great share of attention of the people of Chicago, most of whom had previously been indifferent to what was being done on the Government Square," wrote the *American Architect and Building News.* The four-story building—which included the courts, custom house, and post office—was constructed poorly and began falling apart even before its official debut. Twelve years later, the building was called a "disgraceful old rattle-trap." It was closed in 1896.

Meanwhile, in Circuit Court, Thomas Drummond continued to influence Chicago and Northern Illinois in his role as full-time circuit judge. His first challenge was attempting to save the once-thriving railroads that had fallen into hard times because of financial slumps. Drummond took control of all midwestern railroads that went into receivership following the Panic of 1873 and held them together.

"It has been said by railway officials, of his management, that no experienced railway manager could have done better, if as well, in the guardianship of the interests committed to his keeping," said Judge James G. Jenkins, who served with Drummond on the Seventh Circuit. Drummond ruled that in-

solvent railroads could pay their operating expenses first, before they paid bondholders, so they could stay in business.

"No one decision, I take it, has had greater significance than this, or has been of greater consequence to the country," said Jenkins. "Its correctness was afterward upheld by the Supreme Court of the United States, and is to-day the settled law of the land."

The impact of the Panic of 1873 lasted for years. Railroad workers were discharged and wages were cut. In 1877, workers on the Baltimore & Ohio line voted to strike. Their protest soon spread across much of the nation.

Crowds gather on a public holiday to witness the laying of the cornerstone for the new Chicago Post Office and Custom House on June 24, 1874. It took six years to complete the building, which included federal courtrooms. **CHICAGO HISTORICAL SOCIETY**

Strikers managed to close all five of the nation's trunk lines that connected the Midwest to the East, resulting in bankrupted businesses, closed factories, and violence in many cities. The federal government had never before played a major role in labor disputes, and turned to its courts for a solution.

Drummond was one of several federal judges who swiftly took action. He saw railroads as public highways and was determined to protect them. "A strike or other unlawful interference with the trains will be a violation of the United States law, and the court will be bound to take notice of it and enforce the penalty," he declared. Drummond told marshals to protect the railroads in receivership and asked for federal troops to enforce his decision. He had strikers arrested and then tried them for contempt. Most were sentenced from sixty to ninety days in jail. He also arrested strikers for blocking or delaying the mail.

U.S. Commissioner Philip Hoyne recalled those days when Drummond put down the strike.

> Following the Panic of 1873 there were probably twenty railroads tied up in his court mounting to $100 million in property. All these he was operating through receivers, having more railroad business under his charge than any one man ever attended to either before or since. One day he received a tele-

The city's second Post Office and Custom House was built for the federal court following the Chicago Fire. The building was bounded by Clark, Adams, Dearborn, and Jackson Streets. It opened in 1880 and served the court until 1896. CHICAGO HISTORICAL SOCIETY

gram complaining that the strikers were interfering with the running of trains at Peoria.

A cloud came over his brow and he shouted to old Adam Carey, who was standing in the door.

"Adam, go tell the marshal to come here immediately."

Marshal Jesse Hildrup came in and Judge Drummond ordered him to start for Peoria at once and arrest every man who attempted to interfere with the running of trains. The next day Hildrup returned with a carload of strikers as prisoners.

"I'll show these men how they interfere with the business of this court."

He scared them to their senses, and gave them comparatively light sentences.

The incident was significant, Blodgett recalled, because Drummond's prompt action put an immediate end to the strike. "The simple vigor with which Judge Drummond resented the interference with property in the custody of the court struck terror to the strikers. They had encountered a force they had not calculated on."

Decades later, historian Gerald G. Eggert took a different view, emphasizing the totalitarian nature of Drummond's action. "Though 'devoted to jus-

Street scene across the front facade of the Post Office and Custom House. Although beautiful, the building was an architectural nightmare. By 1892 it was already known as a "disgraceful old rattle-trap." **CHICAGO HISTORICAL SOCIETY**

tice, as he saw it,' Judge Drummond was not a 'conspicuous champion of popular rights,' nor did he especially appreciate the 'vital importance of jury trial to free institutions,'" Eggert wrote. "In 1877 he made generous use of contempt of court proceedings, which involved no juries, against strikers."

District Court Judge Blodgett became the target of the newly formed Chicago Bar Association in 1878. His registrar in bankruptcy cases, Homer N. Hibbard, was accused of failing to report $11,000 in fees and excessive expenses. The association debated filing charges against Hibbard, but eventually took no formal action.

"For a while, the Hibbard case was shoved into the background," wrote Herman Kogan in *The First Century: The Chicago Bar Association 1874–1974*. "But that autumn, charges were carried in several local newspapers and in others elsewhere that Judge Blodgett, who had presided over most of the bankruptcy cases, had conducted himself improperly by engaging in murky dealings with Hibbard and had, moreover, shown gross favoritism toward his friends and exerted severe pressure against his foes, had ruled persistently in favor of railway corporations and big business enterprises, and had con-

ducted his court in a manner that obstructed justice."

Bar association members wrote to U.S. Representative Carter H. Harrison accusing Blodgett of official misconduct. They asked for Congress to impeach the judge. The association split into two groups. Stephen A. Goodwin came to Blodgett's defense. "Is it not wrong that when a gentleman high in official position takes his place upon the bench he should find hissing throughout the length and breadth of the union, charges to his dishonor and against his integrity? Is not this a wrong?" the attorney asked.

"What has he a right to say? He has a right to say that if any gentleman has any such fact against him, let him bring it out in the open day and not smuggle it up to a congressional committee and keep it a secret while the brunt of it went broadcast throughout the land," Goodwin wrote.

Powerful U.S. Senator Lyman Trumbull supported Blodgett, but also wanted the charges against him aired. "Of his purity and integrity I have never known the slightest suspicion," Trumbull said.

A congressional committee held hearings in January 1879. The House Judiciary Committee investigated a slew of official misconduct charges against Blodgett. He was accused of entering into a "dishonest conspiracy" to defraud creditors in bankruptcy proceedings, of improperly attempting to prevent the grand jury from indicting Hibbard for perjury, of borrowing money belonging to the court, and of using his authority to enrich his friends and favorites by appointing them as trustees or receivers in bankruptcy cases. The committee studied each charge and issued a detailed twenty-page report that exonerated the judge.

It was the closest any judge in the Northern District of Illinois ever came to impeachment.

"The results, for all the hullabaloo and fervid meetings, were rather anticlimactic," Kogan wrote. "The prime evidence indicated that Hibbard had lent money to Judge Blodgett presumably out of funds of bankrupt estates under his jurisdiction but that the jurist had made prompt repayment. By March, the investigating committee issued a report to the United States House of Representatives Judiciary Committee mildly censuring Judge Blodgett but recommending that no further action be taken and that all charges against him be tabled."

Blodgett's friends celebrated. They marched the judge by torchlight

Facing page: The 1877 railroad strike as depicted in Leslie's newspaper. The illustration shows the U.S. Cavalry charging a mob of strikers at the Halsted Street Viaduct. **CHICAGO HISTORICAL SOCIETY**

This page: The Illinois State Militia set up tents in front of the city's second federal courthouse during the Great Strike in 1877. *LESLIE'S WEEKLY*

through Waukegan to the Baptist Church to be feted. Once again, Blodgett declared his innocence: "If it was their intention to do what they could to break my heart and to wring from me the utmost anguish that human nature can bear, then they certainly must have been abundantly gratified, for they could have taken no surer means to accomplish that end. The storm came, falsehood did its worst, but finally truth asserted itself and I now stand before my friends without an extra furrow in my face and with my health unbroken!"

Inventor Alexander Graham Bell withstood patent challenges all over the nation, including one in the Northern Illinois District Court. CHICAGO HISTORICAL SOCIETY

A NUMBER OF HISTORIC CHARACTERS passed through Blodgett's court. Some left happy; some left unfulfilled. In 1881, Blodgett confirmed that Alexander Graham Bell invented the telephone.

Bell's patents—Number 174,465, dated March 7, 1876, for an "improvement in telegraphy" and Number 186,487, dated January 30, 1877, for an "improvement in electric telegraphy"—were challenged by S. D. Cushman, who charged that Bell was not the first inventor of the speaking telephone. Cushman declared he was.

Blodgett agreed that Cushman created an electromagnetic telephone years before Bell. The judge wrote that Cushman's device contained magnet coils through which spoken words were transmitted at short distances. But the transmission was faint and the words were difficult to hear. "The attempt to talk through them was often a total failure; and occasionally, when all conditions were favorable, at most only a partial or meager success was obtained," Blodgett wrote.

He ruled: "These considerations compel me to the conclusion that all the testimony, when taken together, falls far short of establishing beyond reasonable doubt the fact that Dr. Cushman in 1851 invented the telephone; that what was done by him must and should be treated as, at best, only an abandoned experiment. I do not think the testimony, when fairly considered, shows that Dr. Cushman produced at Racine or elsewhere, prior to the invention of Bell, a practical operative telephone of any kind. He gave the world nothing."

The public understood the value and importance of Bell's telephone immediately, Blodgett wrote. "It was accepted as a great invention, by the general public, as soon as its operation was seen; and I can see no reason why the public would not as readily have comprehended its advantages and value in

1851, as in 1876, had the machine been so far developed as to give substantial promise of what Bell accomplished."

Blodgett ruled that Bell advanced the telephone to a stage in which it was useful, and so should keep the patent.

In 1882, while serving on the Circuit Court, Judge Blodgett ruled against Mark Twain himself. Samuel Clemens, better known as Mark Twain, charged that Chicago publisher Belford, Clark & Company printed *Sketches by Mark Twain* in 1880 without his authorization. Not only had they used his work but they had printed a preface signed by Twain that he didn't write.

Twain's argument seemed unassailable. Through his attorney, Twain wrote:

> 1. That your orator is now, and has been for about twenty years last past, an author and writer by profession, and that he has been for many years past in the habit of publishing articles, sketches, books, and other literary matter composed by him for publication under the name, assumed by him to designate himself as the author and writer of such sketches, articles, books and other literary matter, of "Mark Twain."
>
> 2. And that the said designation of "Mark Twain" was assumed by your orator about twenty years since, and has been used by him during the last twenty years as his nom de plume, or trade-mark as an author; and that during the said time your orator is informed or believes, no other writer or author has made use of the said name as a designation of authorship.
>
> 3. And that your orator's said writings, articles, books and other literary matter, so published by him under the said designation of "Mark Twain," have acquired a great popularity, and meet with a ready and continuous sale; and writings, sketches, articles, books and other literary matter published under said title, nom de plume or trade-name, are greatly sought for by the public.

Author Samuel Clemens unsuccessfully fought to protect his early stories in Chicago's federal court.
NATIONAL ARCHIVES

The publisher's defense was simple. Clemens had failed to copyright his material.

Blodgett determined that the work had been published previously without copyright, so republishing it was legal. Clemens, however, countered that his nickname was like a trademark, protecting the work. Blodgett did not buy the argument. On January 20, 1883, the judge decided that the use of a nom de plume did not give Clemens any special rights.

"Trademarks are the means by which the manufacturers of vendible merchandise designate or state to the public the quality of such goods, and the fact that they are the manufacturers of them," Blodgett wrote. When Clemens published his work without a copyright, he was dedicating the work to the public. "No pseudonym, however ingenious, novel, or quaint, can give an author any more rights than he would have under his own name."

Blodgett wrote that Clemens would have had more of a legal leg to stand on if he would have made a case against the phony preface.

Clemens's failure to copyright the work reprinted in *Sketches* is mystifying because Clemens was a noted leader in copyright reform.

IN 1887, THE NORTHERN DISTRICT OF ILLINOIS was reorganized by Congress. The counties of McDonough, Fulton, and Tazewell were detached from the Southern District and added to the Northern District, and the district was divided into Northern and Southern Divisions. Cases in the Southern Division were heard in Peoria. Cases in the Northern Division continued to be heard in Chicago.

Thomas Drummond died in 1890. He had served on the Seventh Circuit until his retirement in 1884. Walter Q. Gresham, who succeeded Drummond as the circuit judge, wrote: "I have had relations with many men, and I have no hesitation in saying that, all things considered, Judge Drummond was the most perfect man I have ever known."

In 1913, U.S. District Judge Kenesaw Mountain Landis unveiled a portrait of Drummond in his courtroom, and many came to laud the first judge of the district. President William Howard Taft wrote Landis: "While Judge Drummond was never promoted to the Supreme Court, everyone who came in contact with him felt that he was of the material and timber of which Supreme Court judges ought to be made."

Judge Jenkins recalled how Drummond, during his retirement, was aboard the steamship *Oregon* when it caught fire at sea. As another vessel approached, the captain ordered women and children to lifeboats. He then ordered the eminent Drummond to be the first among men to transfer to safety.

"Let the younger men go first," Drummond told the captain. "They are of more worth to the world. My work is done."

Although the captain's word is law on a ship, Drummond overruled him.

"Happily, every life on that burning ship was saved, but the act was none the less heroic; it was unique," said Jenkins, who called it "the crowning glory of a noble life."

IN 1892, HENRY BLODGETT stepped down as district judge at the age of seventy-one. He was appointed by President Benjamin Harrison to serve as one of the U.S. counsels to help settle the seal fur dispute of the Bering Sea.

Peter Stenger Grosscup was appointed by Harrison as the third judge of the Northern District of Illinois. Grosscup, born in Ashland, Ohio, in 1852, was the great grandson of Paul Grosscup, a member of the 1791 Constitutional Convention in Philadelphia. With a college and law school education, Peter Grosscup twice ran for Congress in Ohio. The first time he was defeated. The second time he withdrew unexpectedly and made a fast exit for Chicago. Rumor had it that he was paid to withdraw, or had become involved in a scandal. But Grosscup quickly made a name for himself as a prominent lawyer. Chicago industrialist George Pullman backed Grosscup for the District Court judgeship and persuaded Harrison to nominate him. He served as a District Court judge for seven years, before being appointed to the Seventh Circuit Court of Appeals by President William McKinley.

Grosscup was a "storm center" of controversy, wrote author Edgar Lee Masters. The judge had a dominating personality that created much ill will when he managed Chicago's bankrupt streetcar system. "He was a man touched in some particulars with great humanity and with notable generosities," Masters wrote, "but he had definite economic leaning and his imperial nature brooked no interference."

Some admired him.

"Judge Grosscup unites more of the qualities of Judge Drummond than Judge Blodgett," wrote attorney Robert Rae. "He is quicker of apprehension, however, than that great judge. One to know him would suppose him to have been a student and disciple of Marcus Aurelius and had taken this great Roman emperor's precepts as his guide. While he has favorites at the bar, he had none while on the bench. He has that quality which will always make him a great and righteous judge. He can refuse with graciousness those who are near him for the sake of many whom he may never know or meet."

Some hated Grosscup.

Union leader Eugene V. Debs, a frequent Grosscup target, wrote articles detailing Grosscup's malevolent political alliances, business deals, and rumors about the judge's sexual life. Debs used no names in backing up his charges in the Socialist publication *Appeal to Reason,* but stood by the accuracy of his articles. "If Judge Grosscup, however, desires to test the knowledge of the writer regarding these transactions, he can bring suit for criminal libel and the whole matter can be heard in court," Debs wrote. Grosscup never took the bait.

Grosscup paid back Pullman in 1894 when he confronted Debs and his nationwide American Railway Union and put down the "Debs Rebellion." The Pullman strike started in Chicago when workers at the Pullman Sleeping Car Company walked off the job. The Pullman company had reduced wages and hours of Pullman workers in an attempt to keep as many people employed as possible following the Panic of 1893. However, Pullman did not decrease the rents he charged for living in the company town of Pullman. After the walkout, Debs's young American Railway Union decided not to move any trains that included Pullman sleeping cars. The strike, like that of 1877, soon threatened the economy of the nation. By late June 1894, only a few trains were running in or out of Chicago. Business at the Union Stockyards was suspended.

Federal judges Grosscup and William A. Woods of Indiana granted an injunction against Debs's union to stop the strike on July 2. When Debs ignored the injunction, Grosscup asked President Grover Cleveland to send federal troops to protect U.S. mail, an act that outraged Illinois Governor John Peter Altgeld, who thought the state militia could handle the matter. Thousands of regular troops were sent to Chicago to protect the few freight trains that were moving. The strike turned violent as railroad yards were torched. About two dozen people, mostly strikers, were killed and hundreds of freight cars were overturned and burned during the resulting melee.

Aging U.S. Commissioner Philip A. Hoyne, still on the job, swore in new deputy marshals hired to protect the mail.

"There were so many persons charged with such offenses, most of whom were apprehended and dealt with by Mr. Hoyne at the same time that he was engaged in the appointment of the special deputies from day to day," wrote Mark Foote, Hoyne's assistant. "The intense application and constant mental and physical labor entailed by the work, which lasted several weeks and involved personal dealings with thousands of animated men, were too much for the veteran commissioner, whose one desire, so far as business was con-

Labor leader Eugene V. Debs insulted District Court Judge Peter Stenger Grosscup in print and challenged the judge to file libel charges against him. NATIONAL ARCHIVES

cerned, had been to round out the forty years of service, with the expecta-
tion of retiring, at the end of the year, for the recuperation which his failing
health and strength demanded. After the unusual and severe strain was
ended, his health failed rapidly and his arrangements to retire were hastened.
In October he departed for a health resort, and lived but a few days after his
return."

The strikes were quelled by mid-July, when workers returned to their
jobs. More than ten thousand troops and three thousand city police were
needed. But Grosscup was not finished with Debs. He called on the grand
jury to investigate Debs and his union. This was the judge's charge:

Gentlemen of the Grand Jury: You have been summoned here to inquire
whether any of the laws of the United States within this judicial district have
been violated. You have come in an atmosphere and amid occurrences that
may well cause reasonable men to question whether the government and laws
of the United States are yet supreme. Thanks to resolute manhood, and to
that enlightened intelligence which perceives the necessity of a vindication of
law before any other adjustments are possible, the government of the United
States is still supreme.

You doubtless feel, as I do, that the opportunities of life, under present
conditions, are not entirely equal, and that changes are needed to forestall
some of the dangerous tendencies of current industrial tendencies. But neither the torch of the incendiary, nor the weapon of the insurrectionist, nor
the inflamed tongue of him who incites to fire and sword is the instrument to
bring about reforms. To the mind of the American people; to the calm, dis-
passionate sympathetic judgment of a race that is not afraid to face deep
changes and responsibilities, there has, as yet, been no appeal.

Men who appear as the champions of great changes must first submit them
to discussion, discussion that reaches, not simply the parties interested, but
the outer circles of society, and must be patient as well as persevering until the
public intelligence has been reached, and a public judgment made up. An appeal to force before that hour is a crime, not only against government of exist-
ing laws, but against the cause itself; for what man of any intelligence sup-
poses that any settlement will abide which is induced under the light of the
torch or the shadow of an overpowering threat?

Debs and seven labor leaders were indicted and put on trial before Grosscup in early 1895. They were charged with conspiring to stop the U.S. mail,
because the work stoppage had stalled at least one train carrying mail. The

lawyer Clarence Darrow, who had recently quit his job as attorney for the Chicago and North Western Railway, and Stephen Strong Gregory defended Debs. Darrow tried to subpoena Pullman, but he left Chicago, so the lawyer interrogated other railroad managers in an attempt to detail how Chicago companies had conspired against Debs.

"Pullman could not be found, and the railroad officials avowed they could remember nothing about what was said at their meetings," wrote Herman Kogan. "In the midst of this, a juror became ill, and Judge Grosscup, over the strong objections of Darrow and Gregory, discharged the jurors—who filed out after shaking hands with the defendants and the two lawyers—and continued the case until May."

The case never restarted. New U.S. Attorney John C. Black argued against continuation of the case because conspiracy to obstruct mail cars would be difficult to prove. Debs ended up serving a six-month contempt

Clarence Darrow
quit as a railroad attorney to defend strikers
against the railroad.
Darrow, an inspiration
for several of today's
District Court judges,
is shown in 1935.
CHICAGO DAILY NEWS

sentence in a Woodstock, Illinois, jail. He appealed the contempt charge to the U.S. Supreme Court but lost. The federal court proved that it could stop Debs, at least temporarily.

Attorney Gregory criticized the turn of events.

"It seems strange to me," he wrote, "except that it has ever been thus that the railroads did not realize as well as public officials how it would disarm Debs to treat him justly—to show that the courts and judges whom he denounced as corporate tools could yet, calm and unruffled, administer the law justly, unmoved by the demand of the wealthy and influential classes for vengeance upon him."

Not all the court's major decisions in the 1890s involved strife and violence.

Chicago's crowning achievement of the age, the World's Columbian Exposition, was the subject of two noteworthy lawsuits. One concerned whether the fair would be open on Sundays. Religious leaders feared a drop in church attendance, but for six-day-a-week laborers, Sunday was the only day they would have an opportunity to witness the wonders along the Midway Plaisance. Congress, which helped finance the fair with the minting of five million Columbian half dollars, ordered the fair closed on Sundays. When fair directors voted to open the gates, the government sued to stop them. The District Court sided with Congress but was overruled by the Court of Appeals. The fair was open for a few Sundays but then closed again—not because of any judicial decision but because many exhibitors decided to give their employees one day off a week.

The highlight of the fair for many was the 264-foot-high Ferris wheel, which along with Paris's Eiffel Tower was one of the engineering feats of the century. The uniqueness of the wheel, which could carry two thousand people, was challenged by the Garden City Observation Wheel Company. It alleged in District Court that G. W. G. Ferris had copied the invention of William Somer, a carpenter from Atlantic City, New Jersey, who had secured a patent for his Roundabout in 1893. Ferris, a civil engineer from Pittsburgh, argued that the Roundabout lacked the technology of his great wheel. "No one has ever tried to experiment in wheels approximating the Ferris wheel in size," his lawyers argued. Ferris prevailed.

DURING THAT TIME, the Northern District Courthouse continued on the move. After the second courthouse was closed in 1896, the District and Circuit courts moved first to the Monadnock Block, at the corner of Jackson and Dearborn, and then to other locations until a new courthouse was completed.

The third Federal Building, at 225 South Clark Street, was a $6 million beaux arts masterpiece, Roman Corinthian in style. The *Chicago Tribune* called it the "granite octopus." It was designed by Henry Ives Cobb, a popular architect of the day, and was dedicated by President William McKinley on October 9, 1899, the twenty-eighth anniversary of the Chicago Fire. Construction actually began in 1898 and continued through 1905, when the federal courts moved into the building.

The Federal Building's two-story base covered the entire block upon which it was built, directly west of the present Dirksen U.S. Courthouse. Four six-story wings rose above the base. A corona-topped dome, one of the tallest and most beautiful structures in the city, soared 275 feet from the center of the edifice. Its rotunda was grand—with marble halls, graceful columns, a terrazzo floor, and brass accoutrements. Six people plunged to their death onto the rotunda lobby during the sixty years of the building's existence.

Four District and Circuit Courtrooms were built in the four wings—each with the grandest murals of their day. Five hundred rooms filled the build-

ing, which was first officially known as the Post Office, Custom House, and Sub-Treasury. That's because the post office was a major part of the building. Some five thousand employees worked there during its peak years.

"Chicago's old Post Office and Federal Building, which occupies an entire square block in the heart of the Windy City, is an ancient and somber pile of stone and iron. Its construction took over six years," wrote attorney Francis X. Busch. "A popular, rollicking song of the Gay Nineties predicted that its side walls, weakened by age and disuse, would surely collapse before the heavily ornamented and domed roof was mounted on them. This dire prophecy was not fulfilled."

IN 1898, INVENTOR THOMAS A. EDISON filed suit in the Northern District's Circuit Court against Edward H. Arnet of Waukegan, for violating his patent on movie cameras. Edison, of New Jersey, argued through his attorney that he was the "original, first and sole inventor of certain new and useful kinetographic cameras." The kinetoscope was the earliest form of motion picture apparatus—a machine that could make motion seem real on a screen.

Facing page: The corona-topped dome of the third Federal Building nears completion around 1900. Scaffolding webbed the dome's rotunda, which crowned one of the city's great interiors. **CHICAGO HISTORICAL SOCIETY**

This page: Chicago's third court building, known as the old Federal Building, opened in 1905 on a block bounded by Clark, Dearborn, Adams, and Jackson. The building's two-story base covered the entire block and formed the foundation for four wings, in which courts were located. **CHICAGO HISTORICAL SOCIETY**

Edison, who received his first patent for the kinetographic camera in 1891, said that Arnet knew about the patent but began making and selling his own device for making photographs of moving objects. Edison asked the court to stop the Waukegan man.

Arnet disagreed that Edison was the inventor. He acknowledged that Edison had received a patent for the movie camera, but argued that the patent was illegal and irregular because the art of making and exhibiting photographs representing the natural movement of objects had long since been accomplished. He also argued that Edison's machine, if constructed, "would be inoperative and useless." After a flurry of charges and countercharges, Edison prevailed. The suit never came to a hearing because Arnet's lawyers withdrew.

Thomas A. Edison came to Chicago's federal court to defend the patent of his motion picture apparatus.
NATIONAL ARCHIVES

WHILE MOST OF THE CASES before the court dealt with commerce, some provided a hint at what living in the Chicago area was like. They were a social history of sorts, telling tales of accidents—and schemes.

When the rigging of a schooner struck the Wells Street Bridge, the court was asked to determine who was at fault. "This bridge was operated by electricity. The failure to stop the bridge upon the centre protection was clearly owing, as the evidence discloses, to the failure of the bridge tender to shut off the current when the bridge had reached the proper position," the newly created Court of Appeals wrote in reviewing the District Court case. As the schooner approached and the bridge began to swing open, the tender apparently lowered an elevated red ball and indicated to the boat that the bridge was open for passage. The bridge quickly swung closed, causing the accident. By city ordinance, the schooner pilot had no right to enter the draw until the bridge was swung completely open and locked.

"The ordinance does not require, nor does common sense demand, that vessels navigating the river shall heave to at each of the numerous bridges that span the river, and critically examine whether the bridge has been swung and whether it has been locked," the court wrote. The accident, it was determined, was caused solely by the inexperienced tender who mistakenly lowered the red ball before the swinging bridge was fully stopped.

Much of the court's work dealt with cases involving fraudulent marriage agencies. At least twenty-three fake marriage bureaus were investigated by the U.S. attorney's office.

Here's how the scheme generally worked.

The bureau would place a pair of ads in the newspaper. To attract women, one ad read: "Matrimony: Wealthy manufacturer wishes congenial, home-loving wife, no objection to lady employed; object matrimony." To attract men, the other ad read: "Wealthy young widow, unencumbered, fine appearance, genial and generous, seeks husband and adviser."

Those who responded were sent a photograph—the same woman to all the men and the same man to all the women—and a full description of their possible paramour. The respondents were solicited for $5 so that the agency could set up a meeting "near your locality" and for membership in the marriage bureau.

Hundreds of men and women sent their money for the initiation fee. None of the new members found mates, because there was no wealthy manufacturer or wealthy young widow. District Court judges and juries ruled against the owners of these firms. "The object of the bureau was not honestly to bring young men and women into communication with each other, that they might have an opportunity of determining whether they suited one another for the purposes of marriage. The sole object was to get the five dollar membership fee," wrote the Court of Appeals, which upheld the convictions.

IN 1899, GROSSCUP WAS ELEVATED to the Seventh Circuit Court of Appeals by President William McKinley—the former Ohio congressman who ran against Grosscup when he suddenly withdrew from the race. Christian C. Kohlsaat was nominated later that year by McKinley to replace Grosscup and serve as the fourth judge for the Northern District of Illinois.

Kohlsaat was the first district judge born in Illinois, in the tiny downstate town of Albion. He came to Chicago in 1867, at age twenty-three, to work as a law reporter for the *Chicago Evening Journal.* He read law and was admitted to the bar in September of that year.

"In 1868 he accepted a position in the county clerk's office, where he wrote all the records of the Cook County court, took the minutes, swore the juries and witnesses, etc., and in fact did all the work that it now requires eight or nine men to perform, even with the assistance of blank records, which were not in use at the time," wrote John J. Flinn in his *Hand-Book of Chicago Biography.* "The work of the county court increased, according to Judge Kohlsaat's estimate, about 2,500 percent."

From there, Kohlsaat worked as a clerk for the Illinois legislature, and then began the practice of law. In 1890, he became a Cook County probate judge and gained political support when his brother, Herman—who had built a huge bakery and lunchroom business—bought control of the *Chicago Inter Ocean* newspaper in 1891. Herman, who served as publisher and manager of the influential paper, became a confidant of President McKinley and pushed for the nomination of his brother to the federal bench. Christian received his commission at age fifty-five and served until 1905, when he, too, was appointed to the Court of Appeals. Kohlsaat was the last Northern District judge to serve alone.

Chicago grew rapidly after the fire. Its population almost doubled during the 1870s and again during the 1880s and 1890s. By 1900, the city had 1.7 million residents. Congress made several changes around the turn of the century that indirectly affected the Northern Illinois District. In 1893, the federal government created the Court of Appeals system, and eventually phased out the old Circuit Court system, making the District Courts the only federal trial courts in America. Congress provided an additional judge in the Northern District in 1904 and the following year created a new Eastern District. The reshaped Northern District consisted of eighteen counties, as it does today. Cases in the western part of the district were heard in Freeport, where a deputy and a marshal were appointed and a judge sat occasionally. The vast majority of cases continued to be heard in Chicago.

Solomon Hicks Bethea and Kenesaw Mountain Landis both received their commissions as Northern District judges on March 18, 1905. Bethea was nominated by President Theodore Roosevelt to fill the district seat vacated by Kohlsaat. Landis was nominated by Roosevelt to serve in the district's new second judgeship.

Bethea, fourteen years older than Landis, was considered the District Court's first senior judge. He was the first U.S. attorney elevated to the court. Born near Dixon, Illinois, in Lee County, in 1852, he read law in 1876 and maintained a country law practice in Dixon. He was active in politics, serving as the mayor of Dixon and as a member of the state House. While serving in the Illinois legislature, Bethea befriended Theodore Roosevelt, then in the New York legislature.

"Mr. Roosevelt, it will be remembered, introduced in the New York legislature one of the earliest state civil service bills, and Mr. Bethea, after some correspondence with Mr. Roosevelt, introduced in the legislature of Illinois the same bill, which was the first measure ever offered in this state providing for civil service," wrote author C. LeRoy Brown. "This was the beginning of a long and close friendship between Mr. Roosevelt and Mr. Bethea."

Bethea was appointed U.S. attorney for the Northern District of Illinois by President McKinley in 1899.

"National attention was challenged by the vigor and efficiency of Mr. Bethea's administration of the district attorney's office," Brown wrote. "He brought the celebrated equity case of *United States v. Swift & Company* and obtained the so-called 'Beef Trust' injunction. He instituted numerous prosecutions of railroads for violation of the interstate commerce laws of the United States, and these prosecutions, though quietly conducted were almost uniformly successful."

The government charged three large Chicago meat packers—Swift, Armour, and Morris—with creating a monopoly when they formed the National Packing Company in 1902. Bethea's case, which charged the companies with trying to take control of packing operations in Kansas City,

Omaha, and East St. Louis, was upheld all the way to the U.S. Supreme Court. But the National Packing Company was not disbanded, and the antitrust battle with the meat packers, based in the South Side stockyards, continued for a decade in District Court.

Bethea became one of Teddy Roosevelt's closest advisers in 1901, when Roosevelt took over as president following McKinley's assassination. Bethea was a natural choice for the seat vacated by Kohlsaat in 1905.

In a memorial for Bethea, Brown hinted at problems Bethea faced on the bench during his four years as a district judge. "Judge Bethea had simple, old-fashioned conceptions of public duty and he was sometimes rather unbending in the carrying out of such conceptions," Brown wrote. "But the bar respected his never failing purpose to act only as the law authorized him to act."

These were particularly difficult years for the District Court judge, ones marked with illness. "The strength and values of Judge Bethea's mental qualities was somewhat obscured by a peculiar diffidence of expression and manner," Brown wrote. "His perception and understanding of the principles of the relationship between the government and the rights of individuals were in advance of the times, and he contributed largely to the national movement to bring the great commercial interests of the country into subordination to the law."

Bethea, considered the court's first senior judge, died in 1909 at age fifty-seven, about six months after he retired due to ill health. The judge bequeathed more than $100,000 to a public hospital that he had helped establish in his hometown of Dixon. The Katherine Shaw Bethea Hospital, named for his wife, survives today.

Landis was the opposite of Bethea. "Though no one ever demanded greater respect for 'the Court' from arguing attorneys, witnesses and court attendants than Landis, some other judges threw up their hands in holy horror," wrote J. G. Taylor Spink in his 1945 biography of Landis. "They accused him of violating the dignity of the judiciary, and some of his most severe critics called him a buffoon, a mountebank, and a man who would do anything to make the front page."

Landis was the son of a Union army surgeon whose leg was amputated during the 1864 battle of Kennesaw Mountain in Georgia. The son was born in 1866, the sixth of seven children of Dr. Abraham and Mary Landis. "Somewhere along the route from Georgia to Ohio, Dr. Landis dropped a letter out of Kennesaw," Spink wrote.

The five Landis boys became distinguished. Walter Landis was a newspaperman and was appointed by Theodore Roosevelt as the first postmaster of Puerto Rico. John Landis became the health commissioner of Cincinnati. Charles and Frederick Landis were both elected to Congress from Indiana.

Kenesaw moved to Chicago and read law in 1891. Becoming a lawyer during those days did not require much effort, Landis later wrote. "All a man needed was to prove that he was twenty-one and had a good moral character." Landis graduated from the Union Law School, which later became part of Northwestern University, and was admitted to the Illinois bar that year.

"He was then just another Hoosier lawyer, in the big town sprawled along the shores of Lake Michigan, determined to make good, but fellow attorneys and the judges before whom he practiced soon learned he was different," wrote Spink. "He wasn't just another country lawyer with hayseed in his hair. He was shrewd, determined, and fearless. If Landis had any trait which stood out more than his inherent honesty it was his absolute fearlessness. Names and reputations meant absolutely nothing to him. He barked and fumed; he appealed to the court to throw out points developed by learned and experienced rivals, and several times just escaped from being held in contempt of court."

In 1893, Landis moved to Washington to help Walter Q. Gresham, the former Seventh Circuit Court judge, after Gresham's appointment by President Grover Cleveland as secretary of state. Gresham, a family friend, asked Landis to serve as his personal secretary. Landis soon made his mark, attending cabinet meetings when Gresham took sick and attracting the attention of Cleveland. Landis stayed until Gresham's death in 1895 but then left the Cleveland administration. Landis later said the president's only fault was that he was a Democrat. Back in Chicago, Landis opened a private law office and became active in Republican politics, running the unsuccessful campaign of Frank O. Lowden for governor.

In 1905, Landis took Room 627 of the Federal Courthouse. "Landis's courtroom was an equally imposing two-story mahogany and marble chamber, festooned with polished brass," wrote Landis biographer David Pietrusza. "On one side wall was a mural of King John at Runnymede, conceding to his barons the Magna Carta. Opposite it was Moses returning from Mount Sinai and about to smash the tablets of the Ten Commandments. Such a chamber was just the spot for Landis's sense of the theatrical. In it he would hold court for nearly the next decade and a half."

On the bench, Landis was an enigma, full of humanity and humiliation. "None of us knows what path Landis will choose and some of us don't recognize it after he has chosen it," wrote attorney Levy Mayer. "Don't make book on him following the law, no matter how clearly it seems written. He calls them as his conscience sees them."

Sometimes Landis was surprisingly lenient. After sentencing a man to Leavenworth Penitentiary, the judge noticed that the new convict was not dressed for the cold of winter. "Here, bailiff, fetch my overcoat and give it to this man," Landis said. Years later, he tossed out charges against a boy accused of stealing $750,000 in Liberty Bonds during World War I. "I am going to set this boy free," Landis declared. "I wish I had the power to jail the men who sent him out with $750,000 in bonds."

The press loved his rejoinders—filled with humor.

One elderly defendant, given a five-year sentence, pleaded with Landis, "But, your honor; I'll be dead long before that. I'm a sick man, and I can't do five years."

"Well, you can try; can't you?"

As Spink noted, "Quite often Landis would take a bored, or pained, look on the bench, or screw up his nose as though he were smelling something odoriferous."

Perhaps the best description of Landis as a judge was written by Jack Lait of the *New York Daily Mirror* following Landis's death in 1944. Lait looked back at his years as a cub reporter in the Federal Building—not with nostalgia.

"Landis was an irascible, short-tempered, tyrannical despot," Lait wrote. "His manner of handling witnesses, lawyers—and reporters—was more arbitrary than the behavior of any jurist I have ever seen before or since. He resented what we wrote: he resented what we did, and probably what we wore. He regarded his courtroom as his personal private preserve and even extended his autocracy to the corridors beyond."

Landis's tyrannical power extended beyond his Federal Building courtroom. Lait recalled watching the judge send a federal marshal out to round up the wife, children, and minister of a difficult witness. Lait wrote of Landis:

He did not subpoena them, mind you. What he said to them he kept off the record. They stood there, terrorized, in tears—simple people who had probably never been in a courtroom before—while he harangued them and the witness.

I have seen him order a marshal to take a witness, who would not testify as Landis wanted him to, and order the marshal: "Hold him in my chambers while he thinks it over." No order of arrest, mind you. That would have been illegal. But confinement—sometimes for hours, with no charge, no commitment. That also did not go on the record. And what ordinary witness would defy a United States judge and court officer, and physically refuse, or resist them? They took it.

I have heard him abuse attorneys and threaten them with contempt because they insisted on getting into the record prejudicial outbursts from the bench which Landis had ordered the court stenographers to delete.

On the other hand, I saw him acquit a young fellow who had confessed that he rifled hundreds of letters, stole money orders and checks, and threw the letters and envelopes into a sewer. This is a penitentiary offense. But Landis declared him not guilty—on the ground that the government paid the boy too little and the temptation was too great. This mercy was as illegal as his severities. But that was Landis.

In 1906, Landis was called to arbitrate a dispute within the Christian Catholic Church, a religious community founded by John Alexander Dowie. Dowie was an astute evangelist, specializing in turning the persecution directed against him to his advantage. Many people were drawn to the fundamentalist minister and to his belief in the power of prayer. Dowie stood flatly opposed to all science, from medical healing to the idea that the Earth is round. After the turn of the century, Dowie created the City of Zion, north of Chicago along Lake Michigan. Thousands of faithful moved there to hear Dowie speak in the huge Zion Tabernacle and join the community. But soon after he created the town, Dowie began to lose support. He declared he was the prophet Elijah and became strangely withdrawn. Financial problems surrounded him and in 1905 he suffered a stroke. When Dowie's religious opponents led a coup, Dowie came to District Court to fight the overthrow.

Landis opposed much of what Dowie and his opponents stood for, especially an oath that required Dowieites to follow his orders above family and government. Landis ruled against those who wanted to overthrow Dowie, but suggested that the church change its policies. He appointed a businessman to serve as receiver for the bankrupt church, and ordered that the church hold elections for a new leader.

"The crowd, composed mainly of Dowieites, gasped at Landis's blasphemy," wrote Pietrusza. "An uproar arose. Women cried out. Landis gaveled furiously and threatened to clear the courtroom if order was not restored." Eventually, Landis's legal solution to the church's theological dispute was followed to the letter.

IN 1907, LANDIS made a name for himself as one of the nation's most prominent district court judges when he fined Standard Oil $29,240,000 for violating antitrust laws.

The Sherman Antitrust Act of 1890 was the outgrowth of tremendous industrial development in the United States after the Civil War. By the late 1800s, many Americans grew suspicious of huge corporations, holding companies, and trusts such as the American Cotton Oil Trust, National Linseed Oil Trust, and Distillers' Trust. Politicians railed against the concentration of wealth, and muckraking journalists wrote about how trusts took advantage of workers, stripped natural resources, and competed unfairly.

After the turn of the twentieth century, Theodore Roosevelt responded to the antimonopoly sentiment by promising to go after the trusts in court. The Standard Oil Trust, a huge combine of oil companies, was an ideal target because it was one of the nation's largest and was the subject of a series of articles by journalist Ida M. Tarbell in *McClure's Magazine.* The U.S. attorney general accused Standard Oil of violating the Elkins Act, a law that banned rebates on large freight shipments. In 1905, two Chicago grand juries returned ten indictments against Standard Oil of Indiana. It was charged with receiving illegal concessions from railroads for shipping oil from refining plants to shipping centers.

Testimony at the 1907 trial clearly showed that between 1903 and 1905 Standard paid a rate of six cents per hundred pounds of oil shipped by railroad, far lower than the posted rate of eighteen cents per hundred pounds. A jury found Standard guilty of violating the Elkins Act, and Landis began figuring out the damages. When the judge submitted a list of questions to Standard attorneys to help him determine the fine, a defense attorney reportedly replied, "I'll see you in hell first." The attorney's answer was greeted by subpoenas of top Standard officials, including President John D. Rockefeller.

After a highly publicized search for Rockefeller, he was finally slapped with a subpoena on the front porch of his son-in-law's estate outside Pittsfield, Massachusetts.

Rockefeller came to Chicago the following day and met with his attorneys

John D. Rockefeller was the star witness in the government's attempt to fine Standard Oil for antitrust violations. Rockefeller declared he would never pay a cent and was correct.

NATIONAL ARCHIVES

to ask them if he should testify. Author Paul H. Giddens, in his Standard Oil
history, described the meeting, held in a Loop bank building. One by one
the lawyers told Rockefeller to avoid the confrontation and refuse the subpoena. The company's newest lawyer, Robert W. Stewart, did not respond.

Rockefeller nudged him, and Stewart finally replied: "Mr. Rockefeller, in
view of the opinion rendered by the distinguished legal talent present, I hes-
itate to express an opinion."

"I'm paying you to give me your opinion," Rockefeller demanded.

"Mr. Rockefeller, you are no different from any other citizen before the
law, and if I were you, I would appear."

The next day, Rockefeller—given immunity to testify—appeared at the
crowded courthouse. Twenty Chicago policemen used nightsticks to make a
path for the aging entrepreneur. It was high drama, until Rockefeller actually testified. Landis asked Rockefeller nineteen questions, but Rockefeller
revealed little. He told the judge that he had not managed the company for
years and knew little about its present operation.

Landis delivered his decision on August 3 to a filled, but quiet, courtroom.

"From the moment that he began reading an almost breathless silence
prevailed," Giddens wrote. "Landis reviewed the evidence presented, administered a scathing rebuke to Standard for its methods, expressed his belief that the company was no better than a common thief, held the contentions of the defendant weak at every point, emphasized the fact that guilt
had been clearly proven, pointed out that the nominal defendant was Standard of Indiana, a million-dollar corporation, and the real defendant was
Standard of New Jersey, a billion-dollar corporation, and ended by levying
an unprecedented fine of $29,240,000."

Standard, indicted on 1,462 counts of accepting kickbacks from the Chicago and Alton Railroad, was fined $20,000 for each car that received a re-
bate. The $20,000 figure was the maximum penalty allowed by law, and the
total added up to the $29 million figure.

Landis, called by one newspaper the "Man Who Came at Last," was the
toast of the nation for standing up to the giant trust. The *Chicago Tribune*
was pleased, writing in an editorial on August 4, "No judicial act will be
more popular than that of Judge Landis yesterday in fining the Standard Oil
Company. There is no part of the United States where that corporation is
not known and detested."

Rockefeller was told of the huge fine while playing golf in Cleveland. According to his biographer, Rockefeller read a note handed him by a messenger, put it into his pocket and said, "Well, gentlemen, shall we proceed." He ended up shooting a fifty-three on nine holes, his lowest score ever. Later he said, "Judge Landis will be dead a long time before this fine is paid."

Rockefeller was correct.

The Seventh Circuit Court of Appeals overruled Landis on July 22, 1908, and remanded the case for another trial. Judge Peter Grosscup, who wrote the majority opinion, called Landis "arbitrary" and criticized him for three major mistakes in the case. Grosscup said that Landis should have admitted the testimony of Standard's traffic manager, who said the company did not know that it was accepting an unlawful rate. Landis also erred in figuring the number of offenses. The fine, Grosscup wrote, should be based on the number of shipments, not on the number of tank cars. Finally, Grosscup wrote, Landis should not have fined Standard of Indiana for an amount more than its worth. To expect Standard of New Jersey, its holding company, to pay was absurd because the company had not even been named in the indictment.

"How can a sentence such as the trial court imposed, based upon reasoning such as the trial court gave, be a sound sentence?" wrote Grosscup. "Can a court without abuse of judicial discretion wipe out all the property of the defendant before the court, and all the assets to which its creditors look, in an effort to reach and punish a party that is not before the court—a party that has not been convicted, has not been tried, has not been indicted even?"

Teddy Roosevelt bristled at the appellate court's rejection of Landis's ruling. "It is an outrage that a creature like Grosscup should be permitted to sit on the bench," the president wrote.

The Supreme Court decided not to hear the case in 1909. *United States v. Standard Oil (Indiana)* returned to the District Court for a new trial. Both Landis and Bethea refused to hear the case. Bethea told the *Chicago Tribune* "he did not want to get mixed up in it." District Court Judge A. B. Anderson, of Indiana, took on the case and quickly ruled the government had failed to prove that a fixed rate on the railroad line existed. The judge directed the jury to come in with a not guilty verdict. Standard Oil did not pay a cent.

After Anderson's decision, reporters asked Landis for his response.

"I finished my part in the Standard Oil case some months ago and just now I am deeply interested in the hearing of a suit brought by a boy who lost four fingers in an accident," the judge said. "I also am interested in knowing who took a package of tobacco from my chambers yesterday, but as for Standard Oil I can only repeat I have nothing to say."

Although Landis and the government never recovered money from Standard Oil, the company was broken up by the Supreme Court in 1911. The breakup affected Rockefeller in the pocketbook; he made millions. But perhaps Landis felt vindicated.

As William Howard Taft later wrote: "The Standard Oil Company was proceeded against, not only because it had combined into itself various corporate entities, but because it had resorted to unfair practices, such as rebates, preferences, control of pipe-lines, local price-cutting, espionage, operation of bogus independent companies, and a great variety of other unfair and illegal acts."

GEORGE A. CARPENTER was nominated by President Taft in 1909 to fill Bethea's seat and was sworn in the following year. Carpenter, the first District Court judge born in Chicago, received his bachelor's degree and law degree from Harvard University. He served as a Cook County Circuit Court judge for five years before his appointment to the federal bench. He was the dark horse in a large group of candidates for the post.

"In naming Judge Carpenter, President Taft has demonstrated that he meant what he said when he announced that he intended to make personally all selections for appointments to the federal bench," one newspaper wrote. "He gave notice some months ago that the senators of a state would be consulted with reference to the distribution of ordinary appointments, but that he himself would determine who should serve on the bench. It was doubted that the president would be able to ignore the politicians, but now it is admitted that he is carrying out his cherished policy to the letter. In the case of Judge Carpenter, he not only arrived at his decision to nominate him independently of the recommendations of his advisers, but he passed over all candidates proposed by the state's representatives in Congress."

The city's newspapers endorsed the surprise choice.

"This man who is to become a federal judge is a native of Chicago, and has just turned to his forty-second year," the *Chicago Evening Post* reported. "He is six feet perpendicularly, with horizontal and curved lines in proportion—built like an athlete. He has the happy faculty of disposing of large quantities of work easily and without fatigue, and those who know him well

say he generally leaves the courtroom at the end of the day as fresh and vigorous as when he entered it in the morning."

Carpenter's first major case was a 1911 antitrust lawsuit against the city's
largest meat packers. The case had been snaking its way through the District
Court in different forms for almost a decade.

Chicago was the ideal center of the nation's meat-packing industry because it was at the hub of the nation's railroads. By 1849, the city was home
to some 185 slaughter and meat-packing businesses. Fifty years later, that
number was 882 businesses. But Chicago's largest packing houses—firms
such as Armour and Company and Swift and Company—dominated the
industry. Their owners were determined to keep their competitive advantage.

The Sherman Antitrust Act was passed to penalize entrepreneurs who
tried to monopolize trade or commerce. In 1910, a grand jury indicted ten
Chicago packers. They went on trial before Judge Carpenter in late 1911. An
all-star team was assembled to prosecute the packers, including Assistant
U.S. Attorney James H. Wilkerson, who had helped prosecute Standard Oil;
W. S. Kenyon, a U.S. senator from Iowa, and Pierce Butler, who went on to
become a Supreme Court justice.

Jury selection took two weeks. The trial lasted more than three months.

Witnesses described how top officials from the large packing houses worked closely together and met weekly. The packers conspired to create a grand plan to create a worldwide combine.

"There was testimony explanatory of the prices fixed for beef and other packing products; and it was shown that the various branch managers of the various packing corporations were obliged to telegraph daily their respective sales to the offices of the National Packing Company," Edgar Lee Masters wrote in his biography of Levy Mayer, the packers' attorney. "The system of bookkeeping of the various packing corporations and of the National Packing Company was brought out before the jury fully and in detail. There was testimony to the effect that Swift & Company, Morris & Company, Armour & Company and the National Packing Company controlled the killing and dressed-beef industry in the country."

The *Chicago Times* described a typical day in the long trial:

Unnoticed, the jury has filed into its seats at the side of the room. The jurymen are evidently impressed with the importance and the dignity of the duty imposed on them. They are all dressed up. At the start they sit in more or less constrained and awkward attitudes. On these twelve rests the decision as to whether or not the Beef Kings go to jail or be fined. One has been a grocer all

Edward Swift, owner of Swift and Company, watches the trial of the Beef Trust in November 1911. The packers withstood ten years of federal investigations and were found not guilty of violating Sherman antitrust laws. **CHICAGO DAILY NEWS COLLECTION/ CHICAGO HISTORICAL SOCIETY**

his life in a tiny hamlet of fifty people; three are farmers; there is a carpenter, an insurance solicitor, a grocer's clerk, a millwright, a drug salesman, a telephone inspector, and a baker. The most prominent is president of a merchant tailoring company.

The joint wealth of the panel is estimated at perhaps $100,000. J. Ogden Armour alone is credited with a fortune of $100 million. Whatever the outcome of the trial, each of the jurymen will have a subject of conversation for the rest of his life.

The fat bailiff stands up in his brass buttons, and everybody in the courtroom rises with him. "Hear ye! Hear ye!" he intones. Out from his chambers onto the broad platform behind the bench walks Judge Carpenter, a tall, well built man in his early forties, with a smooth-shaven, rather stern face, his eyes looking out through gold-rimmed spectacles. He bows the bar, the defendants, and the spectators to their chairs, then seats himself, leans forward to the bench and rests his chin on his hand, his fingers partly concealing his mouth.

Judge Carpenter is a Harvard man, who is just ending his second year on the Federal bench. He had before that some years of experience as a judge of the State courts. Judge Kenesaw Mountain Landis, his neighbor, transferred the trial of the beef packers to his court across the rotunda, famous for the fine of $29 million he imposed on the Standard Oil Company.

As Judge Carpenter seats himself the jurymen settle back patiently into their chairs. Then, just as Levy Mayer rises to address the court, the swinging doors open and a small man, carrying his black coat over his arm, comes in and slips quietly across the room. There is nothing about him to attract attention but as he nears "Packers' Row" three or four men rise to offer him a chair. Plainly this is a personage of importance who deserves a closer inspection. He is a short, rather slender man, nearing fifty years in age. His brown hair begins to grow thin, his shoulders are a bit stooped. He whispers behind his hand to a man who leans forward eagerly to listen. It is J. Ogden Armour.

After the government's three-month presentation, attorney Mayer surprised everyone in court by not disputing the evidence. He simply argued that the testimony did not show intent beyond legitimate cooperation.

"These defendants have been the object of political, legislative, communistic, and socialistic attacks," he told the court. "When all suspicion and guesswork are eliminated, there is no proof that these defendants purposely and consciously violated the antitrust statute. And, without the evidence, is the court going to suspect these defendants made the prices at which beef was to be sold, or restricted the shipments?

"There has been evidence of an exchange of information among two or three of the defendants. But where is the criminality of this? If the commerce of the country is to be regulated by indictment and merchants are to be threatened by indictment because they have done what is shown to have been done here, I think it is time the business men of the country should know it. These defendants met weekly, according to the evidence, in the offices of the National Packing Company, and discussed their business. They were directors of that company, and surely every man has the legal right to talk about his own business. The exchange of margins, similarly tested cost methods and weekly meetings are not criminal acts and the government cannot hope to convict these men for violating the Sherman law for doing these things."

Mayer, in a bold move, called no witnesses. In March 1912, the jury ruled that the packers had not formed a monopoly to restrain trade. Jurors told reporters at the end of the trial they decided that the price of meat was being determined by supply and demand and not at the packers' meetings. Ten years of prosecution were over.

Carpenter distinguished himself in the meat packers case. But history does not look as kindly on him for his handling of the Jack Johnson case.

Johnson, the first African American heavyweight boxing champion of the world, was convicted in 1913 of violating the White Slave Traffic Act, also known as the Mann Act. Johnson was indicted in 1910, a few months after the act was put into effect. He was charged with a felony for "unlawfully and knowingly causing to be transported in interstate commerce from Pittsburgh, Pennsylvania, to Chicago, Illinois, a certain girl for the purpose of debauchery." Many believe that the charges were trumped up against Johnson to punish him for keeping company with white women.

The trial of John Arthur "Jack" Johnson was spectacular. In the opening statement, Assistant U.S. Attorney Harry A. Parkin hinted at what was to follow:

May it please the court, and gentlemen of the jury: Just a word in outlining what we expect to prove in this case. In the first place, we expect to prove by competent evidence, beyond any reasonable doubt, each and every count of the indictment. It will appear in this case that the defendant Johnson, from the time that he began to engage in pugilistic encounters, had a desire to have company upon his trips across the country. We expect to show that the girl mentioned in the indictment was taken from Pittsburgh to Chicago on October 16, 1910, that being the specific definite charge of interstate traffic in women upon which he is brought. . . .

It will appear in connection with that girl that that was not the only trip in interstate commerce which the defendant Johnson took. Beginning in the year 1909, it will appear from the evidence that he took the girl to New York, Boston, Pittsburgh, Indianapolis, Toronto, Montreal, and a number of other cities, finally ending up at Oakland, California, at the time he had the Ketchel and the Kaufman fights. Subsequent to that, and also subsequent to the time he had the fight at Reno, Nevada, it will appear that he again got into communication with this girl, and required her to accompany him to other places, to-wit, Atlantic City, Boston, back to Pittsburgh, Chicago, and other cities in the United States. So that as we go along there will be interwoven with the evidence on the main charge a great mass of detail respecting the conduct of the defendant with this and other women.

It will appear, for instance, that upon one occasion in one city the defendant had three different white women, each of whom he was entertaining and having sexual intercourse with at the same time while he was exhibiting himself in that city. It will appear that he took these three women from various cities across the country at the same time, sometimes in the same train. Now, I just say this so that you will be prepared, as this comes out, to anticipate it; and I want also to give it to you so that you will not lose sight of the main issue in the great mass of elaborating details in connection with it.

Parkin told the jurors that they must decide whether Johnson transported Belle Schreiber for immoral purposes—to set her up as a prostitute and have sexual intercourse with her. "Another immoral purpose," Parkin said, "is one which is too obscene to mention, almost, to the jury trying the case, the purpose being for the defendant to compel these women to commit the crime against nature upon his body. We will demonstrate that beyond any reasonable doubt to you gentlemen before the close of this case."

As it turned out, Belle Schreiber, the prosecution's main witness, freely admitted she was a "sporting woman." She had been an "inmate" of Chicago's most lavish house of prostitution, the Everleigh Club, in 1909 when she met Johnson. For years, she testified she had met Johnson in towns around America and they had had "immoral sexual relations."

Schreiber told the jury that Johnson sent a telegram to her in Pittsburgh in 1910 to come to Chicago, sent her $75 for train fare, and paid for the rent and furniture she needed to set up an apartment at the Ridgewood, 2730 South Wabash. It was disputed at the trial whether the seventy-unit Ridgewood was occupied only by sporting women and call girls. The manager denied the charge, but one of the women residents testified, "I don't think you could make a mistake by ringing a bell."

Johnson's relationship with Schreiber changed in 1911 when the boxer married another woman, Etta Duryea.

Defense attorney Benjamin Bachrach asked Schreiber on the stand: "I see a picture that was introduced in evidence, and it has written on there, 'To my little sweetheart, Belle, from Papa Jack, with good luck.' Were you his little sweetheart?"

"I suppose I was."

"Were you in love with him?"

"I don't know."

"What?"

Jack Johnson, the first African American heavyweight champion, was convicted of violating the Mann Act. The indictment, he later wrote, was a "frame-up." **DAVE ANDELBERG/*CHICAGO DAILY NEWS***

"I don't know."

"Don't you know now? Did you think you were then?"

"I don't know what love is."

When Johnson took the stand, he acknowledged that he had an affair with Schreiber and that they had sexual relations. "Belle and I were very friendly," he said. "I gave her money and everything else." Johnson said he was not aware of the White Slave Traffic Act in 1910, and he denied he arranged for her transportation. He testified that Schreiber sent a telegram to him from Pittsburgh saying that she was sick and needed $75. He said he sent her money but did not intend for it to be used for travel to Chicago.

Schreiber contacted him when she got to Chicago, Johnson said.

"When I met her at the Hotel Vendome she told me that her sister was going to be sick, that she was pregnant, and that she wanted a place for her mother and her sister, and she asked me would I furnish a flat for her," Johnson testified. "I said certainly, I will do anything to make you happy."

The prosecutor attempted to humiliate Johnson by making him detail his sexual liaisons. The lawyer asked the boxer if he had sexual relations with Schreiber in every town where they were together. "I don't remember, I never kept tab," Johnson replied. "Well, did you skip any?" Parkin asked. "Oh, certainly, everybody skips." And later, Parkin asked Johnson if he had sexual intercourse with a woman after the 1909 Kaufman title fight. "I did not," replied Johnson. "After a man has a fight, he is not feeling like that." The prosecutor accused Johnson of beating his wife as well as Belle and another woman.

When Johnson told the court that he had gone to Washington Park Hospital to visit his wife, Parkin asked, "What was the cause of her sickness?"

"I don't know."

"As a matter of fact that was a sickness caused by blows from your hands, wasn't it?"

Johnson answered no.

"Well, was it caused by blow or blows from your hand?"

"No, no."

"Was it not caused by blows received by Etta Duryea, in Pekin Theater here in Chicago at your hands?"

"No."

"Did you carry her out or have her carried out and put in the automobile and taken to the Washington Park Hospital after you had beaten her up?"

"No, no and I will take an oath on it. No."

The boxer was later asked by Parkin, "Now, you say you were not keeping up with the fast women. You had as many as three at a time, in your travels with you, didn't you?

"No, sir."

"Didn't you have three in Philadelphia?"

"No."

"Didn't you have Hattie and Etta and Belle there at the same time?"

"No."

Despite allowing much extraneous evidence, Carpenter's instructions to the all-white jury were evenhanded.

"Gentlemen of the jury, you must realize, and I shall charge you, that a colored man in the courts of this country has equal rights with a white man," the judge said. "He is entitled to the same kind of a trial and the same laws protect him, and you must return the same kind of verdict in this case as you would render to a man of your own color were he accused as is the defendant."

He told the jurors they should find Johnson guilty only if they believe that he transported Schreiber "for the purpose of having her engage in prostitution or suffer relations with him sexually." Johnson said his intent to send money to Schreiber was good; the government said his intent was evil, Carpenter summarized.

"The law," he said, "does not apply solely to innocent girls. It is quite as much an offense against the Mann Act to transport a hardened, lost prostitute as it would be to transport a young girl, a virgin."

A "debauchery" charge was thrown out before the jury considered the case. Even though Parkin promised the jury they would hear evidence of "crimes against nature," they were never mentioned, so that charge was dropped, too.

Still, the jury convicted Johnson. Carpenter sentenced him to one year and one day in prison and fined him $1,000. Johnson, in his 1927 autobiography, declared that the case was unfounded. "It was a rank frame-up," he wrote. Johnson snuck away from Chicago while free pending appeal in July 1913 by purchasing a private railroad car for the Foster Giants baseball team and skipping town with the ballplayers. He escaped to Canada, leaving the United States because he considered himself innocent. "I am not one to defeat the ends of justice," he wrote. "Had I been guilty of the charge which was hung over me, I would have taken my medicine and said no more about it, but I was stung by the injustice of the whole proceedings and hurt to the quick to think that the prejudice of my fellow men, and of my own country-men at that, could be so warped and so cruel."

Johnson fled to Europe but eventually returned to the United States in 1920. He was arrested and served his sentence at Leavenworth.

CONSIDERING THE FACT that Chicago was once a Native American out-post, surprisingly few cases involving Native Americans have been filed in the District Court in Chicago. The most intriguing case, handled by Car-penter, was a 1912 lawsuit in which the heirs of Native Americans argued that the land created by landfill in Lake Michigan belonged to them.

The Potawatomi, Chippewa, and Ottawa argued that an 1816 Indian treaty ceded land only ten miles north and ten miles south of the mouth of the Chicago River as determined by a published survey. They claimed the tribes never ceded or sold their interests or rights to uplands, submerged lands, and lakes and waters east of the survey area, such as the new Lake Michigan property. Attorneys for the railroads that had created the landfill argued that the tribal rights to occupy the land had been surrendered long ago. The case dragged on for years, until the tribes gave up in 1919. The Na-tive Americans were charged with costs.

This was not the first time that property once submerged under Lake Michigan was the subject of a lawsuit. In 1869, the state legislature passed the Lake Front Act, which gave the Illinois Central Railroad title to one thousand acres of land beneath the lake between the lakeshore and the rail-road's wooden trestle. After the area was filled with debris from the Chicago Fire, legislators passed a law to take back the new land. Illinois Central attor-neys contested the law in District Court and eventually took the case to the U.S. Supreme Court. The justices decided that the property should no longer belong to the railroad.

IN ANOTHER HIGH-PROFILE CASE, Judge Kenesaw Mountain Landis gained attention by his inaction rather than by what he did.

Landis's stand may have saved baseball's American and National Leagues. In 1915, the fledgling Federal League charged Organized Baseball with vio-lating Sherman antitrust laws. The Federal League was an upstart organiza-tion of professional ballplayers set up to rival the established major leagues.

Attorneys for the Federals filed a lawsuit in District Court to thwart attempts by major league owners to stop big league players from playing in the new league.

Landis, at first, appeared to be working swiftly. He called the case almost immediately. His January hearings were filled with stars such as pitcher Mordecai "Three-Finger" Brown and Joe Tinker, of the famous Tinker-to-Evers-to-Chance double play combination.

Both men, former Cubs who had jumped to the new league, testified with others about the tyranny of baseball's reserve clause, which kept players tied to a team, and the mistreatment of ballplayers by major league owners. It appeared that trustbuster Landis would have little choice but to come down hard against the major leagues and break up the closed-league system. But Landis loved baseball, and he made it clear that he would not be easily moved to rule against the status quo. "Both sides must understand that any blows at the thing called baseball would be regarded by this court as a blow to a national institution," he said.

Landis held off a decision for months—through spring training, the baseball season and much of the off-season. Finally, the Federal League owners and major league owners came to terms on their own in December. Both leagues feared Landis's decision. The Federals disbanded, but two owners were allowed to purchase major league teams. Federal League ballplayers were sold back to the majors and the lawsuit was dropped.

Labor leader William D. "Big Bill" Haywood and members of the Industrial Workers of the World faced trial for conspiring to work against the war effort. Haywood is shown in District Court on September 7, 1917, before his 1918 trial. *CHICAGO DAILY NEWS*

LANDIS SAID HE CAME CLOSE to leaving the bench in 1917 but decided to stay on after the United States's entry into World War I because he was convinced that his job as a District Court judge helped the war effort. He became a major foe of all things German and a virulent enemy of any political or social movement that threatened the war effort. In one fiery wartime speech Landis demanded that Kaiser Wilhelm II, his six sons, and five thousand German militarists be "lined up against a wall and shot down in justice to the world and to Germany." His son, Reed, was a flying "ace" in the Great War, having downed twelve German aircraft in aerial combat.

In 1918, Landis went after organized labor when William D. "Big Bill" Haywood, secretary of the Industrial Workers of the World, and a hundred colleagues were brought into his court.

The IWW, or Wobblies, was an idealistic combination of about forty workers groups known as the One Big Union. Wobblies were radical. In their war against capitalism, they had little use or interest in patriotism or the Great War after the United States entered the conflict on April 6, 1917. "Keep a cool head; do not talk," Haywood wrote a colleague. "A good many feel as you do but the world war is of small importance compared to the great class war."

Americans feared the radicals, and accused them of calling strikes to hinder the war effort. One Arizona senator said that IWW stood for "Imperial Wilhelm's Warriors." The Wobblies became a prime target for the government, determined to put an end to dissent during the war. In September 1917, federal agents raided forty-eight IWW halls and offices around the country, gathering five tons of paperwork that the government asserted showed proof of a conspiracy against the war effort. Three weeks later, 165 Wobblies were indicted by a federal grand jury in Chicago and charged with conspiring to work against the war. Although particularly strong in the West, the national headquarters of the Wobblies was in Chicago, so the Northern District of Illinois was chosen to try 101 Wobblies. At the time, it was the largest and longest criminal trial in U.S. history.

The proceedings began in April 1918 and lasted for five months. The trial attracted many radicals, including Eugene Debs, Mary Harris "Mother" Jones, and writer John Reed, who would decades later be memorialized in the movie *Reds*.

Author Reed saw this as a heroic moment, a time when the workers stood united. "As for the prisoners, I doubt if ever in history there has been a sight just like them," Reed wrote. "One hundred and one lumberjacks, harvest hands, miners, editors . . . who believe the wealth of the world belongs to him who creates it . . . the outdoor men, hard-rock blasters, tree-fellers, wheat-binders, longshoremen, the boys who do the strong work of the world."

This was really a proceeding against radicalism. Even prosecuting attorney Frank K. Nebeker admitted, "It is the IWW which is on trial here." The government asserted that the Wobblies wanted to close mines, factories, and munitions plants in an effort to oppose the war. Prosecutors cited the few cases where IWW locals gathered to oppose the draft in Texas and Oklahoma.

The defense argued that only three of the nation's 521 labor strikes declared after the war were IWW strikes. The attorneys for the Wobblies tried to show that the union was not antiwar by calling union members who had signed up for the draft and were serving in the military and by calling IWW workers at munitions factories. The union, however, could not argue that it supported the war effort. As one defendant said, "If you were a bum without a blanket, if you had your wife and kids when you went west for a job and never located them since; if your job never kept you long enough in one place to vote; if you slept in a lousy bunkhouse and ate rotten food; if every person who represented law and order beat you up . . . how in hell do you expect a man to be patriotic?"

Haywood took the stand for three days. He talked about his hopes for America and his dreams for a time when capitalists and wage earners worked together on land that was open to all. Haywood was so calm that the *Nation* correspondent wrote that he should be called "Gentle Bill Haywood."

The labor leaders were surprised by the courtesy and the evenhanded manner with which Landis conducted the Wobblies trial. Even Reed reported that the scene in Landis's courtroom was undeniably amiable.

"When the judge enters the court-room after recess no one rises—he himself has abolished the pompous formality," Reed wrote. "He sits without robes, in an ordinary business suit, and often leaves the bench to come down and perch on the step of the jury box. By his personal order, spittoons are placed beside the prisoners' seats, so they can while away the day with a chaw; and as for the prisoners themselves, they are permitted to take off their coats, move around, read newspapers."

But Reed was suspicious of Landis. "Small on the huge bench sits a wasted man with untidy white hair, an emaciated face in which two burning eyes are set like jewels, parchmentlike skin split by a crack for a mouth; the face of Andrew Jackson three years dead."

The facts were seldom in dispute. The jury's mandate was to determine if the IWW had authorized worker strikes for economic reasons, which was legal, or to slow the war effort, which was seditious. Landis gave fair instructions and both sides expressed confidence as the jury left to deliberate. But the fate of the unionists may have been determined by the November 1917 Bolshevik Revolution in Russia. Americans were scared of radicals. The jury was out only an hour before returning with a guilty verdict for each of the defendants.

Weeks later, mild-mannered Landis returned a changed man.

"When the country is at peace it is a legal right of free speech to oppose going to war and to oppose preparation for war," he declared before announcing sentences. "But when once war is declared that right ceases. After war is declared and before the law was passed to raise the army, it was the legal right of free speech to oppose the adoption of a compulsory military service law. But once the law was passed, free speech did not authorize a man to oppose or resist that law.

"The question before the jury in the sixteen or seventeen weeks of the trial was whether or not there was a conspiracy as charged," he continued. "I am obliged to say that the jury was left, in my opinion, no avenue of escape from its verdict. The express declarations of the leaders of the organization, the correspondence of its district officers, everything on the subject of the frame of mind of the organization, and its purposes with respect to war, cannot be treated as mere abstractions; all point to one ultimate object."

Landis sentenced the 101 Wobblies to a total of 807 years in prison and fined the defendants $2.3 million. The sentences ranged from only ten days in the Cook County Jail for minor participants to the maximum twenty years at Leavenworth plus $30,000 fines for the fifteen top leaders. "Judge Landis is using poor English today," quipped one of the defendants. "His sentences are too long."

Haywood and nine others jumped bail. Haywood, given the maximum, headed to Russia and never returned. He died in 1928 in a Moscow hotel. His remains were buried in the Kremlin Wall, along with those of Reed.

A bomb damages the Adams Street entrance of the Federal Building on September 4, 1918. The blast killed four and injured at least thirty. A second bomb was found in 1921.

NATIONAL ARCHIVES

The other prisoners were all granted amnesty after the war.

Just weeks after the harsh sentences were announced, four people were killed and at least thirty injured when a bomb was detonated in the Federal Building. The Wobblies were suspected but never directly connected to the explosion. Killed were a post office employee, a mail carrier, a messenger for the navy intelligence bureau, and a woman who had just entered the building to mail a letter. A second bomb was placed at the same location in 1921, but defused by police.

Landis himself later received one of thirty-six bombs sent to prominent Americans on May Day 1919. Landis was hearing cases out of town when a package arrived at the courthouse in Chicago. By the time he returned, the news was out that the bombs were packaged in boxes from New York's Gimbel Brothers department store—just like a box that had been delivered to the judge's office. Police took the suspicious package and detonated it.

LANDIS TRIED SEVEN PROMINENT SOCIALISTS in 1918 for conspiracy to violate the Espionage Law of 1917 and the 1918 Sedition Act amendment. The laws made it illegal for anyone to "utter, print, write, or publish any disloyal, profane, scurrilous, or abusive language" about the flag, armed forces, Constitution, or democracy.

The case was the government's attempt to shut down the Socialist movement in the United States. It targeted Victor L. Berger, the nation's only Socialist congressman; Adolph Germer, national secretary of the Socialist Party; William F. Kruse, national secretary of the Young People's Socialist League; Socialist writer Irwin St. John; and Socialist editor J. Louis Engdahl. The men were charged with speaking out against the war and publishing antiwar information.

What was published was simply run-of-the-mill Socialist rhetoric. Germer, for example, was charged with printing twenty-five thousand antiwar pamphlets in 1917, two weeks after the Espionage Law went into effect.

The pamphlets read:

The Socialist Party of the United States is unalterably opposed to the system of exploitation and class rule which is upheld and strengthened by military power and sham national patriotism. We, therefore, call upon the workers of all countries to refuse support to their governments in their wars. The wars of the contending national groups of capitalists are not the concern of the workers.

The Socialists, three of whom were German immigrants, asked for a change of venue when the case was assigned to Landis because they thought the judge could not be impartial. Twice in recent weeks he had showed his bias when he said, "If anybody has said anything worse about the Germans than I have I would like to know it so I can use it," and, "One must have a very judicial mind, indeed, not to be prejudiced against the German Americans in this country. Their hearts are reeking with disloyalty."

The defendants argued that the government was not trying them but was trying the Socialist Party. But once again, Landis was subdued at the trial, bending over backward to be fair. And once again, after the jury returned with guilty verdicts, Landis—who became known as the "Scourge of the Disloyal"—sentenced the five defendants to the maximum twenty years at Leavenworth.

Charlie Chaplin, shown with child actor Jackie Coogan, charged the Essanay film studio in Chicago with diluting the quality of one of his films.

NATIONAL ARCHIVES

The Court of Appeals reversed the jury's decision, stating that Landis was too prejudiced to run the case and should have agreed to the change of venue request. The appeals court also remanded the case back to the District Court because some of the information used against the defendants was from acts prior to the date when the Espionage Law went into effect.

The defendants were never retried. The mood of the country changed after World War I. Government raids against radical groups had engendered some measure of sympathy for political outcasts. Even Eugene Debs, the target of so much negative attention, was welcomed at the White House during the 1920s.

LAWSUITS IN CHICAGO'S FEDERAL COURTS always reflect the city's business climate. During the early 1900s, Chicago was an important center of the silent film industry. The heart of the city's film production was the Essanay Film Manufacturing Company on the city's North Side. Its major star was Charlie Chaplin.

Between 1915 and 1917, Essanay filed two civil suits to stop the showing of unauthorized copies of Chaplin's films. Chaplin himself filed suit against the studio for padding a two-reel film into a four-reel film. Chaplin sought $670,000 in damages, saying that the new film had garnered bad reviews. He lost. Chaplin won, however, when he filed a lawsuit against another movie company for stealing his dignified tramp persona. The comic argued that he had invented the character and that it could not be used without his permission.

Chicago was also an important center of the African American press. In 1919, black leader Marcus Garvey sued *Chicago Defender* publisher Robert S. Abbott for libel. The District Court case, *Black Star Line, Inc. v. The Robert S. Abbott Publishing Company,* was eventually dismissed, but it gives insight into the rancor between two of the most prominent African American leaders of the era. Garvey, considered a radical, led the "Back to Africa" movement and fought for the advancement of African Americans through independent businesses and organizations. Abbott, a moderate, strove to encourage blacks to participate in white society.

Garvey announced plans to start the Black Star Line, a black-owned and -operated steamship company, in May 1919. Garvey and his associates traveled around America to raise money for the line, which Garvey saw as an important link between black America and Africa. When Garvey came to Chi-

cago to seek support, he was arrested at Abbott's insistence. Law official Edward J. Brundage charged Garvey with violating "blue-sky laws," statutes to stop investment swindling. Garvey was jailed and fined but freed soon after. He returned to New York, but Abbott and his *Defender* were not yet done with him. The newspaper ran a story headlined "Brundage 'Sinks' Black Star Line" that implied Garvey's steamship line was going out of business.

Garvey charged that Abbott was out to destroy his business and reputation. Garvey asked for $200,000 in damages and all costs, complaining that the story, "conspicuously in large and glaring type," libeled him.

Abbott's defense, that the article was truthful, eventually prevailed. Garvey's libel suit was dismissed in District Court by Judge Carpenter in 1921 at Garvey's cost.

IN NOVEMBER 1920, major baseball owners asked Landis to become baseball's first commissioner. The position at that time was "chairman of the National Baseball Commission." After months of discussion, baseball owners met the judge at the courthouse and offered him a seven-year contract at $50,000 per year. Landis was making $7,500 a year at the time as a District Court judge. The owners sought out Landis because he was a strong, national figure who could help the institution of baseball in the wake of charges that eight Chicago White Sox players had thrown the 1919 World Series. Said Will Rogers, "Baseball needed a touch of class and distinction, so somebody said: 'Get that old boy who sits behind first base all the time. He's out there every day anyhow.'"

At first, Landis refused the offer, saying that his court work was more important. But he took the job under the provision that he would remain a federal judge and that he would be given absolute power over baseball.

Landis was criticized for taking on the post, adding this new job to his judgeship role. On February 2, 1921, the day Landis opened his Michigan Avenue baseball office, an Ohio congressman called for an investigation of the judge. Attorney General A. Mitchell Palmer backed Landis, saying he had not broken any laws. On February 14, the House Judiciary Committee

Kenesaw Mountain Landis and the New York Yankees prospered after Landis left the District Court and became the commissioner of baseball. Here he congratulates Yankees manager Joe McCarthy during the early 1930s. Babe Ruth is directly behind Landis. **CHICAGO HISTORICAL SOCIETY**

voted 24 to 1 to investigate Landis. The American Bar Association formally censured him, but Landis was determined to last through the controversy. And he was determined to oversee the investigation—both by Cook County and by baseball—of what would be known as the Black Sox Scandal. Finally, on February 18, 1922, when the clamor for his removal cooled, Landis resigned from the bench. "There aren't enough hours in the day for me to do all the things that I am obliged to do," he said.

Landis worked for twenty-three years at 333 North Michigan. His office door read simply: BASEBALL.

CHAPTER THREE

1922–1941: "I Would Rather Fight Gangsters with Indictments"

Prohibition and the great depression dominated the nation's psyche and attention during the years between the two world wars. Nowhere were the issues they generated more closely examined than in the District Court of Northern Illinois. The cases against Al Capone, king of crime, and Samuel Insull, king of utilities, were among the most publicized and important trials in the nation.

The behind-the-scenes maneuvering for federal judgeships was becoming ever more intense. Newspapers wrote detailed descriptions of the politics behind the appointments. In 1899, the *Evening Post* wrote, "The scramble for the district judgeship has now developed into an out-and-out fight. It is the two senators against the president." In 1905, Solomon H. Bethea submitted hundreds of recommendations, including letters of endorsement from members of the House and Senate, Illinois Supreme Court justices, state and local judges, lawyers, state officials, and top Republicans. At least twenty-one people applied for a district judgeship in 1912.

The most remarkable campaign for a district judgeship came in 1922, following Judge Landis's resignation. Tucked into the records of the National Archive and Records Administration in College Park, Maryland, are hundreds of letters in support of Florence King's campaign to take *her* place on the District Court. In 1913, Illinois had become the first state to allow women to vote. The Nineteenth Amendment, granting women the right nationwide, was signed into law in 1920. Two years later, the push was on for King.

King, a Chicago patent attorney, formally applied for the job to President Warren G. Harding and Senator Medill McCormick on April 19, 1922. "My early education and training were acquired entirely by my own unaided personal efforts," she wrote both men in separate letters. "My established practice speaks for itself as to my success in my chosen field of work—a success, which, at the time I entered the legal profession, was considered an impossibility. This has meant a lifetime of persistent determination, conscientious effort, and an accumulation of knowledge and experience along lines seldom pursued by women."

King, born and raised on a Michigan farm, learned shorthand and became a stenographer in a law office. She worked as a court reporter while studying law in night school and was admitted to practice in 1895. One Washington, D.C., lawyer wrote that King was the only woman at the time to win a case before the U.S. Supreme Court. She was also a public speaker and lecturer at Chicago Law School.

King was endorsed by men and women in Chicago and around the nation. "The time has come for you to recognize the entire justice of this appointment and the intensive demand for it," wrote Chicagoan William J. H. Strong to President Harding. "The last election was bad enough, but worse will follow for the Republican Party if you do not take steps to satisfy more fully the progressive sentiment in the party and the country at large. The appointment of Florence King is one of the most important acts you can now perform. Do not underestimate the magnitude and the strength of the sentiment in back of Florence King."

Louise M. Byers, a Kansas City attorney, wrote that one of the twenty-three new federal judges should be a woman.

"The Democratic party has been making great ado over the negligence of the Republican Party to redeem effectively its promise to its women supporters, and now is the time to come clean and strong for the women who go down the line for its platform."

King failed to get the support of either of Illinois's two senators, but in July, Senator William B. McKinley of Illinois recommended to Harding that she be named to a federal judgeship in the Panama Canal Zone. That, unlike other federal judgeships, would not be a lifetime appointment. She refused the offer, writing Harding: "It is with the deepest regret that I am obliged to inform you of the impossibility of my leaving the country to accept this position, much as I greatly desire to do so. I sincerely trust that this will not deter consideration of my application for a similar appointment in the Northern District of Illinois for which I filed my application some weeks ago."

King lost her gamble. She never received the nomination and has been barely remembered as a footnote in history. Florence Ellinwood Allen, of Cleveland, became the first female federal judge when she was appointed to the U.S. Court of Appeals for the Sixth Circuit twelve years later, in 1934. The first woman to serve on a district court was Burnita Shelton Matthews, who was appointed to the District Court for the District of Columbia in 1950.

Kenesaw Mountain Landis was replaced as a District Court judge by James H. Wilkerson, who also dominated the court during his years on the bench. Wilkerson was no stranger to the District Court of Northern Illinois. He had helped prosecute Standard Oil in Landis's courtroom as a special assistant to the U.S. attorney general and later served four years as the U.S. attorney for the district.

Wilkerson, born in Missouri, moved to Chicago in the early 1890s to start a law practice. He was elected to the Illinois House in 1902 and served as the Cook County state's attorney. During his four years as U.S. attorney, Wilkerson continued the prosecution of meat packers for violating antitrust laws and filed lawsuits against the sanitary district for diverting water from Lake Michigan.

In late 1922, Congress created a third judgeship in the district. President Harding appointed Adam C. Cliffe, of Sycamore, to the District Court. For decades to come, the third judgeship was by tradition occupied by non-Chicagoans. Cliffe, who attended Northwestern University and read law in 1897, created a private practice in Sycamore and won terms in the Illinois House and Illinois Senate before serving as an Illinois circuit judge.

Like King, Cliffe mounted quite a campaign for the federal judgeship. He submitted endorsements from ninety-six lawyers, nine judges, nine banks,

Facing page: Florence King was the first woman seriously considered for an appointment to a federal bench. "She is a woman of remarkable attainments, possessing fine mental poise and true judicial temperament," wrote attorney John P. McGoorty to President Warren G. Harding in 1922. **NATIONAL ARCHIVES**

three newspapers, a host of women's and men's clubs, and Senator McKinley. But not everyone came to his support. One attorney, John E. Hughes, wrote that Cliffe was swayed by local prejudice and shaped by the trends of the day. "With such men upon the bench, the federal bench, instead of becoming a Gibraltar to resist the onslaught upon the government, will become rather as the sands of the Sahara in the winds of a sandstorm," he wrote the president.

Cliffe sentenced the Newton Brothers—Willis, Doc, Joe, and Jess—and their accomplices to the Leavenworth Penitentiary for carrying out the largest train robbery in the nation's history, a daring $3 million heist from a U.S. Postal Service train in the Lake County hamlet of Rondout in 1924. Willis Newton was brought into court on a stretcher, after being wounded in the robbery. After prison, the brothers continued their criminal career, robbing more trains and banks than outlaws such as the James Brothers and the Daltons. But the Newtons did not gain the same level of notoriety because they did not shoot to kill.

Cliffe died in 1928, at age fifty-nine, after only five years on the bench. He was replaced by Charles Edgar Woodward, who was appointed by President Calvin Coolidge, a Republican, in 1929. Woodward, of Ottawa, also attended Northwestern University. He read law in Ottawa and began a practice in 1899. Woodward served as an assistant Illinois attorney general and was president of the Illinois Constitutional Convention in 1920. He served on the District Court for thirteen years.

BY THE LATE 1920s, some six hundred lawsuits totaling $8 million were filed in District Court over the capsizing of the steamer *Eastland*—Chicago's worst disaster in terms of loss of life. An estimated 844 men, women, and children drowned in the Chicago River near LaSalle Street in 1915 after the ship rolled over as it embarked from its mooring to begin a summer excursion for Western Electric Company employees. A federal grand jury investigated the tragedy, interviewed one hundred witnesses, but never issued a report. Lawsuits against the ship's owner, St. Joseph–Chicago Steamship Company, moved slowly through the courts. By 1927, Special Master in Admiralty Lewis F. Mason determined that the *Eastland* capsized because its chief engineer had incorrectly filled the water ballast tanks, leaving the boat too heavy on port side. The company, according to Mason, was not at fault, greatly limiting its liability. A final decree was signed during the 1930s.

The *Eastland* was the second major disaster to wend its way through the
Northern District of Illinois. More than six hundred people lost their lives
in 1903 when a flash fire swept through a downtown theater. Many in the
crowd were trapped because exit doors opened only inward or were locked.
Cases from the Iroquois Theater disaster packed the court docket for years.

Contributing even further to swollen dockets was Prohibition, the federal
government's 1918 "noble experiment" to stop the manufacture and sale of alcoholic beverages. Hundreds of cases were filed against those accused of violating the Volstead Act, which prohibited the sale of alcoholic beverages.
The cases document how the law was enforced, and flouted, in the Northern
District.

In Rockford, for instance, ninety-five illicit stills operating in single-
family homes of the town's Italian neighborhood were seized by police. Per-
petrators of the elaborate scheme bought huge quantities of corn sugar and
yeast, fired boilers, filled bottles, and transported liquor to roadhouses.

"This phase of the enterprise called for the securing of trucks and men to
drive them, of individuals who gave signals, warnings, and directions to such
truck drivers," wrote the Court of Appeals in reviewing the District Court's
decision. "The same enterprise called in part for distributors in the form of
bartenders or salesmen in 'speakeasies' and like places. It likewise needed the
assistance of those who warned against raids, who 'fixed' police officers, etc.
The enterprise also required individuals who paid the various members of
the various enterprises and who acted as salesmen and who protected the
participants against arrest and imprisonment."

In Chicago, officials shut down the extravagant Club Chez Pierre in the
late 1920s. Despite limited visibility, agents had little trouble observing patrons drinking in the crowded restaurant. The place was filled with popping
champagne, intoxicated people, and empty bottles.

"The finding is inevitable that many persons frequented this place with
the idea of seeing theatrical entertainment, dancing, eating and drinking in-
toxicating liquor," wrote Walter Lindley, who was sitting temporarily as a
District Court of Northern Illinois judge. "While warning cards against the
latter were displayed, the patrons continued to use the place for the purpose
of consumption of liquor. From the facts submitted it is impossible to find
other than that the warning was a sham and that the management had no
objection, but tacitly consented, to constant violations by patrons, provided
the latter acted discreetly."

Alphonse Capone
was first on the Chicago
Crime Commission's
Public Enemies List in
1930. He and his gang
ran unchecked, until
stopped by the Northern
Illinois District Court.

The major challenges for the federal courts during the late 1920s were the gangs spawned by Prohibition. Public Enemy Number One was Alphonse Capone, who had won his stripes—and a scar across his face—as a young hoodlum in Johnny Torrio's Five Points Gang in Brooklyn, New York. Capone moved to Chicago with Torrio in 1920 to work with gangster "Big Jim" Colosimo, who sought help in expanding his underworld empire after Prohibition took effect. Colosimo was killed later that year, and Torrio took over his Chicago gang. Installing Capone as a partner, they opened breweries, brothels, and gambling parlors throughout the city and the suburbs.

By the late 1920s, Torrio and Capone had a working cadre of seven hundred employees. Their operations brought in between $2 million and $5 million a year. Gangs fought a deadly war for profits and turf. Between 1923 and 1926, some 135 gang killings were reported in Chicago. The crescendo of violence reached its peak when seven gangsters were lined up in the SMC Cartage Company garage on North Clark Street and gunned down on St. Valentine's Day in 1929. "Only Al Capone kills like that," said gangster George "Bugs" Moran, whose gang was decimated. By then, Capone had expanded his financial network, opening dog-racing tracks and legitimate and illegitimate businesses in several other cities.

Al Capone and his gang ran unchecked.

"So great was their power that all crimes committed by them were ignored or reported by the police as 'unsolved,'" wrote Fletcher Dobyns, a prosecutor and author of the 1932 book *Underworld of American Politics.* "If by mistake one of their number was arrested, Capone gunmen appeared in open court, made their presence known and immediately witnesses forgot everything, bailiffs, jurors, and judges became nervous, and a dismissal or a verdict of 'not guilty' soon followed. Their assassins carried cards issued to them by the Police Department for their protection in cases of emergency. They did not evade the law. They were superior to it."

In 1925, Judge Wilkerson gave the first indication that federal authorities would get tough on gangsters. He found Cook County Sheriff Peter M. Hoffman and Cook County Jail Warden Wesley Westbrook guilty of contempt for allowing two jailed Capone-era gangsters to have the run of the city during their jail terms.

The two gangsters, Terry Druggan and Frankie Lake, had been sentenced to a year in Cook County Jail in 1924 for Prohibition violations. But the two convicted bootleggers received frequent furloughs and other jail privileges after passing around $2,000 in bribes. Their arrangement was discovered when a reporter stopped by the jail to interview the gangsters. "Mr. Druggan and Mr. Lake are out right now," a secretary told the reporter. They were at an appointment, she said, and not expected to return until the afternoon.

Court records showed that Druggan was allowed to go to his dentist ninety times while serving time and Lake was allowed twelve dental visits. Hoffman produced the dentist, who tried to justify the visits by telling the court that his patient was so nervous he could only be worked on a few minutes a day. Druggan would routinely spend about five hours in the dental office—taking lunch and making calls. He also was often allowed to sleep at his lakeshore apartment and at his country home, returning to jail the next day without a guard. During one stretch, Druggan was away from jail for three days.

Wilkerson sentenced the sheriff to thirty days in the county jail and fined him $2,500. He sentenced Westbrook to four months.

Onto the scene came an unexpected hero: George E. Q. Johnson. He was a political unknown when President Calvin Coolidge appointed him in 1927 as the U.S. attorney for the Northern District of Illinois. "George E. Q. is a slender little man with a shock of unruly hair," the Associated Press reported. "Calm, scholarly, somewhat dreamy eyes benevolently peer out through bowed spectacles." Newspaperman Damon Runyon described Johnson as a "forensic looking man."

Johnson was appointed specifically to subdue Chicago's gangs. The challenge was daunting. Previous U.S. attorneys had been criticized by Judges Wilkerson and Carpenter for cluttering up the courts with small-fry indictments. Johnson set his sights on the big boys.

"I would rather fight gangsters with indictments than with interviews," Johnson said when he took over. At first, the going was slow. Johnson and his staff studied organized crime for twenty months before they started filing indictments during the late 1920s. "Yes, George E. Q. is slower than the Second Coming," said Senator Charles S. Deneen, "but he grinds and grinds and grinds all the time."

Chicagoans, and gang members, took notice when Johnson won convictions against Al Capone's brother Ralph and two high-ranking Capone associates, Jake Guzik and Frank Nitti.

"When he brought Ralph Capone to trial for tax evasion, most of Chicago yawned," one newspaper wrote. "Capone, adjudged guilty, was given a prison term. The yawn became a cheer."

Johnson was the first prosecutor to use income tax law against gang leaders. Johnson's effort was directed by accountants and attorneys rather than G-men. "Here we are not emotional," Johnson told a reporter. "We prepare a case as a game of chess. We don't deal in theory or emotion. The work has often been slow and painful, but it has been effective. Our investigators are thorough. They will trace a criminal heck around the world."

Johnson would not be stopped. Not by public pressure, nor by the gangs themselves.

"I do not intend to be drawn into controversy as to whether Prohibition is

a good law or a bad law," he said, "but I do insist that it is the law, and as
long as it is the law the office of the United States attorney is going to enforce it with all the power and all the ability it can command."

Al Capone, he knew, would be a most difficult catch.

"We were confronted with this kind of a situation—that Al Capone was a
very shrewd man in one way," Johnson later told a Senate Judiciary Committee panel. "He kept no bank account. We never could find a bank account. He kept no books. He signed no checks. In all our investigation we
had one check he endorsed. He never did anything first hand. The system
was he was always two or three removed from what happened and it was
nearly impossible to complete the chain leading to him."

So Johnson appointed a squad of federal agents headed by Eliot Ness to
directly confront Capone.

"This squad from the district attorney's office was led by a very capable
young man by the name of Ness, who is a graduate of the University of
Chicago, and he selected the squad," Johnson said. "The plan was to cause
the Capone gang to lose money, and this squad took brewery after brewery,
and something like 35 of these very large expensive trucks, that cost $4,000
or $5,000 each. They developed a system of detecting these violations and
they pursued that relentlessly."

During the investigation, federal agents learned that *Chicago Tribune* reporter Alfred "Jake" Lingle might be able to give inside information about
Capone. Lingle, who may have been on his way to talk to the law officials,
was shot in the back in the Loop in 1930. The city mourned Lingle's death,
until it was learned that he was a gang associate himself.

A federal grand jury eventually charged Capone with twenty-three violations of income tax laws. He was indicted for paying no income tax between
1924 and 1929 and for failure to file a tax return. The government charged
that during those six years, Capone had a net income of more than $1 mil-
lion and had evaded a tax of about $215,000.

"The income tax law is a lot of bunk. The government can't collect legal
taxes from illegal money," Capone was quoted as saying. Despite this, Capone appeared in June of 1931 before Wilkerson and entered a formal guilty
plea to income tax and Prohibition law violations. He had entered into an
agreement with Johnson's office to plead guilty to tax evasion in return for a
three-year prison sentence and a fine amounting to several hundred thousand dollars. But the deal fell through before it was finalized.

"Capone set out upon this course," Johnson told the senators. "The derby came about that time at Washington Park race track and Al Capone has a manner of dressing in vivid colors to attract attention to himself.

"Then he went across the lake to Benton Harbor. There he took a whole floor in a large hotel and disported himself. Then he went to a baseball game and shook hands with the famous players and pictured around him were these bodyguards.

"Now all these things were blazoned in the newspapers constantly during that time and Judge Wilkerson called this to the attention of the officers of the court and asked them to consider whether it would be advisable to deprive him of liberty and take him into custody."

Wilkerson was so incensed by Capone's arrogance that the judge refused to accept Capone's plea. The judge ordered Capone to stand trial. The gangster changed his plea to not guilty and went to trial.

Spectators jammed Wilkerson's court on October 6, 1931, Capone's first day on trial. "Capone arrived for the opening session fifteen minutes ahead of time, which is said to be a record in punctuality for him," wrote reporter Damon Runyon. "A big crowd was gathered on the Clark Street side of the

Brash Al Capone leaves the federal courthouse on October 7, 1931, with two police officers—Lieutenant William L. McCarthy (to his right) and Sergeant John Howe. CHICAGO HISTORICAL SOCIETY

dingy old building waiting to see him, but Al popped out of an automobile and into the building like a fox going into a hole. Not many of the curiosity-seekers got a good peek at him.

"He entered the courtroom alone and was quickly surrounded by a crowd of reporters, male and female, who began bouncing questions about his ears. They asked him if he was worried, and he replied, logically enough, 'Who wouldn't be worried?'"

But Capone looked confident. He had a reputation of being able to dodge most criminal complaints because he allegedly owned state and county judges in Chicago and kept juries in fear. Capone knew his gang had been busy bribing or threatening prospective jurors. What he didn't plan on was Wilkerson switching jury panels at the last minute, resulting in an entirely rural jury.

"A fragrant whiff of green fields and growing rutabagas and parsnips along with echoes of good old Main Street, crept into the grime-stained Federal Building here today as your Uncle Sam took up the case of Al Capone and gathered a jury in what you might call jigtime," Runyon wrote.

Three grocers, two painters, a pattern maker, a real estate broker, a sta-

Jurors in the Capone case take a break during the proceedings. These jurors were substituted at the last moment to prevent tampering.
CHICAGO HISTORICAL SOCIETY

tionary engineer, a hardware merchant, an insurance agent, a farmer, and a clerk were chosen by midafternoon to sit on the jury at the trial's first day.

Accountants led the government team against Capone. They audited Capone's records in an attempt to prove that the high-living gangster was not paying his fair share in taxes. Agents had spent two years looking into Capone's business records, and persuaded Capone associates to talk.

"This trial brought together a judge and lawyers of exceptional competence," wrote attorney and author Francis Busch in *Enemies of the State*. "A contemporary newspaper account of the trial referred to the presiding jurist and the attorneys, for both the government and the defense, as 'the cream of the bar.'"

Michael J. Ahern and Albert Fink served as Capone's attorneys. U.S. Attorney Johnson and his assistant, Dwight H. Green, headed the government's team. Green, who would later be elected governor of Illinois, had masterminded the strategy of using income tax laws against gangsters.

The prosecution called dozens of witnesses in its attempt to show that Capone was a man of means. Former Capone employees were called to testify about profits made at Capone's gambling houses. Others were called to testify about Capone's spending habits. Spectators cooed when a salesman told the jury about Capone's preference for "glove silk" underwear. A Marshall Field's coat fitter recounted how Capone asked that "the right-hand pocket in all overcoats be made larger and stronger." The implication was that the custom pocket would hold a handgun.

Prosecutor Green told the jury that Capone did all his business with cash and other people's checks. "Carrying on his business in this manner was part of the scheme of the defendant to conceal and cover up his income," Green said. The attorney reminded the jury that the government needed only to prove that Capone had earned taxable income during at least one of the six years during which he paid no taxes.

The proverbial smoking gun against Capone was a 1930 letter his attorney had prepared to work out the compromise agreement with the government. Capone had hired a tax consultant, Lawrence Mattingly, to help in his defense. Mattingly's letter to the government stated that Capone had earned $75 a week from Johnny Torrio in 1924 and 1925, had earned no more than $26,000 in 1926, no more than $40,000 in 1927, and no more than $100,000 in 1928 and 1929.

"There was indisputable confirmation of the government's earlier testimony that Capone had never filed an income-tax return and had earned a taxable income," wrote Busch. So Capone's lawyers forcefully objected to the use of the document.

"They protested that the letter and Capone's and Mattingly's oral statements had been made in a bona fide attempt at a compromise of a pending, disputed claim, and that as such both the written and the oral statements should be privileged and not used as evidence," Busch wrote.

The government argued that its agents had warned Mattingly and Capone that everything they said might be used against Capone in a later trial.

"There were long disputes on the admissibility of the evidence out of the presence of the jury," Busch wrote. Wilkerson finally ruled that the letter could be admitted because no compromise had been worked out.

During one trial session, Capone's bodyguard, Philip D'Andrea, was hauled into Wilkerson's chambers. He was searched by marshals and found to be carrying a loaded .38 caliber revolver and loose bullets. Capone's law-

Facing page: Al Capone in court with his lawyers, Michael Ahern (left) and Albert Fink. "The income tax law is a lot of bunk," Capone reportedly said. "The government can't collect legal taxes from illegal money." *CHICAGO DAILY NEWS COLLECTION/ CHICAGO HISTORICAL SOCIETY*

yers told the judge that D'Andrea did not know he was prohibited from carrying a gun into the Federal Building. Wilkerson was not moved. The bodyguard was held in custody until the Capone verdict was handed down.

By the time the prosecution rested, Capone's only chance was to show that he did not make the money that his own papers indicated he did. His attorneys attempted to make a case that Capone's net income was far below government estimates because the gangster had gambled away his fortune. The defense called a handbook operator to testify that Capone was a chronic loser on horses. Several of Capone's bookies were called to detail the major losses Capone's bookmaking operations had suffered over the years.

The defense strategy particularly piqued Runyon, who had made a national reputation as a broken-down gambler.

"Your correspondent cheerfully yields the palm he has borne with such distinction for lo these many years as the world's worst horse player to Mr. Alphonse Capone," Runyon wrote on October 14.

"Yes sir, and ma'am, Al wins in a common gallop, if we are to believe the testimony brought up in his support today."

In their closing argument, Capone's attorneys portrayed a man who had suffered great financial losses and had attempted to cooperate with the government. Attorney Ahern argued that the government's evidence had only proven one thing: that Capone was a spendthrift. Attorney Fink argued that his client met with government officials only six days after his release from a Philadelphia penitentiary in an attempt to determine what tax he owed.

"Surely, under this evidence, nobody could find that he had willful intent to evade his tax for 1929. There is no possible verdict on those counts save not guilty—unless, of course, you intend to return a verdict on no evidence at all," Ahern said.

"Capone is charged with evading taxes in 1924, and it is charged that he had an income in that year of $123,000. Where is the proof of it? Is there a scintilla of evidence that he made a dollar in 1924? Isn't it terrible, I ask you, that the government should request you to violate your oaths and bring in a verdict on that count?"

Fink used the same argument for the following years, saying the government did not know Capone's losses, or whether the money he spent was borrowed.

"Is the government merely prosecuting this defendant for evasion of income tax," Fink asked, "or is not this prosecution being used as a means by which to stow Al Capone away?"

Replied prosecutor Johnson, in his closing argument: "Never was there a case in my career where there was a more flagrant violation of the laws of the United States. This is a case which future generations will remember. There is no denying the public interest, but I am not asking you to think of this man as Alphonse Capone. Future generations will not remember this case because of the name Alphonse Capone but because it will establish whether or not a man can go so far beyond the law as to escape the law."

Following more than an hour of instructions from Wilkerson, the case went to the jury. Capone was found guilty on five of the twenty-three counts: two misdemeanors—failing to file income tax returns in 1928 and 1929—and three felonies—attempting to avoid income tax payments in 1925, 1926, and 1927.

Wilkerson sentenced Capone to ten years in a federal penitentiary and one year in the county jail. He was also liable for $50,000 in fines and costs. "I guess it's all over," said Capone following the sentence. He was sent to Cook County Jail immediately, then moved to a federal penitentiary in Atlanta, and later to Alcatraz Island off San Francisco. At the end of his term, he was moved to a prison hospital for treatment of syphilis and released in 1939. Capone returned to his mansion in Palm Island, Florida, where he lived until his death in 1947 at age forty-eight.

Johnson credited his accomplishment to "the absolute unreachability of the federal courts." He said: "They are the foundation of whatever success we have had. I cannot too emphatically praise the high caliber of the federal judges. Some people talk of the harshness of the federal courts, but I have often said if innocent of a crime, I would rather be tried in the federal courts, and if guilty, in the state courts."

The case was not the last to involve a Capone. His brother Ralph appeared in court many times on charges of income tax evasion. Al Capone's wife, Mae; his son, Albert "Sonny" Capone; and his estate later sued Desilu Productions over the television show *The Untouchables,* saying the producers were "unjustly enriched" by using the Capone name without the family's consent. The case was dismissed.

John Dillinger, another notorious Chicago gang leader, escaped District Court, but his associates didn't. Anna Sage, the "Woman in Red" who led police to Dillinger at the air-cooled Biograph Theatre on a hot summer night in 1934, ended up in District Court the following year. Sage, an immigrant from Romania, was fighting a deportation order because of prostitution charges. After helping in the capture of Dillinger, she challenged the order, insisting that the Federal Bureau of Investigation had promised to stop deportation proceedings. Her argument was rejected and she was deported to Romania, where she died in 1947.

Louis Piquett, Dillinger's lawyer and confidant, was tried in Judge William H. Holly's court in 1935. The trial attracted great attention because Piquett was called the "brains of the Dillinger mob." He took the stand and testified that he had told Dillinger to turn himself in. He was acquitted by a jury, to the surprise of prosecutors, who thought they had an airtight case. "Mr. Piquett, you are a very lucky man," said U.S. Attorney Dwight Green, shaking a finger at him. But Piquett was returned to federal court and tried before Judge Philip L. Sullivan on additional charges. "If this isn't double jeopardy, then I don't know anything about law," Piquett declared. He was convicted by a jury, sentenced to two years in prison, and fined.

PRESIDENT HERBERT HOOVER nominated John Peter Barnes in 1931 to a new seat, the fourth, in the Northern District of Illinois. Barnes was born in western Pennsylvania and financed his way through the University of Michigan Law School by doing odd jobs, such as washing dishes. He moved to Chicago in 1907 and became a successful corporate lawyer, making up to $100,000 per year through 1930. That was the year his onetime partner, U.S. Senator Otis F. Glenn, recommended Barnes to Hoover, a Republican, for the new judgeship. "I never rang door bells for any politician in my life," Barnes said of the appointment. Twenty-five years later, at a football game also attended by Hoover, Barnes turned to a friend and said: "You know, he appointed me, but I have never met him."

Barnes, who took office a day after his fiftieth birthday, was affectionately known as "iron pants" because he was a hardworking man who had a reputation for being a terror to lawyers.

"He was deliberately severe so that he wouldn't be accused of being softhearted," Judge William J. Campbell said of him years later.

"I saw him dispense justice promptly and effectively—a bit brusque, perhaps, at times—but justice always," wrote attorney Kenneth F. Burgess.

Burgess knew that Barnes was a different person to everybody who came in contact with him.

"This is because he was a complex personality—a mixture not infrequently of conflicting characteristics," the attorney wrote. "He was dignified, austere, and on occasion seemingly unapproachable, yet his judgments were tempered with mercy, a realization of the frailties of humans, and a sympathy for the friendless and the downtrodden. He had no tolerance whatever for falsehood, evasion or deceit."

Barnes attacked the constitutionality of laws instituted by the Franklin D. Roosevelt administration. These included the National Recovery Act, which provided for government licensing of businesses; the Agricultural Adjustment Act, which restricted farm production in an attempt to stabilize farm prices; and the Wagner Act, which guaranteed the rights of workers to organize.

"He held to be unconstitutional some of the New Deal legislation of the early Roosevelt era, yet he was at heart a liberal and far from the narrow reactionary which uninformed persons sometimes pictured him," Burgess wrote. "His decisions in those cases were made because the statutes in question offended his understanding of the rights of men protected by our Constitution. He believed it not merely better, but imperative, that statutes (although designed to accomplish good) should fall rather than that we should abandon the fundamental protection assured to all citizens, both great and humble, in our organic law."

The judge did sustain social legislation passed during the Roosevelt years when it met the test of law. "But when it went beyond the bounds so as to encroach upon the rights of men and of society, he struck it down," Burgess wrote. "And let us now remember that in those hectic days it took real courage to do this—courage in which Judge Barnes was never lacking."

Barnes's career on the District Court bench lasted twenty-seven years. He directed the bankruptcies that led to reorganization of three major midwestern railroads—the Chicago and Eastern Illinois, the Chicago and North Western, and the Alton Railroad. He was the court's first chief judge, a designation that was adopted in districts throughout the United States in 1948, and played an important role in the court during the 1930s, 1940s, and 1950s. He was widely known as a judge beyond reproach.

GEORGE E. Q. JOHNSON, the U.S. attorney who prosecuted Capone, was appointed by President Hoover in 1932 to fill the District Court's new fifth seat. A year earlier, Hoover had offered him the judgeship, but he said he had to finish up his work as U.S. attorney. The delay proved costly.

Johnson received a recess appointment from Hoover in 1932, which meant he was appointed to the District Court bench pending confirmation by the Senate. The permanent appointment seemed to be a cinch; Johnson had won every case that he had prosecuted, and each conviction had withstood review in the Court of Appeals. About one thousand friends and admirers filled the courthouse to witness the installation of Johnson as a District Court judge and his assistant, Dwight Green, as U.S. attorney. Johnson was expected to be confirmed following the promotion of Wilkerson to the Court of Appeals. The Senate held hearings on Wilkerson, but the confirmation was halted because of strong opposition from railroad worker unions upset about a 1920s Wilkerson ruling. Thus, Johnson's confirmation was derailed, too.

In late 1932, the winds of political change blew strong. Hoover was swept out of office by Democrat Franklin D. Roosevelt. When Johnson was told he would not be supported by the new Democratic president, he vacated the judgeship. Johnson went back into private practice. His 1949 obituary in the *Chicago Times* did not even mention that he had served as a federal judge. Johnson's career on the bench lasted only seven months, the shortest term in the court's history.

THE YEAR 1933 was tumultuous for the court. A special subcommittee of the House Judiciary Committee was sent to the Northern District of Illinois to look into what one newspaper called the "high cost of going broke" in Chicago. Soon after the investigation began, Judge Carpenter retired from the bench, a step that he said he had been considering for years. "I feel the ravages of time, and at my age am disinclined to carry on the daily routine of judicial work and assume the necessary burden of decision in important cases," he wrote Roosevelt.

The hearings, which focused on the way judges in the district handled bankruptcy and receivership cases, were front-page news. Targets of the investigation were Wilkerson, Woodward, and Walter C. Lindley, a judge from the Eastern District of Illinois who often worked in Chicago to help clear the court's docket.

Woodward, who was charged with favoring his son's law firm in bankruptcy cases, was asked to testify in November 1933, but he refused at first. Instead, Woodward sent a letter to the committee:

Dear Mr. Chairman,

I am in receipt of your invitation to appear before your committee, for which I thank you. Inasmuch as all of the facts pertaining to the subject of your inquiry are a matter of public record in the office of the clerk of the court, I am sure that I could not further enlighten your committee by appearing before it.

Furthermore, some of these matters are undisposed of and still pending before me, and I am sure you will agree with me that it would be highly improper for me to discuss them with anyone.

Thanking you for your invitation and with my best respects, I remain, very truly yours,

Charles E. Woodward

Newspaper reporters rushed to Woodward's chambers as soon as the committee recessed and sought an interview with the federal judge. He refused to see them.

The following year, the three-man subcommittee released a highly critical report of the Northern District of Illinois. Wilkerson, Woodward, and Lindley were censured by the subcommittee for their "almost criminal negligence" for appointing former law partners to serve as receivers and attorneys in cases with huge fees. The judges' methods were called a "pure, simple racket."

The subcommittee found that Woodward directed as many as twenty-seven equity receivership cases to the law firm of his son, Harold, who personally appeared in many bankruptcy cases. Harold's firm received close to

Facing page: U.S. Attorney George E. Q. Johnson, shown in early 1932, received a recess appointment as a District Court judge from President Herbert Hoover in 1932 but stepped down in 1933 after his nomination was halted by the new Democrat-controlled Senate. **CHICAGO HISTORICAL SOCIETY**

$300,000 in fees after his father's appointment, and the son's earnings sky-rocketed. Lindley was criticized for his action in a Samuel Insull utilities re-ceivership case.

"Our investigation discloses a condition in Chicago that amounts to al-most criminal negligence in the failure on the part of the courts to properly conserve the property in litigation and in some instances an apparent willing assent to the plundering and sacking of the estate committed to the care and custody of the court."

The subcommittee suggested that referees in bankruptcy cases be ap-pointed by District Court judges with approval of the U.S. attorney general and that the referees' annual compensation not exceed $7,500.

"The outstanding fact which, in our opinion, justifies the severest criti-cism of the courts in the Northern District of Illinois both in equity re-ceiverships and the bankruptcy proceedings is the apparent disregard by the judges of the rights of property of the creditors in the matter of the al-lowances of fees to attorneys, receivers, and the various items of expenses," the subcommittee stated.

On May 23, 1934, the House Judiciary Committee voted 15 to 5 to recom-mend the impeachment of Woodward. The committee vote against the Re-publican judge followed party lines. Democrats voted 11 to 1 in favor of im-peachment; Republicans voted 4 to 4. U.S. Representative John Buckbee, a Republican from Illinois, rushed to Woodward's defense. "He is as clean as a hound's tooth, and besides, he lives in my district," said Buckbee. "I've known Woodward most of my life. He's a poor man now, and he has always been a poor man. He never did anything wrong."

Buckbee accused his Democratic colleague, U.S. Representative Adolph Sabath, of Chicago, of pushing the impeachment process because Sabath wanted to sit on the federal bench. Sabath, who launched the subcommittee investigation, denied the accusation. "I could have been a federal judge a dozen years ago, but not now," Sabath said. "The minute my name would go up for Senate confirmation now, all the big interests in the nation would fight me."

The House Judiciary Committee considered impeachment proceedings against Wilkerson and Lindley, but the full committee refused to recom-mend impeachment. In 1935, the subcommittee recommended that no fur-ther action be taken against any of the three Chicago judges—partially be-cause substantial improvement had been made in the District Court.

"Your subcommittee is of the opinion that the evidence does not warrant the interposition of the constitutional powers of impeachment of the House of Representatives, but in several instances conduct prejudicial to the dignity of the federal judiciary was disclosed," the group concluded.

That was not the end. In 1937, U.S. Senator Harry S Truman recommended that impeachment proceedings be initiated against Wilkerson. Truman charged the judge with fraud and mismanagement while he was in charge of the Chicago, Milwaukee, St. Paul & Pacific Railroad receivership from 1925 to 1928. On the Senate floor, Truman called Wilkerson "the most notorious receivership judge on the federal bench" and said, "Wilkerson had a Milwaukee & St. Paul private car at his beck and call in which to take his pleasure."

Truman's proposal went nowhere, but two years later the senator from Missouri again went on record to say that Wilkerson should be impeached. Nothing came of his one-man campaign.

GEORGE E. Q. JOHNSON vacated his seat in 1933 and was replaced by Philip L. Sullivan, a native of Marengo, Illinois. Sullivan earned his law degree at Loyola University Chicago School of Law and began in private practice in 1911. He served as a Cook County Circuit Court judge from 1921 until his appointment to the District Court. He was a regular Democrat who was the choice of the Chicago machine. Senator James Hamilton Lewis said that Sullivan was the first candidate to meet the Roosevelt administration's requirements for federal judicial appointments. He was endorsed by the local Democratic organization, the state's two senators, and the Department of Justice.

William H. Holly, who replaced Judge Carpenter in 1933, was a registered Democrat but had not been active in party politics for years. He had practiced law with Clarence Darrow, and was considered a Darrow protégé. "Holly was young, intelligent, fine looking, sympathetic," wrote Irving Stone in his biography of Darrow. "Clarence came to love him almost as a son."

Holly's candidacy was pushed by a group of liberals who wanted to change the cast of the Northern District of Illinois court. The group included Darrow and liberal University of Chicago professor Paul Douglas, as well as Harold Ickes, a progressive who was Roosevelt's influential secretary of the interior.

"Chicago liberals have long felt that the Chicago federal court has leaned too much to the right on social questions," the group stated in a 1933 press release. "The famous Daugherty injunction issued by Judge Wilkerson against the railroad employees in the shopmen's strike of 1922 is often cited to show the attitude of the local District Court on social questions."

In 1923, Wilkerson approved a permanent injunction against the Railway Employees Department of the American Federation of Labor, ruling that the union was violating the Sherman Antitrust Act when it went on strike in 1922. "The conduct of the strikers and pickets was aggressive, belligerent, violent, and lawless," he wrote of the strike, during which nineteen were killed. That decision alienated liberals and cost him a seat on the Court of Appeals.

Holly was the last Northern District of Illinois judge who read law. He started in private practice in downstate Macomb in 1891 and moved to Chicago in 1902. He ran a private practice for thirty-one years, except for a two-year stint as an assistant Cook County state's attorney. He joined Darrow as a law partner during the 1920s. Holly's nomination confirmed that Roosevelt was determined to take away the power of local Democratic machine leaders in appointing top federal officials.

"The consensus seems to be that this appointment marks the beginning of a 'new deal' in the local federal courts as one of the outstanding policies for the Roosevelt regime, and probably may be taken as a criterion of the class of men who will be elevated to the federal bench during this administration," wrote reporter Charles N. Wheeler at the time.

Holly took over Room 582, the courtroom of George E. Q. Johnson. "I appreciate this honor," Holly said. "I think it is more than I deserve, but I am going to try to make believe that I deserve it." From the start, Holly was careful not to be typecast as a liberal. "I have no political or economic program," he said. "I just want to be a good judge, fair and impartial."

True to his word, Holly's political stance was difficult to peg on the bench. In his early years, he upheld the right of the government to regulate milk prices and stopped the City of Chicago from closing the stage show *Tobacco Road.*

In 1938, Holly delivered the eulogy for Clarence Darrow at the Bond Chapel on the University of Chicago campus. "Holly went frequently with his chief to the Midway for dinner, where they spent 'companionable evenings together, discussing the ignorance and inhumanity of the world, the men that they admired and approved, those whom they disagreed with and disliked,'" author Stone wrote. Holly and Darrow had agreed that whoever lived longer would speak at the other's funeral. Said Darrow: "Let Judge Holly speak at my funeral. He knows everything there is to know about me, and he has sense enough not to tell it."

In 1939, Holly ruled that the Fair Labor Standards Act, which established the minimum wage, was constitutional. The decision amplified federal power. The following year, he slowed the government's drive against bookies when he ruled that horse race odds could be transmitted between states. In 1942, Holly ruled that the State of Illinois could not keep Communist Party candidates off the ballot. An Illinois statute banned a ballot position to any party "associated, directly or indirectly, with Communist, Fascist, Nazi or other un-American principles." Holly struck down the statute as unconstitutionally vague. He found that state officials had no evidence that the Communist Party was engaged in activities forbidden by the statute and called the decision to leave Communist candidates off the ballot "purely arbitrary." However, he refused to order that the Communist Party candidates be placed on the upcoming ballot because the hearing was held only fifteen days before the fall election and new ballots could not be printed in time.

Despite his efforts to be evenhanded, Holly was ultimately considered one of the court's most liberal judges. In 1940, he was given a portrait of Oliver Wendell Holmes to hang in his courtroom. "It has been said that Justice Holmes wore liberalism and tolerance as if they were daily garments," Judge Campbell said at the ceremony. "It can be said also of Judge Holly."

DAYS BEFORE HIS RETIREMENT as an active judge, James Wilkerson said his most interesting case was the trial of Samuel Insull, the mastermind behind the nation's utilities revolution, and his business associates.

"It was the first case tried here under Section 77-B, and many legal points were involved that were entirely new to bankruptcy proceedings," Wilkerson told a reporter. "The criminal trial in this case was one of the most unusual a judge has ever been called upon to hear. I knew many of the defendants personally, including Samuel Insull. It was a jury case and the jury chose to find the defendants not guilty."

Insull was a symbol of America. His brawny businesses represented the nation's economic boom during the 1920s and its financial collapse during the 1930s. His bankruptcy was the largest business failure in U.S. history to that time.

Insull, born in England, worked for the London agent of American inventor Thomas A. Edison and came to the United States at age twenty-one to serve as Edison's private secretary. Insull became one of Edison's most trusted employees, handling the inventor's financial affairs for eleven years. Insull learned from and translated Edison's innovations with business acumen. When Insull took charge of the Edison General Electric Company in the 1880s, Edison told him, "Do it big, Sammy. Make it either a big success or a big failure." Insull consolidated the company, and three years later left it as a $500 million corporation known simply as General Electric.

He moved to Chicago in 1892 to become president of the Chicago Edison Company, a small firm that provided electric service to only a portion of Chicago. But he dazzled all of America by illuminating the 1893 to 1894 World's Columbian Exposition with ninety thousand incandescent lamps. Insull convinced consumers that electric light was brighter, cleaner, and safer than gas. Once again, Insull consolidated the company with others, including the Commonwealth Edison Company, and soon was providing electric service to all of Chicago. In the late 1890s, he began acquiring electric and gas companies outside of Chicago. In 1902, he created the Public

Tycoon Samuel Insull (left) and his attorney, Floyd E. Thompson, walk through the lobby of the federal courthouse on October 3, 1934, on their way to the second day of Insull's trial. Thompson, who successfully defended Insull, previously served as a justice on the Illinois Supreme Court. HERALD AND EXAMINER/CHICAGO HISTORICAL SOCIETY

Service Company of Northern Illinois to provide light and power to rural communities.

Next, Insull took over the Peoples Gas Light & Coke Company, which provided gas to Chicago and power to mass transportation lines. In 1912, he created the Middle West Utilities Company as a holding company of his far-flung small utilities.

Insull was nothing short of a financial and technical genius. He built the world's largest generating plants of the time and pioneered the use of turbine generators and power lines. But that was only the start. He understood how to streamline the operation of utilities so they made huge profits in monopolistic environments. Investors flocked to buy shares of Insull's new companies. They trusted Insull and reaped the huge profits his companies returned. Insull gained so much trust that he was even able to sell new securities right after the 1929 stock market crash.

But he could not hold his financial empire together. By 1932, several of Insull's investment companies—although not his utilities—were in receivership. Rumors of financial irregularities started to float as his companies collapsed. Thousands who invested with Insull lost money, including Insull himself. One banker said that Insull was too broke to be bankrupt. The stock market was at an all-time low and people were looking for scapegoats. Insull, exhausted from years of trying to keep himself and his companies afloat, resigned from his many directorships and left for Europe. By the end of the year, the U.S. attorney and Cook County state's attorney both announced they were looking into Insull's failed companies. A federal grand jury returned an indictment against Insull, his son Samuel Insull Jr., and fifteen others, charging them with using the mail to further a scheme to defraud the public of $100 million.

By then, Insull and his wife were living in Paris. He tried to avoid U.S. prosecution, but was tracked down in Turkey, extradited, and returned to America.

"I made mistakes," Insull admitted, "but they were honest mistakes."

Insull's trial began in October 1934. He and his codefendants were charged with defrauding the public by selling inflated stock. Their alleged crimes were read to the jury in a fifty-page indictment. The government called eighty witnesses. Few facts were disputed. In dispute was exactly what all the facts meant.

Insull was the primary witness for the defense.

"The old man [he was seventy-five] took the witness stand, calm and as-sured," wrote Francis Busch in his book *Guilty or Not Guilty?* "To the oath impressively pronounced by the clerk, 'Do you solemnly swear . . .' he replied with a ringing 'I do.' He faced the jury and, under the skillful direct examination of his able counsel, told his story—one of the most remarkable ever heard in an American courtroom."

After detailing his rise to success, Insull explained his fall. He testified that he never expected that the stock market crash would result in a Great De-pression. He said that he kept operating his companies until April 1932, but by then most company stock was worthless. Tired and discouraged, he left for Europe. He refused to comply with the state's attorney call for his return, but said he intended to return after the 1932 elections. Then, he believed, his chances for a fair trial might be better. Now he had no income or property, and was depending on friends for his existence.

Insull remained dignified and spoke with pride during his testimony. Asked if his annual salary had reached as high as $500,000, he responded, "Yes, and I was worth every penny of it." He told the jurors he had nothing to hide and had conducted his business with honesty.

"Insull had made a remarkable witness," Busch wrote. "John Healy, attorney for one of the codefendants, a former state's attorney and a lawyer of sincerity and outstanding ability, summed up the general impression when he declared in his argument: 'I have sat in the prosecutor's chair, and I have sat on the defendant's side of the table, and in my almost fifty years of experience I have never seen a more remarkable exhibition on the witness stand than you gentlemen witnessed when Samuel Insull was upon that stand. This old man, now on the rim of the dying day, with the courage of a lion, fought for the only thing he has left—his honor and his good name.'"

Insull's attorney, Floyd E. Thompson, argued that Insull was not to blame for the sins of the speculative boom. "Why had the government brought this charge against Insull?" Thompson asked the jury. "Insull's name had become a symbol—the symbol of an era, a tragic era in which people had gone speculation wild and money mad, in which millions of dollars had been risked and lost. Something, figured the government, had to be wrong somewhere."

Insull, said the attorney, believed in himself and in his companies.

"Gentlemen," he told the jury, "you have had a description here of an age in American history which we hope never will be repeated. We are trying that age. There is no proof here that anyone had any wrongful motive. There is proof that these men believed implicitly in the business venture in which they were engaged, and they poured their own fortunes and their own good names in it."

In his closing argument, Thompson reminded the jury of Insull's benevolence and his civic leadership. Thompson rattled off a long list of Chicago institutions that Insull was instrumental in creating, including the Chicago Civic Opera, and told the jurors that Insull's civic and charitable contributions approached and sometimes exceeded his lofty salary.

Legend has it that the jury took just five minutes to decide. So as not to appear biased, jurors took cake and coffee and returned with their not guilty verdict two hours later.

Insull's tribulations were far from over. He and his brother, Martin, were tried in Cook County Criminal Court in 1934 for embezzlement and found not guilty. Insull and others were tried again in the Northern District of Illinois in 1935, charged with transferring money before his bankruptcy. Judge John C. Knox, of the Southern District of New York, was assigned to hear the case in Chicago. He stopped the trial following the government's presentation, telling the jury: "The proof offered by the government is not of a quality which would, if the case were submitted to you, enable you to find the defendants guilty beyond a reasonable doubt."

Insull was judged not guilty, but the uncontrolled speculation on his securities paved the way for federal government regulation, such as the Securities and Exchange Act. After three trials, Samuel Insull had been judged more a product of his times than an instigator.

IN 1938, U.S. ATTORNEY MICHAEL IGOE was appointed by President Franklin D. Roosevelt to the bench to fill the court's new seat, its sixth. Big, brawny Igoe was the consummate politician who rose up the ranks of the Democratic Party. Born in 1885 in Minnesota, Igoe graduated in 1908 from Georgetown University Law School in Washington, D.C., and came to Chicago to start a practice. Politics interested him from the start. He was a member of the Illinois legislature from 1917 to 1930, serving most of those years as the Democratic leader of the House. He worked as first assistant U.S. attorney from 1915 to 1916 and served on the South Park Commission, helping to bring the Dempsey-Tunney "Long Count" heavyweight championship to Chicago's Soldier Field in 1927.

That same year, Igoe seconded the Democratic presidential nomination of Alfred E. Smith of New York. But Igoe proved he was no lockstep party man when he fought the control of Chicago Mayor Anton Cermak, the state Democratic Party leader. Igoe eventually broke with Cermak, saying the political boss was "attempting to become party dictator of Illinois." He tried to lead an insurrection against the Cermak machine in 1932, running for the Democratic nomination for governor, but was defeated.

"Igoe has been a petty and noisy cog in the old Sullivan-Brennan machines and was simply a Tammany politician run amuck," attorney Fletcher Dobyns wrote in 1932. After Cermak was assassinated, Igoe won a seat in the U.S. House in 1934, but resigned the next year to take over as U.S. attorney in Northern Illinois. In 1938, Igoe lost in his bid for the Democratic nomination to the U.S. Senate. He was rewarded when Roosevelt named him to the District Court.

To signify the change in his life, Igoe reportedly gave up cigars and liquor and sipped only an occasional glass of wine during his twenty-nine years on the court. Igoe was best known for the years he spent helping Judge Wilkerson reorganize and unify the city's failing public transportation companies.

In 1947, Igoe helped supervise the bankruptcies of the Chicago Surface
Lines and Chicago Rapid Transit companies and oversaw creation of their
successor, the publicly owned Chicago Transit Authority. At age eighty, Igoe
was the nation's oldest federal District Court judge working full-time. He
assumed senior status that year and continued to work part-time to dispose
of three hundred civil and criminal cases on his calendar. He became such a
fixture in the courthouse that his nameplate remained on his courtroom
door years after his death in 1967.

"Some have said that I've been severe in determining sentences for the
guilty," Igoe once told a reporter, "but I've always tried to put myself in the
position of the defendant. I've always sought an explanation for his actions,
and then I've ruled. The cases involving young people have been the ones
that have gone directly to my heart. They have been the ones I've really
struggled with. I'm now convinced that almost all our juvenile crime is the
result of one parent failing to be in the home for the youngster, either because of divorce, separation or death."

IGOE'S SUCCESSOR AS U.S. ATTORNEY, William J. Campbell, was nominated to the District Court in 1940, succeeding Wilkerson, who took senior
status at the end of 1940. Campbell, at thirty-five, was one of the nation's
youngest district judges. He grew up on Chicago's West Side and attended
St. Rita High School and St. Rita College. His first major legal client was the
Roman Catholic Archdiocese of Chicago.

Campbell attracted Roosevelt's attention when FDR was governor of
New York. Campbell was a national leader of the Young Democrats, an organization formed by Roosevelt.

"Campbell got on the bench after an astute combination of politics and
Catholicism," stated Joseph Goulden, who wrote about the court in the re-
vealing book *The Benchwarmers* during the 1970s. "After graduating from
Loyola Law School in Chicago in 1926 he set up a ho-hum law practice and
got into Democratic machine politics, which in those days was closely
aligned with the local Catholic hierarchy. Campbell became very friendly
with the liberal-minded Bishop Bernard J. Shiel and helped him found the
Catholic Youth Organization. Campbell so impressed Shiel that he soon became a de facto nuncio to President Roosevelt on behalf of Chicago Cath-
olics. By one account, Campbell 'managed to enhance himself in the eyes of

the president by emphasizing his friendship with the bishop, while he improved his situation with the bishop by implying a similar friendship with the president.'"

Roosevelt first appointed Campbell the Illinois administrator of the National Youth Administration, then U.S. attorney for the Northern District of Illinois. At that time, Campbell had represented only one person in federal court, the owner of Rosie's Snake Pit, a Loop speakeasy. "All the Cook County judges could be found there almost any afternoon," Campbell recalled in a 1984 oral history.

As U.S. attorney, Campbell prosecuted Moses Annenberg, publisher of the *Daily Racing Form* and *Philadelphia Inquirer,* for income tax evasion. Annenberg pleaded guilty and went to jail for two years. Campbell also arranged for the release of Al Capone after Capone had served most of his prison term. Campbell said Capone was ordered never to return to the Northern District of Illinois as part of the terms of his parole. Campbell also refused to allow Capone to leave prison until he had paid his entire back taxes. Capone delivered the tax due, $10,000, with truckloads of pennies. "It took them a few days to get the pennies and it took us a few days, of course," Campbell said. "I kept him right in the clink until we counted every one of them."

Campbell said he was appointed to the federal court because as U.S. attorney he went after "the wrong people": "I was indicting the local branches of the Kelly-Nash machine that were working hard with the local bookies and there was quite an organization going. Now you must remember that Roosevelt was coming up for his first reelection and he needed the Kelly-Nash machine to carry Illinois."

Actually, Roosevelt was seeking his second reelection in 1940. The Chicago machine—composed of Mayor Edward Kelly, a Roosevelt confidant, and Patrick Nash—took command of Democratic politics in Chicago after the death of Cermak. They later helped engineer the movement to draft Roosevelt for a third term at the Democratic National Convention at Chicago Stadium.

Campbell sat on the bench as an active judge for thirty years, longer than any judge in district history. He exerted a tremendous impact on the court during those years.

"I can still recall that bright October day in Chicago in 1940 when after a beautiful and inspiring induction ceremony in his ornate courtroom in our

old courthouse, the Senior Judge (this is what the Chief was called in 1940) took me into his chambers and flippantly tossed me a sheaf of papers listing over two hundred cases as my calendar," Campbell wrote years later. "He casually observed that I might find myself a courtroom wherever I could and begin a call of the calendar since several cases thereon had not been called in over ten years!

"I resolved then that if ever I was in a position to do anything about it, some better method of 'breaking in' a new federal judge would be devised," Campbell wrote.

The District Court was far different then. Judges had no clerks; attorneys called surprise witnesses. Judge Wilkerson devised a system to create an even distribution of bankruptcy cases because all the judges wanted bankruptcy assignments, Campbell said. These were plums because judges could use them to throw lucrative receivership jobs to their friends.

Each judge operated in his own manner, Campbell said. "I used pretrial, for example. No other judge did," he said. "Then Judge Holly came to use it. Wilkerson resigned without ever having held a pretrial conference."

The volume was overwhelming during Campbell's early years, he wrote. Although bank robberies grabbed the headlines, there were more post office robberies. "For some reason or other, the robbers thought the post office was an easier pushover and I guess it was because most of the banks had guards whereas most of the post offices had none."

To operate efficiently, Campbell accepted agreements in many criminal

Federal judges honor Judge William H. Holly on his eighty-first birthday in 1950. They were (from left) Walter J. LaBuy, William J. Campbell, John Peter Barnes, Philip L. Sullivan, Holly, Thomas W. Slick, and Michael Igoe. Slick was a retired District Court judge from Indiana.
CHICAGO TRIBUNE

cases. "I participated in plea bargaining unless the defendant absolutely refused, and that was rare," he said. "I would always agree to a lower sentence if they pled guilty, somewhat to the chagrin of the United States attorney. But I figured it was the only way of keeping current with the criminal calendar."

THE FBI SHADOWED the court, keeping close tabs on each of the judges. In 1934, FBI Director J. Edgar Hoover wrote a memo about the close relationship between Judge Wilkerson and U.S. Attorney Green. In another memo, FBI agents noted that Judge Barnes was "very complimentary toward the work of the bureau" but later "severely criticized the bureau in open court." The memo took special note of Barnes's criticism of prosecutors, including his advice to a defendant "that if he were the subject he would 'see who I could sue.'"

An April 4, 1939, FBI report showed how much gossip, both positive and negative, was being gathered by Hoover:

On Wilkerson: "This judge was formerly mentioned a number of years ago in connection with a bankruptcy scandal in Chicago. As senior judge he has permitted bondsmen to solicit business in the corridors of the Federal Court Building."

On Sullivan: "He is possessed of judicial temperament and is a competent and very able judge."

On Barnes: "He is the best qualified judge in the District Court."

On Holly: "He appears, however, to lack experience and is never inclined to impose a jail sentence. Practically all prisoners brought before him are placed on probation, whereas for the same offense a like prisoner before one of the other judges would receive a penitentiary sentence."

On Woodward: "This judge was investigated several years ago in connection with a bankruptcy ring and the receivership racket. . . . Rumors are still occasionally heard in Chicago with respect to his possible connection with such a bankruptcy ring."

On Igoe: "He is not, however, possessed of a judicial temperament. He is primarily a politician, is inexperienced as a prosecutor and his training is not up to the standards formerly required for appointment to the bench."

Finally, the memo noted: "There is considerable dissension among the various federal judges on the bench in Chicago in that they are divided into cliques and do not get along together at all."

CHAPTER FOUR

1941–1963:
"Our Titanic Struggle against the Enemy"

WORLD WAR II dominated the Northern District of Illinois for years following the bombing of Pearl Harbor. The court was a domestic battleground over the issues of the draft, loyalty, and government control. After the war, the court increased in size and diversity as two judgeships were added and the first Polish American, African American, and Jewish judges were appointed.

World War II set the stage for this new era. Judges heard hundreds of Selective Service cases, which they dispatched with efficiency. U.S. Attorney J. Albert Woll wrote that by mid-1943 the District Court had a standard-issue approach to Selective Service complaints. Of the 161 indictments returned during the previous year, only one person was acquitted.

"I can say that under the law no one can beat the Selective Service Laws from a legal standpoint," Woll stated. "The courts of the entire nation—the Supreme Court as well—have unanimously upheld the action of the local Selective Service boards in classifying registrants. They have consistently and without exception held that once a registrant has been classified 1A—and the appeal board has affirmed its action—that action is final, and may not be challenged in a trial upon an indictment for failure to obey the action of the board. Indeed, the trials have now been reduced to a simple formula. Has the defendant been classified 1A? Has the appeal board confirmed that classification? Was the defendant ordered to report? Did he report? If he did not—then he is guilty, and there is no power in the court or in the office of the United States attorney that can change or alter that decision."

One of the government's primary targets was the Nation of Islam, founded by Elijah Muhammad.

"Perhaps the outstanding accomplishment in this field was the entire annihilation in this district of a ring of slackers who called themselves the 'Nation of Islam,'" a U.S. attorney's report stated. "Of this group, sixty-three were indicted and all convicted and sentenced to terms ranging from three to five years."

In 1942, a federal grand jury indicted Muhammad, whose national African American Muslim community would later be known as the Black Muslims. A bench warrant was issued and bond was fixed at $10,000. Muhammad and some of his followers were charged with conspiracy to cause insubordination, disloyalty, mutiny, and refusal of duty in the U.S. military and naval forces.

Muhammad, who was born Elijah Poole, entered a not guilty plea in early 1943. His indictment was based on statements that he allegedly made in Chicago at his Allah Temple of Islam, 104 East Fifty-first Street, after the United States declared war against the Axis powers. According to the government, Muhammad told his followers, including men of draft age, that they were not U.S. citizens and that the only flag they could call their own was the flag of Islam. Muhammad also allegedly said that blacks owed no respect to the United States because they had been oppressed, beaten, and lynched under the American flag.

The indictment showed that government agents attended many Nation of Islam gatherings. They reported that Muhammad told his congregation that the Japanese were fighting to free blacks.

"The Japanese are the brothers of the negro and the time will soon come when from the clouds hundreds of Japanese planes with the most poisonous gases will let their bombs fall on the United States and nothing will be left in it," Muhammad was quoted as saying.

Muhammad was acquitted of sedition charges, but was found guilty of failing to register for the draft at age forty-five and failing to comply with Selective Service rules. He served four years in prison.

THE COURT'S MOST SENSATIONAL CASE during World War II was against Hans and Erna Haupt, Walter and Lucille Froehling, and Otto and Kate Wergin.

"Ladies and gentlemen of the jury: The government intends shortly to disclose to you in this courtroom a picture of treason," announced U.S. Attorney Woll in his opening statement on October 26, 1942.

First, Woll discussed the charge.

"Treason," he said, "according to the Constitution, is practically the same as that in the criminal code. In effect it is either levying war against the United States or adhering to the enemies of the United States, giving them aid and comfort." The six defendants were indicted for giving aid and comfort to Herbert Haupt, a Chicagoan who had returned to the United States from Nazi Germany on a German U-boat with plans to sabotage the U.S. war effort. Haupt, twenty-two, was the son of German immigrants Hans and Erna Haupt, the nephew of Walter and Lucille Froehling, and an acquaintance of Otto and Kate Wergin. The six were charged with thirty-three overt acts to help and shield young Haupt.

Close to eighty people testified at the jury trial before Judge William J. Campbell. The FBI spared no expense in bringing people to Chicago to

The 1942 treason trial in the courtroom of District Court Judge William J. Campbell. From left are Marshal William H. McDonnell and defendants Kate Wergin, Erna Haupt, Lucille Froehling, Otto Wergin, Walter Froehling, and Hans Haupt. Across the table is U.S. Attorney J. Albert Woll. GARY SHEAHAN/ CHICAGO HISTORICAL SOCIETY

document Herbert Haupt's sabotage mission and the couples' role in aiding him.

The government's first task was to show that Herbert Haupt was a foreign agent. Ten weeks before the Chicago trial began, Haupt was executed in Washington, D.C., for his role in the plot, along with five would-be saboteurs. Two other saboteurs, who had turned in the others to the FBI, were spared. One of those two, Ernest Peter Burger, was the government's star witness at the Chicago trial. Haupt, he said, had reported in April 1942 to a Nazi sabotage school outside Brandenburg, Germany. There, Haupt and his coconspirators were trained. The eight saboteurs were taught how to manufacture and use explosives, Burger testified. Their main goal was to damage Alcoa factories that produced the aluminum skin of warplanes. But they also had a long list of other targets, which included the Hell Gate Bridge in New York City, the hydroelectric power plant at Niagara Falls, locks on the Ohio River, important railroad tracks and stations, even department stores.

After weeks of training, the eight men were taken to Berlin, where they were given German uniforms, U.S. currency, fake Social Security and draft registration cards, explosives, and sabotage devices. They were separated into two groups before heading across the Atlantic Ocean to the United States on submarines.

Both U-boats trolled off the coasts of America and surfaced so that the saboteurs could board life rafts for the final leg of the journey. One group landed on Long Island, New York. Haupt's group landed June 17 near Jacksonville, Florida. Herbert arrived in Chicago by train two days later. Within hours, he met his parents and the Froehlings. The following day, he met the Wergins. On June 27, Haupt was arrested by the FBI.

U.S. attorneys called FBI agents and officials to trace Herbert Haupt's trail from Jacksonville. The government called neighbors and friends in Chicago to detail Herbert Haupt's nine days in the city. The government also relied on wit-

MRS. GERDA MELIND
On the Witness Stand
Sketched in Federal Court Oct. 3 1942

nesses who testified about the defendants' pro-German, anti-Semitic attitudes. One woman told the jurors that Hans Haupt, Herbert's father, told her that his U.S. citizenship was meaningless. Another woman, who employed the Haupts during the late 1930s and early 1940s as domestics, testified: "They said that [Adolf] Hitler was a godsend to the people over there." These statements, made before Pearl Harbor and the U.S. declaration of war against Germany, were admitted into evidence despite protests from defense attorney Paul A. F. Warnholtz. Years later, Campbell said that Warnholtz was a poor choice because of his heavy German accent.

The government presented fourteen "voluntary statements" signed by the defendants. Their attorneys argued unsuccessfully to bar the confessions, saying they were given under duress.

The defense called no witnesses. Their attorneys argued that treason—as defined by the Constitution—had not been proven. Defense attorney Warnholtz stated that the defendants were acting out of love and friendship. The Wergins' son, Wolfgang, had accompanied Herbert from Chicago to Germany but had not returned. Warnholtz argued that the Wergins could not turn in Herbert because he was the only link to their son. Warnholtz also argued that the three couples did not fully know Herbert's mission. He said they knew young Haupt had gone to Germany and returned on a submarine, but did not comprehend that he returned with a plan of sabotage.

The jury deliberated for about six hours and found all six defendants guilty of treason in November 1942. Following the decision, and prior to sentencing, Campbell received many letters asking for mercy.

"As an American who has always been proud of my country I see nothing but race persecution in the so-called trial of Haupt's parents, the aftermath of their love for a child who died for not committing sabotage," wrote Charles Dormner, from New York City. "May I tell you and the rest of our law enforcement body that any natural father or mother would do the same thing and I say as a free thinking American that you have in this case clownish efforts to outclass Hitler in utilizing hate instead of justice."

Campbell sentenced Hans Haupt, Walter Froehling, and Otto Wergin to death by electrocution. Erna Haupt, Lucille Froehling, and Kate Wergin were sentenced to twenty-five years in prison and fined $10,000.

"In pronouncing sentence upon these six men and women, this court is constrained to give full consideration to the fact that our nation, and every

Facing page: Gerda Melind, the girlfriend of saboteur Herbert Haupt, testifies at the trial. She told the court that Herbert proposed marriage to her following his return to Chicago in 1942. **GARY SHEAHAN/CHICAGO HISTORICAL SOCIETY**

man, woman and child in it, are engaged in a global death struggle against forces of tyranny and evil unprecedented in the history of mankind," Campbell said.

Campbell said that the severity of the sentences would serve as a "timely and solemn warning" to all who would attempt to commit the smallest act of sabotage or treason. He was careful to separate the defendants from the German American population in Chicago.

"This court does not for a moment believe the prisoners to be representative in the slightest degree of the mass of our German-born citizens," he said. "These citizens should not in any way be subjected to harassment, unfairness or prejudice as a consequence of the acts of the defendants in this case."

Campbell rejected the plea from defense attorneys that he show mercy to the women. He did not sentence them to death, he said, because he felt they were less complicit than their husbands in the plot to help Herbert Haupt.

"In weighing the mercy pleas for the women here involved, it also has been incumbent on the court to consider the millions of suffering mothers of boys who are fighting this war for us, and the mothers who toil in aluminum and powder plants or on production lines in constant danger from saboteurs—mothers who have equal rights to consideration with the prisoners here. These defendants by their acts have thus forfeited any rights to consideration as mothers."

The stiff sentences made Campbell something of a national hero. *Newsweek* magazine wrote: "Seldom has a judge so young given a more complete and eloquent summary of a case in passing sentence than that delivered by Federal Judge William J. Campbell, which concluded the trial of the six Chicago traitors found guilty of aiding an enemy agent."

Campbell received dozens of letters and telegrams. Almost all congratulated him.

James F. McElwee wrote from Peoria: "From the general reaction of the public in this part of the state—and I believe the feeling is the same all over the United States—the name of 'Campbell' will go down in history."

E. McNamara, of San Antonio, Texas, sent a Western Union that asked: "May I be the first member of W. J. Campbell for President Club?"

Campbell received, or kept, only one critical letter. "I think Judge Campbell would send all German men of the city to the Electric Chair, relating this to the verdict in the Haupt and Relatives case." It was signed "An American."

SEVEN MONTHS AFTER THE SENTENCE, the U.S. Court of Appeals for the Seventh Circuit reversed Campbell's decision and remanded the case for a new trial. The judges criticized Campbell for admitting the defendants' statements, for trying all six at once, and for giving confusing jury instructions.

The fourteen statements were inadmissible because they were all made before any of the defendants were arraigned before the U.S. commissioner. The government contended the six had waived those rights because they freely and voluntarily signed a written waiver of custody. The appeals court disagreed.

Without the statements, the treason case against the six was much more difficult to prove. The government made deals in 1944 with five defendants. Lucille Froehling and Kate Wergin were unconditionally released. Walter Froehling and Otto Wergin pleaded guilty to a lesser charge and were given five-year terms, much of which had already been served. Erna Haupt was interned for the duration of the war and denaturalized. She was deported to Germany after the war.

Prosecutors decided to bring Hans Haupt back to trial, possibly because they had the most evidence against him. Warnholtz, his attorney, told the court that Haupt had attempted suicide twice, once in the Winnetka Police Jail and once at the Cook County Jail. He asked that Haupt undergo a sanity test. Haupt passed the test, and his jury trial began in May 1944 in the courtroom of Judge John Peter Barnes.

"Although he was occasionally given to hasty judgments, critics and friends alike acknowledged his outstanding legal ability, his probity, courage and fairness," attorney Francis Busch wrote of Barnes in the book *They Escaped the Hangman.* "It was generally conceded that in the trial of criminal cases he 'leaned over backward' to avoid doing an injustice to even the meanest of the unfortunates who appeared before him."

Most of the same witnesses were called in the second trial. Once again, the government called Burger to the stand to establish Herbert Haupt's role as a saboteur. Once again, prosecutors called FBI agents, friends, and neighbors to reconstruct Herbert Haupt's week in Chicago and establish Hans Haupt's pro-Nazi sentiment. Shortly before closing arguments, the Allies landed at Normandy and the great "Invasion Day" was proclaimed all over Chicago. Haupt's lawyer vainly argued that the excitement and patriotic fervor drummed up by the Allies' advances made it difficult for a jury to be fair.

This time, the jury deliberated for twenty-eight hours without sleep.

Again, Haupt was convicted of treason. Barnes said his instinct was to sentence Haupt to death.

"As the time to impose sentence on the defendant, Hans Max Haupt, approaches, I find myself impelled to speak in explanation of the sentence," the judge said.

"Thirteen years experience in imposing sentences on persons who have pleaded guilty or been convicted of the commission of crime has taught me that, when I feel impelled to speak at a time such as this, the sentence under consideration does not square with my conscience. If I feel impelled to speak of the enormity of the defendant's crime, I know that the sentence under consideration is too severe; if I feel impelled to speak in extenuation of the crime, I know that the sentence under consideration is too light; and it is only when I feel that I may remain silent that I know that the proposed sentence squares with my conscience. Now the sentence to be imposed forces me to speak."

Barnes said the verdict of the jury was fully justified by the evidence.

Punishment, Barnes said, should attempt to reform a person and prevent him from repeating a crime. It should protect society by deterring that person and other criminals.

"Hans Max Haupt is fifty years old, and, in spite of the fact that he has lived in this country since 1923 and was naturalized in 1930, is, and for a long time has been, a fanatical Nazi," Barnes said. "He willingly, and apparently gladly, sacrificed his only child to the Nazi cause. The court does not believe that Hans Max Haupt can be reformed. He is and always will be a Nazi.

"The court does not believe that it need by punishment try to prevent Hans Max Haupt from committing treason again. Still the court believes that the defendant's mental faculties are unimpaired, his spirit is broken and he is not likely to commit treason again.

"What punishment is necessary to be imposed in order to deter other like-minded persons from committing like crimes? My conscience tells me that there is but one answer to that question and that answer is death. That would be the sentence and there would be no oral or written observations thereon by the court were it not for the facts hereinafter set forth."

But, said Barnes, after the jury had rendered its verdict, the foreman handed him a note. It read:

Your Honor, Judge Barnes:

Realizing fully that our function terminated with the rendering of our verdict, we, the jury, are moved humbly to beseech Your Honor's consideration in dealing mercifully with this defendant.

In conformity with your Honor's instructions, neither pity nor sympathy has entered into our deliberations. In this plea we express only what is in our hearts.

Respectfully, signed twelve jurors

"The twelve men and women who signed that communication share with the court the responsibility for the fate that shall overtake Hans Max Haupt," Barnes said. "Not until after they rendered a verdict of guilty did a duty rest on the court to impose sentence. They are reasonable men and women and listened carefully to the evidence. They heard all that the court heard. They know all that the court knows. They desire, as does the court, to do right. In deference to the request of these men and women, whose judgment may be better than mine, the sentence will be life imprisonment and, because the statute requires it, a fine of $10,000."

Eighteen months later, the Court of Appeals affirmed Barnes's ruling. Hans Haupt was imprisoned and deported to Germany in 1957.

U.S. Attorney General Francis Biddle was contemptuously called a "New Dealer" after he ordered the federal takeover of Montgomery Ward during World War II. **NATIONAL ARCHIVES**

FREE ENTERPRISE AND THE NATION'S WAR EFFORT went on trial in the Northern District of Illinois in 1944. Just before 11 P.M. on April 27, Judge William H. Holly issued a temporary restraining order prohibiting Montgomery Ward board chairman Sewell L. Avery from blocking the government's planned takeover of Ward to settle a labor dispute. The ruling led to the ouster of Avery from his own headquarters and one of the most famous photographs taken on the home front.

Avery appeared defiant in his office at 619 West Chicago the morning after the order was issued. He declared that the government had no legal right to seize the company. He refused to obey Holly's injunction and ignored an order from Wayne C. Taylor, undersecretary of commerce, to let the government run his business.

"After further discussion, we asked him to leave the office—we could not let his presence interfere with the government's possession," U.S. Attorney General Francis Biddle later wrote in his book *In Brief Authority.* "He said he would do no such thing—'to hell with the government.' There was a pause. . . .

"I was shocked. This reckless old man was paralyzing the national war effort that had been built up with such infinite pains," Biddle continued. "Turning to Taylor, I said, 'Take him out!' Avery looked at me venomously, summoning the most contemptuous words he could think of; and finally—'You New Dealer!'"

Two U.S. soldiers picked up Avery, in sitting position, and carefully carried him out of his office as photographers snapped away. "The picture did more to rouse the country to Avery's defense than any argument on the merits of the controversy," Biddle wrote.

The Ward company and the government had been at odds for years. President Franklin D. Roosevelt had ordered striking Ward employees back to work. In return, the president expected company officials to extend the

Sewell Avery, the chairman of Montgomery Ward, is carried from his office by soldiers in 1944 after he defied President Franklin D. Roosevelt and the War Labor Board in a labor dispute. The District Court approved the takeover. WILLIAM PAUER/ *CHICAGO SUN-TIMES*

workers' contract temporarily, but Ward officials refused. The company ignored directives from the War Labor Board, which had been created to iron
out disputes between labor and business during the war. Biddle, who
pleaded the government's case in District Court, argued that Roosevelt had a
right under war powers to seize Ward or any business that refused to abide
by the labor board's decision and by doing so hurt the war effort. Ward had
government contracts to provide clothes and material to the military.

Ward attorneys stated that if the government could seize Ward it could
seize little stores, or even an individual's property. Ward attorney Harold A.
Smith said that Biddle had "failed to mention the Bill of Rights or the rights
of citizens in wartime." He said the government's seizure was unlawful.

Holly, who went on senior judge status in 1944, was pushed center stage
in the dispute when he was called upon to make the temporary restraining
order permanent. But the government returned the company to Ward officials in May 1944, only hours before the expected ruling. Holly had made
copies of his long decision. After the settlement, he announced that his decision—never made public—would be destroyed. He told his bailiff to return
the copies, each in a sealed envelope, to the printer.

"The decision was a literary gem," bemoaned his secretary, Betty Druggan.

Avery returned to his office on May 11. He shook hands with employees
and accepted several dozen roses.

Because the dispute was settled, at least temporarily, Holly never determined whether the president's seizure was legal. Biddle admitted that the
seizure was "unnecessarily melodramatic," and wrote, "No act of mine as attorney general caused more sharp resentment and blame than the part I
played in connection with the seizure by the government of the Chicago
plant of Montgomery Ward & Company."

Seven months later, when Ward officials again balked at following federal
orders, Roosevelt ordered another seizure of the company. The War Department took over the property again on December 28, 1944. This time, Judge
Philip L. Sullivan ruled against the government. Pending appeal, however,
the government was allowed to continue its seizure. The Court of Appeals
ruled in the government's favor, saying that the president had the power to
take over Ward.

"There was hardly mention of the decision in the papers; and an issue
which had rocked the country a year before quietly sank into oblivion," Bid-

dle wrote. It was the last major World War II case the District Court decided.

AFTER HOLLY'S RETIREMENT as an active judge, a push was made by Chicago politicians to appoint a Polish American to the Northern District of Illinois court. Attorney General Biddle supported state Representative Benjamin S. Adamowski. Chicago Mayor Edward Kelly supported Cook County Circuit Court Judge Walter J. LaBuy. When Adamowski was drafted into the army, LaBuy became the choice in 1944.

LaBuy was born in 1888 near Beaver Dam, Wisconsin, and came to Chicago as a boy to live with his uncle. LaBuy received his law degree from DePaul University College of Law in 1912 and started in private practice in Chicago. He served as a member of the Cook County Board from 1930 to 1933, when he took the bench as a Cook County Circuit Court judge. He was named chief judge the following year.

A *Daily News* editorial memo stated that LaBuy was the nation's only federal judge of Polish ancestry, and perhaps the first ever.

"The elevation of Judge Walter J. LaBuy to the federal bench is tangible evidence that in this, our country, persons regardless of ancestry, origin, or creed may attain high positions of trust and service in our government with the approval of both Democrats and Republicans regardless of party if they are qualified, able men of character and of good record in public service," the memo stated.

LaBuy ruled on several significant business cases during the 1940s and early 1950s. He dismissed an antitrust suit against Yellow and Checker cab companies, a decision that was later overruled by the U.S. Supreme Court. In 1949 and 1950, a jury in LaBuy's court heard the government's case against Preston Tucker, the innovative automaker who was the subject of the 1988 movie *Tucker*. U.S. Attorney Otto Kerner Jr. and his staff spent twelve weeks putting on seventy-three witnesses to prove that Tucker attempted to defraud investors in building his avant-garde Tucker '48 cars at his Southwest Side factory. Tucker and colleagues were acquitted on all counts, but the company was finished. Tucker sued Kerner and other government officials for malicious prosecution, but the suit was tossed out.

In one of his most publicized cases, LaBuy acquitted James Caesar Petrillo, head of the American Federation of Musicians, who was trying to pre-

serve musicians' jobs at radio stations as recorded music became more popular. Petrillo took on a Chicago radio station after officials there refused to hire more musicians to play live music on the air. The Lea Act—directed against Petrillo—had been passed by Congress to prohibit "feather bedding," forcing employers to hire people they didn't need. Petrillo was charged with illegally interfering with the station. But in 1946, Judge LaBuy found the Lea Act unconstitutional. He wrote that Petrillo had a right to picket the station, to direct union members to walk off their jobs, and to direct other union members not to work for the station.

"There is in this case no charge of violence in picketing and therefore the placing of a picket must be regarded by this court as peaceful picketing," the judge found.

Petrillo, the object of numerous lawsuits during his long, stormy reign as the musician union czar, was delighted. "Thank God for the federal court," he said, "where they preach and practice democracy when they say the Constitution applies to musicians as well as to the National Association of Broadcasters, and where they say that Congress cannot discriminate against two hundred thousand musicians."

James Caesar Petrillo, leader of the American Federation of Musicians, is serenaded by colleagues. Petrillo called several strikes against TV and radio stations in his fight to keep jobs for musicians. *CHICAGO DAILY NEWS*

PRESIDENT ROOSEVELT NOMINATED Elwyn Shaw to the District Court on the same day he nominated LaBuy. Shaw, a Democrat from Freeport, was the personal choice of Senator Scott W. Lucas of Illinois. Shaw filled the court's "rural seat," which was vacated when Charles Edgar Woodward died. Shaw, born in Lyndon, Illinois, received his law degree from the University of Michigan Law School and started in private practice in Freeport. He served on the Illinois Supreme Court from 1933 to 1942, including two years as chief judge.

The Senate Judiciary Committee deferred action on Shaw in March 1944. The nomination was opposed by two labor leaders, but Shaw was approved by the Senate in May.

Shaw heard only a few significant cases during his six years on the bench. But he did take a strong stand against conspiracy trials. In December 1944, after hearing a case against 105 corporations and individuals charged with fixing the price of cheese, Shaw told a *Tribune* reporter, "Ever since Prohibition, there has been a general tendency of the government to try conspiracy cases. They put everything into a sack and toss it at the jury. That theory is faulty."

Shaw died while still an active district judge in 1950 at age sixty-two.

IN 1949, THE SIX JUDGES of the district wrote federal officials asking for two more judges. The court had been falling behind in hearing civil cases since 1944, when it had only 1,105 civil cases pending. By 1949, the court had 2,354 civil cases pending.

"Since the coming into the court, in 1933, of Judges Holly and Sullivan, the judges of this court have handled the business of the court without substantial assistance from the outside, and we think we may be permitted to say that, for a metropolitan community of the size of ours, this is a somewhat extraordinary record," the judges wrote the Senate Judiciary Committee.

The judges were not worried about criminal cases because three-quarters of all defendants pleaded guilty, or bankruptcy cases because all but large reorganization or receivership cases were being handled by assistants known as bankruptcy referees.

In February 1950, J. Earl Major, chief judge of the Seventh Circuit Court of Appeals, followed up on the request. "There is an acute situation here which the present judges are wholly unable to cope with, and it seems almost impossible to procure the assistance of outside judges," he wrote the

Judiciary Committee. "I need not bother you with statistics, all of which I
assume are available in the administrator's office; however, I point out that
there are now pending 41 antitrust cases, several of which are ready for trial
and which alone are sufficient to require the attention of the entire court for
months to come."

Two new judgeships were approved in August 1950, but the judgeships,
and the Shaw vacancy, were not filled for almost three years because of political wrangling. In July 1951, President Truman nominated Judges Cornelius
J. Harrington and Joseph Drucker to fill two vacancies on the court, but Democratic Senator Paul Douglas opposed the choices because they were not
run past him for approval. He rejected both nominations in committee.

The rural seat was finally filled by Democrat Joseph Sam Perry, who lived
in west suburban DuPage County. Perry was born at Carbon Hill, Alabama.
He began working at age thirteen in a coal mine and continued mining,
farming, and teaching in country schools until 1917, when he enlisted in the
navy. After his discharge in 1919, he returned to Alabama and graduated
from high school. Then his academic career took off. In 1923, Perry graduated from the University of Alabama as an honor student and in 1925 earned
a master's degree from the University of Chicago. Two years later, he graduated with a law degree from the university.

Between 1928 and 1951, Perry practiced law in Chicago and Wheaton. He
served as a state senator from 1937 to 1943 and as the DuPage County public
administrator from 1949 to 1951.

In a speech at a Chicago Bar Association meeting in 1951, Perry gave a
rambling but detailed description of the road he took from DuPage County
to the Northern District of Illinois bench. "To begin with, if you want to be
appointed to that office in Illinois, you almost have to be a Democrat," he
said. That, for Perry, was not an easy choice. Born in a rare corner of Alabama that was staunchly Republican, he was converted to the Democratic
Party as a boy. After his University of Chicago education, he once again almost "backslid" to the Republican Party after moving to Republican Du-
Page County. His speech, one of the most candid accounts of the politics
needed to get appointed to the federal bench, explains in part why Joseph
Drucker was never confirmed as a District Court judge. The text was published in the 1961 book *Courts, Judges and Politics*. Perry told the audience:

> I will be frank about it. At first I talked around amongst the Republicans
> about doing some work—there was no Democratic Party out there—but the

Republicans didn't need me. Well, after I became converted to the Democratic Party again, or was saved again, so to speak, I proceeded to organize the Democratic Party out there and to make it tough for the Republicans. The result was that we finally had the framework of a party. Later, with the aid of the late Governor Henry Horner and a few other good Democrats, I landed in the legislature and kept working along and served my term there. Then I got out of politics and came back and practiced law.

And then I gambled. I saw a man—Paul Douglas—who looked as though he might be elected to the United States Senate. I backed him and as a result I had his support. My political friendship with my good friend Scott Lucas, in the meantime, had grown bit by bit and Scott was not mad at me.

Since we are talking confidentially I will be perfectly frank with you folks in admitting that I tried to obtain this appointment seven years ago and learned then that it requires not one but two senators. At that time I was out of politics and they did not need me. Therefore, I decided that this time if I wanted that appointment I had better get back into politics—which I did.

When I learned, as I soon did, that everyone shoots at the top man—that he is everyone's target—I went to each of the senators and said, "Listen here, if you are going to back me, for heaven's sake don't make me number one. Be sure to back me and get me on the list but don't make me number one."

As it turned out that proved to be pretty good strategy because everyone else was shot off and, no use lying about it, I helped to shoot them off. The result of it was I landed on top. I have the job now and I am going to stick.

IN 1952, THE DISTRICT COURT again came under a cloud because of its handling of bankruptcy cases. A subcommittee of the House Judiciary Committee held hearings into alleged irregularities in bankruptcy cases before Judge Philip L. Sullivan. The hearings were held after the *Chicago Sun-Times* ran a series of articles alleging that Sullivan's brothers and associates had won control of the $10 million Lott hotels after they were reorganized in Sullivan's court. The North Side hotels included the Belden-Stratford, the Webster, and the Parkway. They went into receivership in 1928 and emerged in 1949 in a trusteeship established by the federal court. Principal stockholders in the hotels turned out to be attorneys Harold E. and George D. Sullivan, the judge's brothers; Charles A. McDonald, who heard the case as master-in-chancery; and Byron Cain, who served as federal trustee to manage the hotel during its period of reorganization.

A subcommittee was to determine whether the House Judiciary Committee should start a full investigation.

Public hearings were held in Chicago in July 1952, but the three-member subcommittee, with two Democrats, never issued a report to the full committee. Sullivan, appointed in 1933, was a Democrat. The committee was reorganized after Republicans gained control in the 1952 election. This time the subcommittee was controlled by two Republicans. It met in 1954, but again did not issue a report.

AS THE 1950S UNFOLDED, the District Court took on an increasingly important issue in America: civil rights for African Americans. In 1952, six officials of the town of Cicero were indicted for allowing mob action against a black family that had attempted to move in to the all-white suburb west of Chicago. Judge LaBuy freed, by directed verdict, the Cicero town president and fire chief. Then a jury found the police chief, town attorney, and two police officers guilty.

"The jury's decision obviously came as a stunning surprise to the other four," wrote the *Sun-Times.* "They had been laughing and joking with their families and watching a fight on television in a courthouse office while the jury was deliberating. All had big smiles on their faces when they went into the courtroom to hear the decision. These quickly faded as the verdict was read."

At the trial, Harvey E. Clark Jr., a Chicago Transit Authority bus driver, testified that police blocked him when he first tried to move into town. The family rented an apartment, paid the first month's rent, and arrived with their belongings on June 8, 1951. They were stopped by police officers, one brandishing a revolver, who asked Clark to show a permit allowing him to move into town. He was told to wait for Police Chief Erwin Konovsky, who arrived and, according to Clark, told him, "I am not going to jeopardize the lives of 19 white families for the likes of you."

Clark testified that cops grabbed and shoved him and his helpers. A crowd cheered as police told him to leave town forever, Clark said. One person gave him a kick.

The following week, Clark filed a civil action in federal court seeking police protection to move into the apartment. District Court Judge Barnes signed a preliminary injunction against Cicero on June 26, telling town officials they must not stop the move.

The family tried again on July 10. Clark showed up with his wife, Johnetta, two young children, a friend, and movers. Again a crowd formed.

"They were gesturing and making remarks that they didn't want niggers out there, and cockroaches and bringing filth and indecency into the community," Clark testified. "And every move that was made there was some nasty crack made about it, and they laughed at my belongings, and there were rhythmic claps when they would see a musical instrument, and one fellow spat at me. One fellow threw a cigarette in the car and set the back seat on fire. And they took sharp instruments and disfigured the whole right side of the car and wrote 'Cicero' on it, and 'KKK' and Xs. And there was just a complete confusion. One woman hit me on the arm as I walked to the door, and told me I would be sorry that night."

The Clarks drove back to Chicago. By nightfall, the crowds had turned ugly. Thousands surrounded the apartment building, throwing rocks and smashing windows. The rioting, which lasted for three nights, shocked the nation. Years later, Martin Luther King Jr. would call Cicero the "Selma of the North."

Witness Ralph Harsough testified that he saw one Cicero police officer at-

tempt to stop rock throwers, but generally, he said, "They were standing in a rather disorganized fashion along the south side of the building."

He testified: "This officer told me that there were colored people moving into, or had leased the apartment on the third floor, and when I asked him why there was nothing being done to stop the vandalism, he said, 'Our chief has warned these niggers to stay out of here.'"

Harsough was asked: "What did the police officers do?"

"They did nothing."

Defense attorney Floyd E. Thompson said the police department did everything possible to move the family in peacefully and hold back the crowds that first night. Every available Cicero officer was called to the scene, he said, and other police departments served as backup. On the second night, crowds broke the lines and invaded the building. "Soon articles of furniture came flying out the window and onto the apron of the alley and on the sidewalk alongside of the building," Harsough said.

Rioters piled up the Clarks' furniture, doused it with fluid, and set it afire. The family never returned.

Thompson argued that the police department did not start or encourage the riot. It was "utterly overwhelmed," and could not control the situation. The National Guard was eventually called in to stop nights of riots.

"We will show you that the officers of the Town of Cicero are the victims of a situation which they had nothing to do with creating, and that they were now being charged with a crime because they couldn't accomplish the impossible," Thompson argued.

The jury found Konovsky, Town Attorney Nicholas Berkos, Sergeant Roland Brani, and police officer Frank A. Lange guilty. The decision was later reversed by the Court of Appeals and remanded to the District Court. The appeals judges said the evidence was adequate to sustain the verdicts, but that "highly inflammatory" photos of the riot, which did not link the individuals in the case to the event, should not have been shown. The four Cicero officials were never retried. Wrote the *Chicago Defender:* "This farcical conclusion of the incident is an indictment of the local police, the FBI which talked loudly of investigating the situation at the time and the courts which have found some grounds to clear everyone of blame."

IN 1954, JUDGE JOHN PETER BARNES freed gangster Roger "the Terrible" Touhy from prison. He determined that Touhy was the victim of an intri-

Facing page: National Guardsmen relax in front of the embattled apartment building at 6139 West Nineteenth, Cicero. The July 14, 1951, caption reads: "Expecting more trouble after sundown, troops have been ordered to 'keep 'em moving' to prevent a mob from forming again." Three nights of violence subsided after the soldiers arrival in the western suburb. **BILL KNEFEL/ CHICAGO SUN-TIMES**

cate gangland frame-up that had denied him his federal constitutional rights and had cost him decades of freedom. Touhy, a rival of the Capone gang, had been convicted of the 1933 kidnapping of John "Jake the Barber" Factor, who was wanted by British authorities for defrauding stock investors of $7 million. Factor, who had an international reputation as a confidence man, was the half brother of makeup mogul Max Factor. John Factor told police he had been beaten, held for twelve days, and released only after he paid $50,000 with a promise of $20,000 later. But the story, after being believed for decades, turned out to be a hoax made up to prevent his extradition.

"The Factor kidnapping, which led ultimately to the extermination of the 'Terrible Touhy' gang, is one of the gaudiest and most bizarre criminal cases on record," wrote Melvin Purvis, once head of the Chicago FBI office, in his 1936 book *American Agent.* "There was a queer odor about the affair from the start. As a news event, it was of international interest. It had color, mystery and an odd murky undercurrent of uncertainty."

Touhy had originally been sentenced to ninety-nine years in prison, but Barnes ruled that Factor faked the kidnapping and he ordered Touhy's release. The judge was standing up for a reviled gang leader and attacking local law enforcement officials. Barnes wrote in his six-hundred-page ruling that Touhy was the innocent victim of a "diabolical" frame-up. "Perjured testimony was knowingly used by the prosecutor to bring about Touhy's conviction," the judge declared.

The ruling drew immediate condemnation from those who had taken part in the original prosecution. Cook County Circuit Judge Thomas C. Courtney and Superior Judge Wilbert F. Crowley, who had served as Cook County state's attorney and the chief prosecutor in the 1930s case, were indignant at Barnes's charges and accused the federal judge of misconduct.

Barnes's ruling, which he called the most memorable in his long career, was short-lived. Two days later, the Court of Appeals returned Touhy to Stateville prison. The appeals judges determined that Barnes, who had taken years to make the decision, did not have jurisdiction in the case because Touhy had not exhausted his state remedies.

Touhy was released on parole in 1959. Twenty-three days later, he was shot to death gangland style.

Factor, on the other hand, came to a better end. The "kidnapping" helped him escape extradition. After serving six years in federal prison for mail fraud, he moved to Los Angeles, where he amassed a fortune as a real estate developer and a reputation as a do-gooder, contributing to many causes, including the redevelopment of the Watts neighborhood following race riots there. Pardoned in 1962 by President John F. Kennedy, Factor lived to about ninety. The headline on his obituary in the *Los Angeles Times* read: "John Factor, Noted Philanthropist, Dies after Long Illness."

JUDGE BARNES HELPED the court recover from the bankruptcy scandals that had plagued it for decades. Barnes, who developed a reputation as the court's conscience, was quite the individual. He grew a beard in 1944 after a heart attack, because it saved him from shaving. "Two things I've disliked most in life are dressing and shaving," he said. "Suddenly it dawned on me I could get rid of shaving." That beard became a symbol of justice in the Chicago courts. Wrote *Chicago Sun-Times* reporter Ray Brennan: "He

Soprano Maria Callas rages after being served a summons by Deputy Marshal Stanley Pringle (left) and Deputy Sheriff Dan Smith at the Lyric Opera of Chicago in 1955. "I will not be sued," cried the diva. "I have the voice of an angel!" The breach of contract lawsuit was first heard by District Court Judge John Peter Barnes but later transferred to U.S. District Court in New York and settled out of court.
CHICAGO DAILY NEWS

trimmed it at medium length, cut off squarely beyond the chin and resembling—as one prominent Chicago lawyer said after an unnerving time in Barnes's courtroom—the business end of a bulldozer."

Although Barnes seemed stern on the bench, he closely guarded the constitutional rights of prisoners and often sided with the underdog. "He could broil, fry and boil a hypocritical defense lawyer or a too-eager prosecutor with incendiary language," wrote Brennan. "An hour later he might be conferring sympathetically with an out-of-work, wife-expecting-a-baby, young husband charged with stealing from mail boxes."

In 1939, Barnes placed on probation a teller of a small suburban bank convicted of stealing $2,749. "If you are going to pay a man such a small salary, it is dangerous to let him handle money," Barnes said. "This defendant had to feed and shelter a family of five on that amount or steal more."

When it was discovered that Illinois prisoners were being thwarted in their attempt to file writs of habeas corpus, Barnes threatened wardens with jail terms if they hindered the flow of the writs to the District Court.

"Hundreds of convicts promptly petitioned Barnes for relief," Brennan wrote. "Many of the applications obviously were preposterous and others had no standing in law. A small percentage of the petitioners received hearings in court and most of them were turned down. A magazine writer wrote that, of the applicants, only seven were freed as falsely convicted. Judge Barnes read the comment and was aghast.

"'What does he mean by only seven?' the judge asked. 'If only one had been freed, it would have been worth the effort. And if not one justifiable case had been found, these men still should not have been denied their constitutional rights.'"

Barnes was beset by family tragedy. His son Darr died at age ten of diphtheria. Two other sons, Paul and Hugh, were killed in action during World War II in 1944.

Campbell informed Barnes of each of his son's deaths. "The second time that I went up to him, he fainted in my arms coming down from the bench," Campbell recalled.

But Barnes persevered.

"He met this blow as he did all others—seeking solace in his work and with his family—dependent more than ever upon Mrs. Barnes who, throughout the 51 years of their married life, sustained him and gave him an

Facing page: Found guilty of violating the Smith Act, Communist leader Claude Lightfoot (left) leaves U.S. District Court with his attorney John J. Abt Jr. on January 26, 1955. **DAVE MANN/*CHICAGO SUN-TIMES***

added stability such as few wives were able to do," said his friend, attorney
Kenneth F. Burgess. "Although he gave other reasons, I always felt that he
grew the beard which distinguishes his later years as a part of a self-protective
effort to change his personality—at least outwardly—and in a measure to
assuage the sorrow that was in his heart."

Barnes resigned from the court on the last day of 1958 and died four
months later.

FOLLOWING THE END of World War II, America found itself with a new
enemy—the communist empire. Dozens of cases were filed concerning the
residency status of immigrants from commu-
nist nations. Other cases concerned the basic
rights of communists living in the United
States.

Claude Lightfoot, chairman of the Illinois
Communist Party, was the first person tried
and convicted of violating the Smith Act,
which made it a crime to belong to an organization that advocates the violent overthrow of the
government. The jury deliberated for ten hours
before finding Lightfoot guilty in 1955. The
Chicago Herald American declared the decision
"the heaviest legal blow at Communism this
nation has ever seen."

Assistant U.S. Attorney James Benton Parsons, who like the defendant was African American, called the verdict "a major victory toward
the security of the nation." He told a reporter:
"I don't like to see the vicious exploitation of minority groups. I don't like to see my people sold
down the river with some trumped-up ideas that
had origin in other countries.

"I don't like to see communists using our race
to destroy something fine that our race helped
to build."

Lightfoot was fined and sentenced to five

years in prison by Judge Sullivan. His decision was reversed by the Supreme Court, which found that the law was an unconstitutional infringement on free speech.

Being called a communist was a serious condemnation. In 1957, a Slavic refugee named Sveta Maric sued an acquaintance for slander after he was allegedly labeled as a communist while attending a meeting at a Serbian Orthodox Church on the South Side. Judge Perry ruled that the statements were indeed slanderous and made with malice. Maric said that he was unable to find work in his community following the remarks. As a result, Perry ordered that $1,500 in damages be paid.

In one of the most notable legal decisions in court history, Chicago attorney Elmer Gertz sued the publisher of the John Birch Society magazine for calling him a leader of the communist movement. A District Court jury awarded Gertz $50,000 in damages in 1970, but the verdict was set aside by District Court Judge Bernard Decker, who dismissed the case. Gertz appealed to the Court of Appeals and the U.S. Supreme Court, which sent it back for retrial. Gertz won in the second round and was awarded $400,000.

JUDGE LABUY'S BIGGEST AND LONGEST CASE during the 1950s was the antitrust trial of the E. I. duPont de Nemours & Company. The case was the most complex federal antitrust case ever tried up to that time.

In 1949, the government charged that the duPont company had formed a cartel to restrain trade by buying huge amounts of stock in the General Motors and U.S. Rubber companies so it could control the companies and increase its revenue. DuPont, the government charged, forced General Motors and U.S. Rubber to buy only duPont products. A trial against duPont began in early 1952 and lasted through most of 1953.

LaBuy issued a 220-page opinion in 1954 that was delivered to court by printers under guard of four armed men. LaBuy disagreed with government attorneys. He called the duPont stock purchases good business. "The government has failed to prove conspiracy, monopolization, a restraint of trade or any reasonable probability of restraint," he ruled. The duPonts owned 33 percent of General Motors and 18 percent of U.S. Rubber, so they could not control the companies, LaBuy wrote. The government's contentions, he wrote, were supported only by "suspicion and conjecture."

The Supreme Court overruled LaBuy in 1957, declaring that duPont did hold illegal control over General Motors. "Well, they could only rule one of two ways—for me or against me," LaBuy said. "They went against."

The court returned the case to LaBuy with instructions to hold hearings on how duPont should untangle itself from the two companies. Finally, in 1962, LaBuy ruled that duPont must get rid of its GM stock within three years. That concluded thirteen years of litigation.

THE NORTHERN DISTRICT COURT OF ILLINOIS finally did expand again in 1953, when two new judges—the first Republican appointments since 1932—were nominated and confirmed. They were named to resolve the long-standing dispute between President Truman and Senator Douglas. After Douglas blocked the appointment of two Truman choices in the early 1950s, he inadvertently closed the door on Democratic nominees as Republican Dwight D. Eisenhower assumed the presidency.

Winfred G. Knoch was named by Eisenhower to fill the court's seventh judgeship, and Julius J. Hoffman was nominated to fill the eighth judgeship. About seven hundred people attended the investiture of the two judges in LaBuy's courtroom. "The room was filled with roses, lilies and applauding Republican politicians," the *Chicago Daily News* reported.

Knoch, a Republican powerhouse, was born in Naperville and spent most of his life in the western suburb. He earned his law degree from DePaul University in 1917, joined the army, and returned to Naperville to start a private practice. He was an assistant DuPage County state's attorney during the 1920s and developed a reputation as a tough prosecutor. He served as a DuPage County judge during the 1930s and as a state judge from 1939 until his appointment to the District Court. During the Depression, Knoch organized the Naperville National Bank and assumed the precarious loans of many residents in the western suburb. He considered this to be his greatest civic contribution. Knoch served as board chairman or president of the bank for thirty-five years. He sat as a District Court judge until 1958, when he was appointed to the Seventh Circuit Court of Appeals. In his later years, Knoch was something of a country squire; he lived on a 250-acre farm known as Knoch Knolls, which is now part of the Naperville Park District.

Hoffman, the city kid, was born in Chicago, attended Northwestern University and Northwestern University School of Law, and ran a private practice from 1915 to 1947. He then took a seat as a judge on the Cook County

Superior Court. "Before the [1968 Democratic Convention] conspiracy trial Hoffman was noted for two characteristics: his foul temper and his antipathy to the United States government in tax cases," wrote author Joseph Goulden.

By 1956, all but two of the eight district judges wore robes regularly in court.

"The one robe I have is too heavy. It wears me out," said Barnes.

"They say I don't wear it for the sake of the Irish—because it harks back to the English system," said Sullivan.

By the end of the decade, however, the judges decided that robes should be their standard dress.

A report by the Administrative Office of the U.S. Courts sketched a picture of the busy court during the 1950s.

"The metropolitan character and other factors peculiar to the district leave their mark on the types of civil suits commenced," the report stated. "As the largest railroad center in the world the district receives many Federal Employer's Liability Act cases, which have averaged about one hundred per year for the last ten years. Because of peculiarities in the law of criminal procedure in the State of Illinois, a great many habeas corpus cases have been filed by state prisoners. A few years ago this district had more federal question habeas corpus cases than all other districts combined. For the last three years they have averaged about 90 per year. In 1947, 238 were filed. Considerable patent litigation arises in the district; cases of this nature have numbered between 50 and 75 yearly for the last ten years. This gives each judge a patent caseload three times greater than the average for the [then] eighty-six districts."

Two more Republicans were nominated by Eisenhower in 1958. Julius H. Miner filled Barnes's seat and Edwin A. Robson took Knoch's seat when Knoch was elevated to the Court of Appeals.

Miner was born in Lubon, Russia, and moved to the West Side of Chicago at age seven. He earned degrees from Chicago-Kent School of Law in 1917 and Northwestern University School of Law. He was in private practice until 1924, when he took on the role of master in chancery of the Cook County Circuit Court. In 1940, Miner was elected to the Cook County Circuit Court and was later named chief judge of the court. In 1951, he ran for a seat on the Illinois Supreme Court but was defeated. He appeared in the

Chicago Bar Association Christmas show in 1951 and proclaimed: "To think that only a year ago I was known as Julius the Just and now I'm just Julius."

Miner was an innovator. While on the Circuit Court, he required a sixty-day cooling-off period for spouses in divorce cases, an idea that was adopted by several other states. In the federal court, Miner came up with a way to streamline civil procedure. He called for the appointment of an impartial medical examiner for civil cases so that judges would not have to decide between dueling doctors giving testimony. And he separated civil cases into two phases. The first determined liability. If necessary, the second determined compensation.

Robson was born in Chicago, grew up in the Englewood neighborhood, and graduated from DePaul University College of Law in 1928. He was in private practice for seventeen years before being elected in 1945 as the youngest sitting judge in Cook County. Robson presided in Divorce Court, which was swamped after World War II because, as the *Chicago Daily News* noted, it was "catching the aftermath of long war separations and the result of the economic independence conferred on women by high war wages."

Robson made national news as a prominent Divorce Court judge. He installed a nursery so that children of divorcing couples could be cared for while their parents were in court. He became something of a commentator on the social problems caused by divorce.

"Since August to the end of today's court call, I will have heard two thousand divorce cases," he wrote in January 1946. "I point to this with no pride. In fact, I point to it with shame; shame for the people of my county, state and country." Later that year, he granted a divorce to ice skating sensation Sonja Henie from millionaire sportsman Dan Topping. They told the judge they sought to go their own ways, which Robson decried. He told his packed courtroom that society was at fault for a "lack of respect" for marital obligations. Robson had been named chief justice of the Cook County Superior Court in 1950 and served on the court until the following year, when he was named by the Illinois Supreme Court as a state appellate judge. He served until 1958, when he was nominated and confirmed as a federal District Court judge.

IN 1959, WILLIAM J. CAMPBELL took over as the chief judge of the Northern District of Illinois. Barnes had been named the court's first chief judge in

1948, when the position was created by statute nationally. The title has always been determined by a formula based on seniority. Barnes did not like administration, and according to Campbell he passed off most of his administrative duties to Campbell. In 1957, Philip Sullivan was named the district's second chief judge. Sullivan enjoyed supervising the grand jury, one of the functions of the chief judge, but he, too, was not interested in administrative work. So by the time Campbell was officially named chief, he had already established a national reputation among judges. He was in charge of determining the federal judicial budget requests and he was used to testifying before Congress in Washington, D.C. Campbell was also recognized for upgrading the district's Probation Department to a level that was seen as a standard for the country. During the 1950s, Campbell had hired Ben Meeker from Indiana University as the district's chief probation and parole officer. Meeker professionalized the Probation Department, setting up academic qualifications for probation officers and creating a model office.

One of Campbell's first acts as chief was to defend the Northern District of Illinois, which was denounced in 1959 by federal investigators for its case assignment system. The staff of the Senate Appropriations Committee criticized the court's long-standing practice of assigning the "old cats and dogs" of the calendar—difficult, protracted cases—to new judges.

"From the record, it would appear that the administration of this court needs improvement," the report stated. "It is apparent that the caseload has been inequitably divided and nothing has been done about it. This situation should not be permitted to prevail."

The report said that when Miner was appointed to the court in 1958 as one of eight District Court judges, he was given one-fourth of the court calendar, including the oldest cases and most demanding patent and antitrust cases.

"Although, at the time of the appointment of Judge Miner, some one or two of our judges assigned to him lengthy cases they might better have kept themselves, nevertheless such inequities were promptly corrected when called to the attention of the executive committee of this court," Campbell said.

The report also criticized the Northern Illinois judges for their lack of uniformity in disposing of cases. Some judges, investigators found, were two or more years behind other judges. The fastest District Court judge disposed of an average case in 16.6 months. The slowest took 38.4 months. "The result is that one set of litigants in these courts obtains trials within a relatively short time, while another group in the same court, purely because their cases happen to be assigned to a judge who . . . had a larger number of trials or protracted cases, must wait several years," the report stated. Campbell, who bristled over the report, nonetheless said he was reorganizing the court to address the inconsistencies.

Campbell became the first Northern Illinois judge to be awarded the national Edward J. Devitt Distinguished Service to Justice Award, the most prestigious award given to federal judges. He was honored for his Chicago work and his national accomplishments, such as helping to create the Federal Judicial Center in Washington, D.C., the federal court system's research and education agency. When he died in 1988, Campbell was the nation's longest-tenured federal judge, with forty-eight years on the bench. Campbell, long considered arrogant and unyielding, softened in his later years.

FOR DECADES, THE NORTHERN DISTRICT OF ILLINOIS—like other federal courts—had been determining moral standards in its community.

In 1959, Columbia Pictures applied to the Chicago police commissioner for permission to show the film *Anatomy of a Murder*. The commissioner declined to issue the permit because the film was "immoral or obscene." Columbia officials took their case to District Court to get an order directing the city to issue the permit. Judge Miner agreed. "Taken as a whole, the film cannot be placed in the category of the obscene or immoral, because its dominant effect does not tend to excite sexual passion or undermine public morals," Miner wrote. "The infrequent mention of 'rape' or 'contraceptive' in the film is not likely to so much arouse the salacity of the normal and average viewer as to outweigh its artistic and expert presentation. In fact, the criminal assault upon the murderer's wife has the effect of arousing pity and revulsion rather than desire or sexual impure thoughts."

In a similar case decided just a few months earlier before Judge Sullivan, Paramount sought a declaration that the censorship statute was unconstitutional as an unreasonable prior restraint of free speech. Paramount's lawsuit came after the city ruled that the movie *Desire under the Elms* could be shown only to adults over the age of twenty-one. Sullivan took issue with the vagueness of the statute. He disagreed that the statute's reference to "children" would or should include all persons up to the age of twenty-one. He also disagreed with the notion that a film could be just "sort of" obscene. "A picture is either 'obscene' ('offensive to taste; foul; loathsome') or it is not,"

VIRTUE TRIUMPHS!

*The look of alarm
On this bundle of charm
May stir up some foolish illusion,
Her state of attire
'Neen rather sparks overdesigns,
Perhaps you've surmised
That the girl's been surprised
By a callousious man of a lower-
But, brother, you're wrong,
'Cos in here wrong right along—
It wasn't a wolf ... but a mouse!*

**PAINTING BY VARGA
VERSE BY PHIL STACK**

Sullivan wrote. "None of these criteria can change with the age of the beholder." Sullivan acknowledged that the city may, under its police power, limit free speech to prevent an evil, but any restrictive action, he said, must be reasonable and not capricious. He ruled that the censorship statute did not meet those criteria.

Morality was only slightly on trial in 1948 when *Esquire* magazine sued its famed artist, Alberto Vargas. Vargas was accused of copyright and trademark infringement after he produced sexy paintings of women and captioned each as a "Varga Girl," the name used in the magazine. Vargas was no stranger to the District Court. He had previously sued *Esquire* and publisher David Smart to void the exclusive contract he signed with the magazine. But Vargas had lost in the Court of Appeals. *Esquire* now considered all of Vargas's work its own since the contract was valid. Judge Campbell took due deliberate notice of each of Vargas's paintings presented into evidence. He noted that Vargas's portrayal of "clothing" was as "concealing as the ordinary window pane" and wrote that Vargas's artistic talent was limited to the portrayal of the female figure in varying degrees of undress. "His success in this line of endeavor can undoubtedly be attributed to the remarkable physical characteristics of his finished product, e.g., the exaggerated torso and the subtly curved but unduly long leg. It is apparent from the testimony that this is all he has ever drawn and seems to be all he ever will draw. It follows, therefore, that all his future drawings will bear some similarity to his previous work." Campbell ruled that Vargas was entitled to draw his women for other publications but could not use the Varga Girl moniker.

Artist Alberto Vargas fought *Esquire* magazine publisher David Smart for years in District Court. Vargas sought to take his Varga Girl from the magazine and publish it independently.

BY THE 1950S, THE FEDERAL BUILDING had fallen on hard times.

Attorney Francis X. Busch wrote in 1954 that the old Federal Building and Post Office had become "an ancient and somber pile of stone and iron." In his book, *Enemies of the State,* Busch described what had become of the once-grand building.

The place is scarcely inviting. The huge central rotunda and the three wide passageways leading to public streets are usually littered with fragments of letters from the "general delivery" boxes and the wrappings of candy bars and other confections sold at the news and general-supply stand on one side of the spacious inner circle. Two banks of dingy, wobbling, creaking elevators, operating at the whim of the individuals in charge, carry persons to and from the upper floors.

Of the numerous rooms on the upper floors, those provided for the District Courts are alone impressive. They are spacious, airy, solidly furnished and regularly cleaned. In the older courtrooms superb murals depict the Blind Goddess of Justice holding her scales, Moses handing down the Twelve Tables of the Law, King John signing the Magna Carta at Runnymede, and the delegates to the Constitutional Convention signing a report of its proceedings, and other scenes illustrating the development of supremacy of the law.

These courtrooms ordinarily have no lure for sensation hunters. "Court fans" seek the state courts where they may chance upon a murder or rape trial or a sensational divorce case. The cases tried in the federal courts are, for the most part, dry and uninteresting to the layman: on the civil side, bankruptcies, receiverships and damage suits against nonresident corporations; on the criminal side, prosecutions for dope peddling, mail frauds and violations of the antitrust, liquor or internal-revenue laws.

A man prepares to jump from the seventh floor of the Federal Courthouse in January 1964. The man was caught in a net spread across the rotunda lobby following a long attempt by police to talk the man down from his perch. Six others leaped to their death during the building's history. **BOB KOTALIK/ CHICAGO SUN-TIMES**

By the late 1950s, discussion about tearing down the courthouse for a new building became more commonplace. Judge LaBuy hoped to save the old building, and disagreed with Mayor Richard J. Daley about the need for a new facility. In January 1959, LaBuy wrote the General Services Administration suggesting that the building be renovated with new elevators and escalators. The Seventh Circuit Court of Appeals had long since left the courthouse. LaBuy suggested consolidating the courts in one building again and selling the U.S. Court of Appeals Building, on North Lake Shore Drive, to raise much of the $2.5 million needed for the courthouse rehabilitation.

Campbell, who became chief judge of the district in 1959, had different plans. He had been working for years with his Senate friends, Republican Everett M. Dirksen of Illinois and Democrat Lyndon B. Johnson of Texas, to gather federal money to construct a new courthouse. Money for construction was part of President Eisenhower's farewell budget.

WITH THE ELECTION of John F. Kennedy, the Democrats roared back to political power. Democrats returned to the District Court as well. In August 1961, Kennedy nominated Richard Austin to fill the seat vacated by Walter

The old Federal Courthouse looms over the stores on Jackson Boulevard in 1957. GLENN E. DAHLBY/CHICAGO HISTORICAL SOCIETY

LaBuy and nominated James Benton Parsons to fill the seat vacated by Sullivan.

Austin, a lifelong Chicagoan, attended the University of Chicago Law School and sat next to Richard Loeb in class the day after Loeb joined Nathan Leopold in the sensational 1924 murder of Bobby Franks.

Austin received his law degree in 1926 and flip-flopped his legal career, working for years as a private attorney and as an assistant state's attorney between 1926 to 1952. As a special prosecutor, Austin helped convict Michael Moretti, a state's attorney policeman accused of murdering two children, and serial killer William Heirens. Austin ran a surprisingly good campaign for governor on the Democratic ticket in 1956. As a last-moment fill-in, he almost pulled off an upset win against seemingly invincible Governor William G. Stratton. Austin lost, but he won support from Daley, who, after Kennedy's victory, was the power behind Democratic federal judgeships in Northern Illinois. Austin served as a Superior Court and Criminal Court judge from 1953 to 1961, including two terms as the court's chief justice, before he was nominated to the District Court.

Austin was tough. On his wall was a plaque that read: "Yea, though I walk through the valley of the shadow of death, I shall fear no evil, because I'm the meanest SOB in the valley." His obituary in the *Chicago Tribune* described him as "a short man with a towering brow and a jutting jaw." In 1971, *Tribune* reporter Dorothy Storck wrote, "He has one of those faces in which everything is pronounced. Large nose, large mouth, large eyes behind bifocals. In court his head rises a touch gargoylelike over the bench, ferocious looking even. But ferocity is not part of Richard Austin's makeup. Sarcasm, perhaps, an acerbic wit. Certainly a good deal of understanding."

Three days after nominating Austin, Kennedy chose James Benton Parsons to serve on the Northern District of Illinois. Parsons was the first African American in the nation's history to receive a lifetime appointment as a District Court judge. "He was the Jackie Robinson of the federal District Court system," explained District Court Chief Judge Marvin Aspen at a seminar in 2002 for young practitioners of the court. Less than half of the new lawyers present that day knew who Parsons was.

Born in Kansas City, Missouri, Parsons grew up in downstate Decatur and got his bachelor's degree from Millikin University. He taught music at small colleges in Missouri and North Carolina, and joined the navy in 1942 as a bandmaster. Following the war, he was accepted at the University of

Chicago, where he received a master's degree in 1946 and his law degree in 1949. "Even in law school, it was generally known he was to become the first African American federal judge in the continental United States," said his classmate, Milton I. Shadur, who also later became a Northern District of Illinois judge.

Parsons served Chicago as an assistant corporation counsel from 1949 to 1951. He was then hired as an assistant U.S. attorney, where he distinguished himself by winning sixty-three consecutive convictions against draft resisters. When he was being considered for the Cook County Superior Court, District Court Judge Perry wrote Daley of Parsons: "He is positively the most fair and able prosecutor that it has been my privilege to know." Parsons served on the Superior Court from 1960 until his District Court appointment.

The elevation of Parsons gave the District Court judges a new perspective almost immediately. In September 1961, during his first month on the federal bench, Parsons was denied member-guest privileges at the Union League Club, the dignified social club near the courthouse that had admitted district judges as honorary members for decades. Parsons's new brothers—Judges Campbell, Igoe, LaBuy, Perry, Hoffman, Robson, Miner, and Austin—handed in their memberships and marched to the rival Standard Club, which welcomed them all.

Parsons's resume, on the surface, looked like that of many new federal district judges: graduate of a prestigious law school, work as a public prosecutor, and appointment as a local judge. But Parsons brought quite a different background to the court.

One of his grandmothers had escaped moments before being sold into slavery; his other grandmother was the daughter of a slave.

"I remember lying on the floor every week with a coal oil lamp and reading a newspaper called the *Chicago Defender,* reading about people like myself," Parsons recalled years later in an oral history. "We were called colored people then. There were pictures of them, getting in and out of automobiles with chauffeurs in Chicago. Beautiful mansion houses in which they lived. Magnificent attire, parties, all of these social pictures, social pages, very much like the things that you read about in the literature of the period. I didn't see any of that in Decatur."

Decatur, though, was a fine place for a young African American boy to grow up, Parsons said, because he seldom felt discrimination. Nonetheless, he remembered being called "Sambo" on his first day as a waiter at a Rotary Club banquet. He recalled what happened when his father, who had earned money from church work and real estate, wanted to buy a Packard. A salesman first directed the elder James Parsons to the garage to show him used models. When his father explained that he wanted a new car, and made the deal, the salesman started to tell him how he could take out a loan.

"Then he took out of his pocket a clean beautiful white envelope and pulled out and counted out twenty-eight $100 bills," Parsons recalled. "He told my brother, 'JB and I are going on back. You bring the car. You stay here and get it and bring it on home.' I wanted to stay with my brother, but I was proud of my father so I walked with him."

Parsons also recalled watching a movie in the balcony of the Abraham Lincoln Theater in Springfield on a field trip with his white school friends. When the lights went on, an usher noticed young Parsons and told him he would have to sit on the other side of the aisle.

"Then I said, 'Why do you say that?' And he said, 'Colored are supposed to sit over there and white are supposed to sit here.' I said, 'Why are you telling me that for, I'm not colored.' I remembered saying that. I guess I didn't know what to say. He said, 'Well I'm sorry sir, but you look like you are.'

"So I said okay, and went on over there and sat down and then all my buddies came over there, everybody." The usher went to get the manager. "And some of the rest of us had, I didn't but I wish I had, Boy Scout knives or new knives and took a little slice of this piece of leather of the seats and raced out of there."

Parsons, who graduated third in his high school class and was the class orator, announced to his family that he wanted to be a lawyer. While he was in high school, his older brother Mason asked him for legal help. Mason had bought a suit from his boss, but their father ordered Mason to return it because he didn't want the family buying anything on credit. He returned the

Facing page: James Benton Parsons was the first African American bandmaster in the U.S. Navy. Parsons conducted an all–African American navy band that performed in the States and in the Pacific theater during the last months of World War II. **NATIONAL ARCHIVES**

suit, but his boss continued to garnish his wages. Mason wanted out of the deal, so James went to the public library and started to look at statute books.

"So, I sat down and I wrote out this lengthy dissertation with a lot of 'Whereases, my brother, etc., etc., Whereases, whereas, and whereas.'"

Parsons's brother agreed to show it to Rudolph Lorenz, the justice of the peace, who worked in the Masonic Hall at the end of East Main Street. James skipped school to accompany his brother.

"I stayed behind him while he threw over the papers and said, 'Here it is, sir.' There was a man standing to the side of him, tall fellow, very well-dressed, handsome fellow. Judge Lorenz read what was on the paper and read it a second time. He said to my brother, 'Who wrote this?'

"My brother said, pointing to me with his thumb over his shoulder, 'He did it.'

"I was frightened. I tried to hide farther behind him. Judge Lorenz called me around and said, 'You did this?' I said, 'Yes, sir.' Then he handed it up to this fellow standing beside him at the desk and he said, 'Manny, it looks like the kid beat you.'"

Parsons said:

> I knew that as soon as my father got in, and I didn't know when he would get in, he would doubtless find out about it. He always found out about everything and I would really get a whipping. I would get killed for that because Pop wouldn't want me to do a thing like that. That was doubtless violating the law. It was acting like a grownup. It was condoning my brother not telling his father what he had done.
>
> No, so I hid and sure enough as evening came on I heard my father yell up from downstairs. I heard these voices down there, these heavy male voices and he called me JB, that's for James Benton. He yelled at me, "Come down here." So I got myself together and thought if there were some way I could be sure I wouldn't get [a whipping]. See Pop would never hit me in his life that I could remember. Well, I could let him whip me, I could take it.
>
> Well, I came down the stairs reluctantly and I saw them standing there in the center, Judge Lorenz and this fellow Manny, later known as Rosenblum. Pop was smiling and I came up and I saw him smile at me so I came up closer and he put his arm around my face. This Manny fellow patted me on the head and said, "Look, there is a box out in the car. Go out there and bring it in." I went out to his car and here was a big sort of wooden box, I mean sort of big. It looked big to me then and it was heavy enough that I couldn't carry it and I had to drag it on the end, pull it up by a board, pull it up the steps, and

pull it into the front room, which was the parlor, right there on the carpet. Set it down and it was full of books. He told me, "Read them, young man, and reread them. You are going to be a lawyer one of these days." They were old law books. They seemed to relate to everything. They didn't relate to any one thing. I knew then that I was going to be a lawyer. The decision was already made.

President Kennedy gets credit for appointing the first African American to a federal District Court judgeship, but perhaps the honor should go to President Ronald Reagan. It was Reagan who saved Parsons as a boy.

Years after his appointment to the bench, Parsons met Reagan, then governor of California, in Los Angeles. They talked about their Illinois years (both were born in 1911), and determined that they had both attended the same Boy Scout encampment downstate at Starved Rock. Parsons tried for his swimming badge, but had to be rescued from the Illinois River.

"You mean you were the one who had to be pulled?" Reagan asked. "What was your name? Were you Jimmy? Don't you know who pulled you out? I was the one who pulled you out."

"Pleased to meet you, Mr. Governor," Parsons replied. "You were the one."

Parsons was greatly helped along his career path by his friend, John Sengstacke, publisher of the *Chicago Defender,* which Parsons read as a boy. Sengstacke got him his job as assistant corporation counsel and as assistant U.S. attorney and convinced Parsons to run for the Superior Court. Sengstacke was in Kennedy's office, along with Parsons's old law professor Senator Paul Douglas, when the president made the call to Parsons requesting that he serve on the District Court.

"Aye, aye, sir," said Parsons, a former navy man.

"Carry on," said the president.

IN SEPTEMBER 1961, one month after the nominations of Austin and Parsons, Kennedy nominated a third University of Chicago Law School graduate to the District Court bench. Hubert L. Will was born in Milwaukee and worked his way through undergraduate and law school at the University of Chicago as an assistant to university President Robert Maynard Hutchins. "I did a little of everything for Dr. Hutchins, including shining his shoes and pressing his pants," said Will, "although there were some jobs of higher intellectual content." More important, perhaps, was that Will was the roommate of Senator Paul Douglas.

After graduating in 1937, Will moved to Washington to serve as an attorney for the Securities and Exchange Commission, as a clerk for the Senate Committee on Banking and Currency, and as a special assistant to the U.S. attorney general. During World War II, Will worked for the Office of Strategic Services as chief of the counterespionage branch for the European Theater of Operations. He returned to Chicago to work as a member of corporate law firms from 1946 to 1961, but his Washington work was never far from his heart. He kept two photos on his Chicago law office wall: a picture of William O. Douglas, who was Will's boss at the Securities and Exchange Commission and later a U.S. Supreme Court justice, and a picture of General William Donovan, his boss at the OSS.

Will, who filled the district's new ninth judgeship, had excellent credentials for the job. He was a high-flying, liberal LaSalle Street lawyer with powerful political alliances. Will was a charter member of the Douglas for Senator Committee in 1948, the year Paul Douglas won his first term, and a charter member of the Volunteers for Daley organization in 1955, the year Richard J. Daley won his first term as mayor.

"He was our prince," said Olga Claesson, administrative assistant to the chief judge. "He was absolutely fearless. We got the sense there was nothing he could not take on."

Will grew up in the second floor apartment above the Louis E. Will Drug Store on West Twenty-fourth in Milwaukee. His father was a pharmacist who ran an all-night drugstore that boasted the first tiled soda fountain in Milwaukee.

"I would say to my mom that it was always interesting, never a dull moment living above the drugstore," Will recalled. "We lived above about half a dozen different flavors of ice creams, all kinds of chocolate, all kinds of medicines."

Will's father sold Will's Cough Syrup and provided liquor for medicinal purposes during the Prohibition.

"My father could get bonded whiskey, using prescriptions from cooperating doctors. So a relatively small but very lucrative business was selling bonded Kentucky bourbon at good prices with the doctor furnishing the prescription. My father had the bourbon customers and got the whiskey. So if you were a good friend of the pharmacist you could throw a very good party."

Years later, Will became the second District Court judge to be awarded the Devitt Award, making the Northern District the first in the nation with two Devitt winners. Will won because of his court innovations and his skill on the bench. He considered judging an art and once said: "Every good judge wants to preside over the perfect trial."

Will drafted one of the nation's first pretrial order forms, final order forms, and the applications used by prisoners to file habeas corpus petitions. In a 1993 interview, Will said that all of his ideas came from his desire to take control of the judicial process. He said his first District Court trial, a minor traffic accident, took ten days to play out in his courtroom.

"I said to my law clerk, 'I made a bad mistake, Jimmy. I bought myself a lifetime ticket to an endless series of unprepared, badly acted amateur theatricals, the result of which is supposed to be justice. It's not going to work.'" So Will started preparing pretrial forms to help lawyers and himself determine issues, set time limits, and encourage early settlement.

"Trial is a contest," he said. "Somebody has to be there to enforce the rules. I think the art of judging—the art of aggressive refereeing, among other things—has come a long way in the thirty-two years I've been a judge and the twenty-five years before that when I was a practicing lawyer. In my youth, sometimes the better actor won. Frequently the better jury picker won. Now I think it's the better prepared lawyer who usually wins."

IN 1963, KENNEDY nominated Bernard Decker, a Republican, to fill the District Court's tenth judgeship. Decker was born in Highland Park and graduated from the University of Illinois at Urbana-Champaign. He received his law degree from Harvard Law School in 1929. After running a private practice in Waukegan from 1929 until 1951, he was elected a Lake County Circuit Court judge.

Decker had first been seriously considered by Kennedy for a District Court post in 1962. He was approved by the Justice Department and by the American Bar Association Committee on the Federal Judiciary, but was rejected by Senator Douglas. A page 1 article in the _New York Times_ on April 30, 1962, stated that Kennedy's nomination of Decker demonstrated how hard it would be to confirm appointments based on merit rather than appointments based on political weight. Decker had the backing of Republican Senator Everett M. Dirksen and Republican U.S. Representative Marguerite Stitt Church. Douglas understood Kennedy's desire to appease the powerful Dirksen, but he disliked Decker. "I do not regard this appointment as being in any way distinguished," Douglas said, "and I bear no responsibility for it." The senator suggested attorney Albert E. Jenner Jr. or former Illinois Supreme Court Justice Charles W. Davis if the president was determined to appoint a Republican. Dirksen, however, prevailed. Decker received a recess appointment in late 1962 and his commission in 1963.

Kennedy's final appointment to the District Court was Abraham Lincoln Marovitz, who filled the seat vacated by Miner in 1963. Marovitz received his law degree from Chicago-Kent School of Law in 1925 and worked as an assistant state's attorney from 1927 to 1933, when he went into private practice. He was a member of the Illinois Senate and was elected judge of the Cook County Superior Court in 1950. He served there until 1963, when he went to the District Court.

"You can't place him in the system," said Seventh Circuit Court of Appeals Judge Ilana Diamond Rovner, who worked with Marovitz on the District Court. "He is a legend. He is a legend because he is an original. He is apart, not like anybody else."

What set Marovitz apart were his social relations. Almost every night, Marovitz, a bachelor, dined out with people he met. He considered himself a friend to everyone he came in contact with—from the pope to the precinct

Judge Abraham Lincoln Marovitz (center) and a friend pose with Jimmy Durante (right) in the entertainer's dressing room. "You can't place him in the system," said Judge Ilana Diamond Rovner of Marovitz." He is a legend. He is a legend because he is an original. He is apart, not like anybody else." **DISTRICT COURT COLLECTION**

cop. His office was filled with hundreds of signed photographs of notables
such as Joe E. Brown and Eleanor Roosevelt, Frank Sinatra and Jack Dempsey, Jimmy Durante and Carl Sandburg, John Glenn and David Ben-Gurion.
And he never once failed to talk to a messenger, or waiter, or taxi driver he
met.

"I never, I don't think, I've never lost a friend once I made one," he said.
"Making friends is an art; keeping them is a greater art."

His installation ceremony October 1, 1963, gave the court a hint of the
man who would be known for decades as "Uncle Abe." The place was so
packed with grammar school friends, Marine buddies, monsignors, rabbis,
and the politically powerful that Campbell announced, "Although I am very
gratified at this tremendous turnout on behalf of our new Brother Marovitz,
I am constrained to make the suggestion that possibly he should have run
for some elective office."

The story of how Marovitz got his name, a story he told hundreds of
times, is legend. When he was born in Oshkosh, Wisconsin, his mother,
Rachel, named him after Abraham Lincoln because, Abe always said, "She
heard Lincoln was shot in the temple and saw pictures of him with a beard,
so she figured she was naming a son for a great Jewish hero."

His father, Joseph, moved the family to Chicago, where he worked as a
tailor. "My father was the most honest man I knew," Marovitz said. "He'd be
pressing a guy's pair of pants and find a dime, nickel, quarter, or dollar bill
and he'd say to us in Yiddish, 'That's that man's money, it's not mine.' Then
he'd put the money in an envelope and write the man's name on it in Yiddish, to return it to him."

Marovitz was shaped by his parents. His mother would ask him, "Have
you done your mitzvah, your good deed, for the day?" His father told him,
"You must stand for something in this life."

Marovitz graduated from high school, drifted from job to job, became an
amateur featherweight boxer, and attracted the attention of attorney Levy
Mayer, who had defended the beef trust in District Court. Soon, Marovitz
found himself working as an office boy with Mayer, Meyer, Austrian &
Platt. Partner Alfred S. Austrian took a particular interest in Marovitz and
told him that the firm would pay his tuition to Chicago-Kent School of
Law, $120 a semester, and deduct $2 per week from his paycheck. The firm
paid three years of tuition and never deducted a cent. Without ever attending college, Marovitz graduated law school at age nineteen. He had to wait

almost two years to take the bar exam because state law required lawyers to be twenty-one.

Marovitz became the youngest lawyer in the state's attorney office, and eventually opened a law office and began work as a criminal attorney. He picked up an array of unsavory clients, including gangsters Frank Nitti, Murray "the Camel" Humphreys, and Gus Winkler, who was believed to be the machine gunner at the St. Valentine's Day Massacre. He soon received lucrative retainers from six unions, which set him up financially for life.

Despite representing mobsters, Marovitz kept his reputation intact.

"I've never taken a dime in my life," he once said. "People call me up for a favor, and they can get it because that's the way I operate."

In 1938, with the help of powerful Democratic Party boss Jacob "Jack" Arvey, Marovitz was elected to the Illinois Senate, the first "professed" Jew in the Senate, he liked to say. It was there that he became friends with young Richard J. Daley.

"At our inauguration our parents were there and sitting next to each other," Marovitz said. "We became very, very close friends. We did a lot of walking and talking to each other in Springfield. Many of the fellows did things down there that they wouldn't do in their hometowns, but Dick and I walked a lot and talked about legislation and other things. We visited all the historic sights and were together practically every night."

As a member of the state Senate, Marovitz could have avoided serving in World War II, but he enlisted in the Marines and served in the South Pacific.

Marovitz always played up his boxing background. He liked to say that he was the least-educated judge on the bench. "To make up for what the good Lord took away from me upstairs in the brain department, I think maybe he gave me a little extra in the heart department," he once said.

IN MAY 1964, Austin convened the trial of Teamsters President James R. Hoffa and seven others for conspiracy and fraud. Hoffa came to Chicago after being sentenced in Chattanooga, Tennessee, to eight years in prison for jury tampering. Both trials were part of a decade-long campaign by the government to stop the growth of organized crime in labor unions, particularly in Hoffa's International Brotherhood of Teamsters.

Some 130 witnesses testified at the thirteen-week trial. During the first few days of jury selection, the trial drifted out of control as lawyers tested Austin. He asserted his authority by displaying a large gavel and announcing, "For the first time since I have been on the bench, I have this."

Government lawyers argued that Hoffa and his seven codefendants got kickbacks by approving a loan from the Teamster pension fund. The trial continued peacefully until its conclusion, when somebody called the courthouse and said that Austin was going to be killed. That did not deter the judge, but he did send the jury to the Great Lakes Naval Training Center in North Chicago for extra protection at night. The jury deliberated for three days and found Hoffa guilty of fraud against the pension fund. Hoffa was sentenced to twenty years in prison, a term that was to follow his eight-year term from Tennessee. When Hoffa's attorneys asked if he could serve the terms concurrently, Austin refused, saying: "The sound of the clanging of the jail house door has a salutary effect, not only on the defendants, but on others who might commit similar crimes."

Three years after the conviction of Hoffa, Austin was presented with a predicament. The U.S. solicitor general alerted him that agents of the FBI had, prior to the trial and conviction of Hoffa, overheard conversations among the defendants and their lawyers through the use of illegal wiretaps. Austin, after examining transcripts, ruled that the government obtained no

Teamsters leader James R. Hoffa was found guilty by a Northern Illinois District jury of defrauding the union pension fund. He began serving his prison term in 1967 but retained the Teamsters presidency until 1971, when he resigned. His sentence was commuted that year by President Richard Nixon. Hoffa disappeared in 1975 and was later declared legally dead. **NATIONAL ARCHIVES**

new information from the conversations. He overruled the defendants' motion for a new trial. Hoffa was released by President Richard M. Nixon after serving five years in prison. He was reported missing in 1975, and has never been seen since.

MEANWHILE, PLANS CONTINUED for a modern federal complex in Chicago with respected modernist architect Ludwig Mies van der Rohe. Mies's sketches for the federal complex changed dramatically throughout the years before construction began. The Chicago Plan Commission rejected a first proposal as being too grandiose. Finally, a scheme was approved in 1960 for a thirty-story courthouse skyscraper, with dark tinted glass and black-painted steel, rising east of Dearborn Street. A *Tribune* reporter wrote, "Plans for the building include air conditioning, and if conditions warrant, atomic bomb shelters."

The new courthouse was to be part of a two-block, $100 million federal plaza that would include a taller skyscraper office building and low post office west of Dearborn. "In few other buildings did Mies achieve a more thoroughly unified monumentalism, possibly carried to the point of an almost inhuman exactitude," wrote architecture historian Carl Condit.

Construction of the courthouse building began in 1961 and was completed three years later for about $40 million. The site, on the western half of

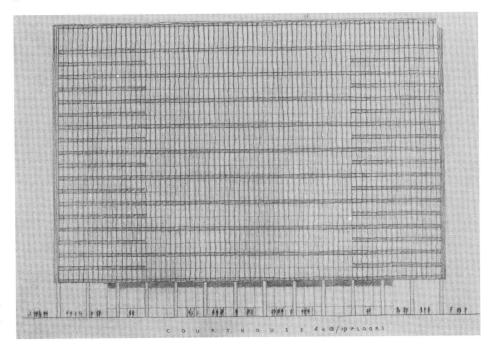

An early sketch of the Federal Building by architect Ludwig Mies van der Rohe. The building, and the entire surrounding Federal Plaza, is based on an intricate four-foot-eight-inch grid. Each beam of the Federal Building is twenty-eight feet apart.

the block bounded by Dearborn, State, Jackson, and Adams Streets, directly
east of the old courthouse, included the seventeen-story Great Northern
Office and Theater Building, the seventeen-story Majestic Hotel, twenty-
five-story State-Quincy Garage, several one-story stores, and a twenty-five-
foot vacant section of the Berghoff Restaurant. They were torn down starting in January 1961. Construction, aided by mild winters, was ahead of
schedule. The first matte-black steel beams were put in place in March 1963,
and the building was officially topped off six months later.

Just before the frame was completed, three African Americans sued to
stop work at the courthouse, contending they had been denied apprentice-
ship jobs because of their race. Campbell ordered that the men be placed on
a list to be hired as apprentice iron workers on future projects. "The union
has continually discriminated against the rights of negroes to learn and earn
a living in this trade," he wrote.

The new U.S. Courthouse and Federal Office Building at 219 South
Dearborn was officially dedicated in late 1964. Among the speakers at the
ceremony was Illinois Governor Otto Kerner Jr., the former U.S. attorney
who would later be tried and found guilty in the building. The District
Court held its last session in the old courthouse that same November.

The new Federal Building boasted a simple exterior but complex interior.
Space for nineteen two-story courtrooms was imbedded in the building,

The new courthouse
rises in front of the old
building. This view
looks west from Quincy
Court. **JOHN MCCARTHY/
CHICAGO HISTORICAL
SOCIETY**

*Using a giant wrench,
Mayor Richard J. Daley
ceremonially tightens
a bolt on the first steel
girder in the superstruc-
ture of the new Federal
Building at Jackson and
Dearborn. Looking on
are Cook County Crimi-
nal Court Judge Erwin J.
Hasten (from left), Rep-
resentative John C. Klu-
czynski, Chief District
Court Judge William J.
Campbell, and Rep-
resentative Roman C.
Pucinski.* **RALPH WALTERS/
CHICAGO SUN-TIMES**

away from any windows. From the start, Campbell wanted to create a building with majestic courtrooms. "The average citizen who comes in either as a
juror or witness or wanders in off the street sits in the back benches," Campbell said. "I'll tell you, that's what impresses them. And the administration of
justice must be more than pure justice. It must appear to be justice, and it
can't appear to be justice in cracker box surroundings."

The courtrooms were the height of 1960s elegance, with walnut walls and
benches, black leather chairs, and aluminum ceiling grills. "One view holds
that these walled-off cells symbolize the repressive injustices of the police
state," wrote Condit. "Another that they represent a reflective justice uncon-
taminated by the prejudices and passions of the marketplace."

This was Campbell's courthouse. He was involved in every detail, from
the finances to the architectural details. His favorite place was a grand courtroom, known as the ceremonial courtroom, where Campbell could gather
his court family for major occasions. He insisted that the architects change
their specifications for the judges' washrooms adjacent to that room. The
plans called for only a men's room.

"One day," he told the builders, "there will be women here."

CHAPTER FIVE

1963–1977: "This Is No Longer a Court of Order"

A CEREMONY ON NOVEMBER 30, 1964, marked the Northern District of Illinois's first day in the new courthouse. All twelve district judges looked regal peering down from the sweeping en banc bench of the ceremonial courtroom as U.S. Marshal Joseph N. Tierney initiated the event.

"Hear ye, hear ye, this honorable court is now in session pursuant to adjournment," the marshal announced. The words were familiar but the setting new. "God save the United States and this honorable court."

The ceremony was a celebration, recognizing the accomplishments that occurred in the old courthouse and courting the prospects in the new building. Partners from the four architectural firms were introduced before Dominic Tesauro, regional administrator of the General Services Administration, officially turned over the building to Chief Judge William J. Campbell.

"May the honorable judges of this court continue to be blessed with the necessary strength, courage and enlightenment to cope with the conflicting claims of stability and progress in a complex and changing world," Tesauro said.

Campbell was nostalgic about the "cherished quarters across the street," where he had served as an attorney and judge for a quarter of a century. But he reminded those present how difficult the building was to work in during the summer. With open windows, the heat and dirt of Chicago made the courthouse a sweatshop. Judges took months off; employees were sent home, or stayed at home. "So," he said, "you will pardon me if I do not join some of the bleeding hearts who have so recently found so many lines in the daily press in shedding any great tears about leaving the old courthouse."

Judges of U.S. District
Court and U.S. Court of
Appeals join in a cere-
mony marking the start
of court sessions in the
new U.S. Courthouse
at 219 South Dearborn
on November 30, 1964.
The caption reads:
"The picture was taken
through a courtroom
window, the taking of
pictures in federal courts
being prohibited."
CHARLES KREJCSI/
CHICAGO DAILY NEWS

The significance of the new building went beyond bricks and mortar—or, in this case, steel and glass. The judges were rooted in the past. Judge Michael Igoe, for instance, had been a practicing lawyer since 1908. But, whether they realized it or not, the judges were embracing the future by moving into the Miesian-modern skyscraper. Unlike any other court building that had ever been built in the United States, Chicago's new Federal Building was monumental in a minimalist manner. Space and simplicity connoted power here, rather than the ostentatious, ornate details and flourishes of the past.

The U.S. District Court for the Northern District of Illinois—like the building itself—demonstrated innovation and efficiency. During the late 1960s, the District Court of Northern Illinois became the first federal court to routinely conduct civil trials with fewer than twelve jurors. It boasted of being the most efficient urban court in the nation, as it still does today. Campbell was determined that the court be a model. He gave an annual report about the judges every June, before the court recessed for the summer, to prod the judges into working harder.

"One or two of them were a bit lazier than the others and I incurred their ill will by reporting that at the end of the year to the press. I never had to re-port it more than once," he said. "I'd just say, 'Well, Judge So and So wasn't up to par this year and it is obvious, whether for illness or personal reasons, he didn't spend the time in chambers and on the bench, and as a result the backlog is apparent in his caseload.' And they printed that usually on the front or second page. Well, no judge wants to have that for two years in a row, so they phoned me up. They'd say, 'Why the hell did you do that?' I said, 'Well, after all, you did it, I didn't. Well, if you want me to give you some praise next year, go to work.'"

The court, like the new Federal Building, was Campbell's. Known as "the Chief," Campbell mechanized the clerk's department and consolidated the offices of the court clerk and bankruptcy clerk. He knew he was autocratic, and he knew that he was not a "pinup boy with some of my fellow judges." But Campbell was an adroit political animal, both locally and on the na-tional scene. His secret, he said, was never letting a matter come up in a meeting unless he knew he had enough votes to prevail.

"I would always say, 'Between now and the last meeting, gentlemen, I have done thus and so. You can either repudiate me or you can approve it; but if you repudiate me, I am going to have enough votes to win,'" Campbell re-counted years later in an oral history. "And then in that way I ran the court."

He had little opposition.

The old courthouse is torn down just west of the new courthouse in 1965. The old building was demolished to make way for another Fed-eral Building and the post office on the Fed-eral Plaza. **CHICAGO HISTORICAL SOCIETY**

"Oh, Judge [Richard] Austin used to lead the pack once in a while," Campbell said. "He thought that I was interfering too much in the patronage of the bankruptcy system, I think. He caused me a little trouble, but I always was sure I had enough votes to beat him before I called a meeting."

Asked in his oral history if he had any problems with other judges, Campbell replied: "Yes, each is a prima donna. Each one is a law in himself."

In 1965, Sam "Momo" Giancana, Chicago's reigning gangster, was sent to Cook County Jail by Campbell when Giancana refused to answer grand jury questions after being granted immunity. Campbell had expected that his decision to jail Giancana would be the first step in the government's attack against organized crime. He figured that several other leading criminal figures would be brought before grand juries in a similar manner and would be pressured to talk. It never happened. The government failed to move against organized crime. Its investigation stalled while Giancana was in jail. One year later, at the end of the grand jury's term, Campbell released Giancana and apologized for the government's lack of action. It was a missed opportunity for the government, he said. However, during his year in jail, Giancana lost control of the syndicate.

Campbell's most important legacy, perhaps, is the establishment of the nation's first Federal Defender Program. The innovative plan was an outgrowth of the Supreme Court's 1963 Clarence Gideon decision, in which justices ruled that defendants accused of crimes were entitled to capable representation in federal court. The Chicago program was set up to have two functions: to represent defendants unable to obtain an adequate defense and to give law school students trial experience by working with mentor attorneys. Some of Chicago's most outstanding lawyers of the day—Philip Corboy, Albert E. Jenner Jr., Don Reuben, William Barnett, and George Cotsirilos—were appointed to the first federal defender advisory panel. During the first years of the program, up to 150 students from the city's six law schools were assigned annually to help the panel's lawyers.

The Chicago program served as a model nationwide. The federal defender office in Chicago now has 19 full-time lawyers and 130 lawyers who serve on an appointment panel, according to executive director Terence Mac-Carthy. The office defends about nine hundred cases a year.

DURING THE 1960s, the decade of protest, the courthouse became a fortress. New rules were created in an attempt to keep the judicial process working with as little outside interference as possible. In June 1964, Campbell banned demonstrations inside the courthouse.

Campbell's order prohibited anyone from "congregating, interfering with the orderly administration of justice or dispatch of business, causing a disturbance, or in any way creating a nuisance within the court house building." Marshals and law enforcement officials were instructed to remove from the building anybody intent on demonstrating. If protesters refused to leave, they were to be taken before the chief judge immediately for a hearing on contempt of court charges. Anyone was entitled to enter the building during business hours, Campbell said, "as long as they remain orderly." His proclamation was posted on doors and bulletin boards.

The rules followed a series of sit-ins in the fourth-floor office of U.S. Attorney Edward Hanrahan in the old courthouse. The protesters were demanding that federal troops be sent to Mississippi to protect civil rights demonstrators. One day, about a dozen demonstrators were forcibly removed from Hanrahan's office, including Marion S. Barry Jr., who would later become the mayor of Washington, D.C. Barry was arrested and charged with criminal contempt of court. Barry, a field representative for the Student Non-Violent Coordinating Committee, appeared before Campbell the following day, but his case was continued. That afternoon, Campbell, in robes, came down and confronted a group on the fourth floor.

"Don't force me to place you all in contempt," Campbell told the twenty-three demonstrators. "This is my courthouse."

After a face-off, the demonstrators agreed to leave. Campbell rode down the elevators with them and stood, with folded arms, in the doorway as they exited the building.

Campbell also prohibited television cameras inside the building after 4:30 P.M. because he said television crews encouraged demonstrators. He permitted picketing and parading outside the building.

More demonstrations followed in the new building. In February 1965, nine civil rights protesters were arrested after commandeering several elevators and staging a sit-in on the first floor. Dominic Tesauro of the General Services Administration called it "a new high in interference in public business."

For years, Northern District of Illinois judges had wrestled with the question of how open the courts should be to the press. Judges threatened reporters with banishment several times after reading articles that they considered inaccurate. At one judges' meeting, Will went so far as to suggest that the press and the public could be excluded from criminal trials at the request of a defendant. Judge James Benton Parsons calmed Will down, saying that he did not think the court could get away with muffling the press.

In late 1965, the District Court judges passed a local court rule that banned photographic and broadcasting equipment from the courtroom areas where trials were held. The judges also adopted a policy that banned out-of-court statements by lawyers on pending cases. They said that attorneys, including the U.S. attorney, could comment on cases, but only in court, later raising the stakes by saying that lawyers risked discipline if they talked about pending cases.

Just before the high-profile trial of Democratic National Convention protest leaders was to begin in 1969, Campbell upped the ante by prohibiting photographers and broadcasters from the entire Federal Building and the plaza. His rule was reversed the following year by the Seventh Circuit Court of Appeals, which found the rule violated the First Amendment.

IT SEEMS THAT EVERY DECADE has one case that never goes away. The duPont antitrust lawsuit lasted throughout the 1950s. The krebiozen case, heard on different levels by several District Court judges, lasted throughout the 1960s.

The controversy came to a head in 1965 when Judge Julius J. Hoffman presided over a jury trial to determine the value of krebiozen, a drug that was touted to cure cancer. The drug's makers were charged with mail fraud and conspiracy in promoting a substance that the government considered worthless. The case was a particularly difficult one because of the life-and-death emotion it raised in cancer sufferers and their families. The *Chicago Daily News,* before the start of the trial, stated the krebiozen case was "expected to be one of the great dramas in the history of Chicago's federal court." It turned out to be one of the longest trials in District Court history.

Krebiozen had a wide following among people desperate for a miracle. Hoffman received dozens of heartfelt appeals from cancer patients and their loved ones, pleading to make the drug available. One such was from Dan Jacobsen of Clarks Summit, Pennsylvania, who said his wife began to regain her health while on krebiozen but had started to fail rapidly now that the drug was banned.

"Your honor, before God I do not exaggerate," he wrote.

The Food and Drug Administration banned interstate shipment of the drug in 1963, after its creators refused to submit the drug for full government testing. Prosecutors said the drug was merely creatine, a common material found in animal tissue, and of no help in treating cancer. They presented 103 witnesses, showed one thousand exhibits, and created 11,949 pages of testimony in making the case against krebiozen.

The drug's defenders—producers Stevan Durovic; his brother, Marko; Dr. Andrew C. Ivy, krebiozen's chief medical sponsor; and William F. P. Phillips, a general practitioner who prescribed the drug—argued that government tests were inadequate to show the active substance in krebiozen.

Weeks after the start of the trial, Hoffman, in an unprecedented move, announced that enough evidence had been put on record to create a case for the existence of a conspiracy among the defendants. "His ruling, which granted a government motion, instructed the jury that all prior testimony and most exhibits introduced against certain of the defendants could from that time on be considered against all the defendants as evidence of the conspiracy charge," a *Denver Post* reporter wrote.

After six days of deliberation, the jury returned in January 1966 and acquitted the four defendants. Hoffman, apparently upset at the verdict, did not even extend the courtesy of thanking the jury for its months of work. Later that year, Judge Bernard Decker dismissed a lawsuit by the makers of krebiozen against the Food and Drug Administration that would have repealed the FDA's ban on the interstate shipment of krebiozen. So the drug never became available to the nation.

PRESIDENT LYNDON B. JOHNSON nominated two Democrats to the District Court in 1966. William J. Lynch was appointed to fill the seat vacated by Michael Igoe and Alexander J. Napoli was named to establish the district's eleventh judgeship.

Lynch's political pedigree was clear. He grew up with Mayor Richard J. Daley in the Bridgeport neighborhood on the South Side and was Daley's law partner for several years. He received his law degree from Loyola University Chicago School of Law in 1931 and worked as the chief attorney for the Chicago Transit Authority, as an assistant Cook County state's attorney, and as a member of the Illinois Senate. He was rated as well qualified for the District Court judgeship by the American Bar Association and was approved by both Democratic Senator Douglas and Republican Senator Dirksen.

Lynch was more than just a politician. He was street smart and canny, and could hold his own intellectually with any judge on the bench. And he wasn't as tough as his demeanor suggested. "We always had a problem with Judge Lynch," said H. Stuart Cunningham, who was clerk of the court. "I would get calls from the warden. 'We've had this guy here for three days and we don't have any damn paperwork on him.' So I'd call Judge Lynch's chambers. Here is this hard-as-nails political appointee, who doesn't have to worry about a damn thing. He knew that until his name was signed on the judgment and commitment, that the guy wasn't actually committed and judged. He did every psychological trick in the world to avoid signing the judgment and commitment. He was a softy."

Alexander Napoli was a Chicago success story. His first diploma, at age twelve, was from the Tri-City Barber College. Napoli, who lived in Chicago's Far South Side communities of Roseland, Pullman, and Kensington, worked his way through college and law school by laboring in his father's barber shop. He received his law degree from the University of Chicago in 1929 and started in private practice. He worked as an assistant state's attorney and as a judge in the Municipal Court, Superior Court, and Circuit Court. As chief judge of the Cook County Circuit Court, Napoli took mass murderer Richard Speck's not guilty plea at Speck's 1966 arraignment.

"It has been suggested that Judge Napoli's nomination is intended to refurbish the image of Italian-Americans, an image supposedly tarnished by the Cosa Nostra," wrote the *Sun-Times*. "Such an effort is quite unnecessary, of course."

Napoli sentenced Danny Escobedo to twenty-two years in prison for selling and possessing narcotics and other charges in 1968. Escobedo made U.S. legal history after his murder conviction was thrown out by the U.S. Supreme Court in 1964 because police wrongly refused his request to see his attorney. Escobedo returned to the District Court and Cook County Circuit Court several times on various charges.

Napoli overturned a 1933 city ordinance and ruled in 1970 that fathers could be present in the delivery room when their wives gave birth.

THE YEAR 1968 was a particularly momentous one in Chicago. In April, the West Side turned into a riot zone after the assassination of Martin Luther King Jr. In August, Vietnam War protesters attempted to upset the Democratic National Convention. These acts called for extra security at the court. During the height of the West Side violence, Campbell told the judges he

had requested closed-circuit TV cameras for the private corridors outside
the judges' chambers, as well as electric door locks and panic alarms for the
judges and their secretaries. Campbell told the judges the system would cost
$100,000 and that he would find the money for it. The judges voted 5 to 4
for the proposal.

Campbell also drafted a letter that year to the U.S. attorney general requesting a federal detention center be established in Chicago. Court prisoners were housed in the federal tier of the Cook County Jail. It was crowded and lacked proper medical facilities, especially for narcotics addicts, alcoholics, and epileptics. The attorney general promised Campbell the center would be built.

Two well-known sports figures competed in federal court in 1968.

Boxer Muhammad Ali, the former Cassius M. Clay Jr., filed a lawsuit against a company that produced a series of fictionalized fights in a single-elimination tournament broadcast to 380 radio stations around the country. The company, Woroner Productions, supposedly used a computer to determine the action in these realistic-sounding bouts between all-time heavyweight champions. On the computer, Ali lost to boxer Jim Jeffries in the quarterfinals.

In real life, Ali had never been defeated as a professional, and his attorneys argued that losing the computer matchup tarnished his reputation. "Plaintiff is the world's most famous professional boxer; he is the greatest," Ali's attorneys noted. Ali, who had won the heavyweight championship in 1964, was not paid for use of his name. The radio "fights" had earned about $3.5 million in advertising revenue, according to the lawsuit, and his lawyer argued that Ali was entitled to part of it. He sued Woroner for $1 million. The suit asked that Woroner not rebroadcast the fights, and that the firm pay the boxer for use of his name.

Ali settled out of court before the case, to be heard by Judge Parsons, came to trial. Ali was paid $10,000, or 10 percent of net proceeds of an upcoming computer fight between him and Rocky Marciano.

Baseball manager Leo Durocher also sued to protect his name. He named actress Zsa Zsa Gabor for $1 million in a contract dispute. Durocher had been paid $6,000 for a series of commercials for Aamco automatic transmissions. After his contract ran out, Durocher said the company aired a new set of commercials that concluded with Gabor telling the TV audience, "Say that Leo sent you."

When Gabor refused to appear in Chicago to give a deposition in the case, Judge Will threatened her with contempt. The *Chicago Sun-Times* headline writers asked, "Must Zsa Zsa Go to Zsail?"

Gabor sent needed information in lieu of the deposition and Will dismissed the contempt charge—and the lawsuit. "This probably was among the 10 least important cases I have heard, and it has received the most publicity," the judge said.

ONE OF THE MOST IMPORTANT CASES in the court's history grew out of events surrounding the 1968 Democratic National Convention. Thousands of demonstrators converged in Chicago to protest against the Vietnam War, racism, and poverty. Their skirmishes with Chicago police culminated on August 28 when police stormed the demonstrators near the Conrad Hilton Hotel on Michigan Avenue.

Less than two weeks after the convention, Campbell swore in a grand jury to determine who was at fault. The jurors indicted eight policemen and eight demonstrators, "outside agitators" who had come to Chicago to "tear Pig City apart." Most of the police officers were charged with depriving citizens of their civil rights by inflicting summary punishment. Seven of the officers were acquitted in District Court. Charges against the other were dropped.

The eight demonstrators—Yippie leaders Abbie Hoffman and Jerry Rubin; Black Panther Party leader Bobby Seale; David Dellinger, Rennie Davis, and Tom Hayden of the National Mobilization Committee to End the War in Vietnam; and Students for a Democratic Society members John Froines and Lee Weiner—were charged with violating a 1968 "antiriot act," a law that made it a federal offense to cross state lines with the intent to incite, promote, encourage, or participate in a riot. They were also charged with conspiracy, despite the fact that some had not met each other before the convention. From the start, it was apparent this was going to be unlike any other trial held in the district. On the day the indictments were handed down, Davis and Weiner held a press conference in Chicago to announce they would use the trial as a national forum on political issues. Rubin, Hoffman, and Dellinger held a press conference in New York to say they were proud to be indicted. Rubin called the indictments the "Academy Award of protest." Seale wondered why he was included. He had given two speeches to peaceful audiences during the week and had flown back to Oakland, California, before the convention violence began.

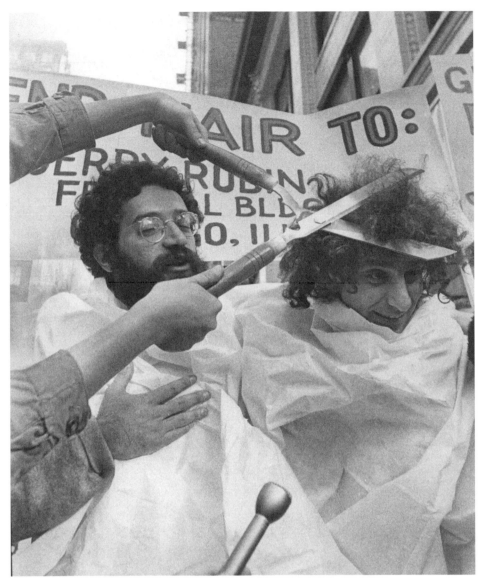

The trial, *United States of America v. David T. Dellinger et al.*, was originally set before Campbell, but was transferred to Hoffman before the arraignment of the defendants. The trial began on September 26, 1969, and lasted for nearly five months. Two hundred witnesses were called and twenty-two thousand pages of testimony were recorded.

"It was interesting every day," said William Snyder, who clerked for Judge Hoffman. Security was tight, with checkpoints in the lobby and many armed marshals in Hoffman's twenty-third floor courtroom. Hoffman was a strict courtroom judge, demanding of and demeaning to lawyers. "He was taken by the majesty of the judicial system and the law, and he felt he had something to live up to," Snyder said. "Most every lawyer had a Judge Hoffman story. Most were critical."

But out of court, Hoffman was charming, a sought-after socialite and an excellent boss. In chambers, he was respectful of his staff, challenging, even gossipy. He would grumble about weekend speeches made by the Conspiracy Eight defendants, but was impressed by Abbie Hoffman's intelligence and referred to him as Cousin Abbie, Snyder recounted.

Judge Hoffman chose the jury in half a day. He asked the potential jurors about their families and jobs and ignored a list of forty-four questions submitted by attorney William Kunstler, who along with Leonard Weinglass represented the defendants.

Among Kunstler's questions were:

Do you believe that people who protest publicly against the war in Vietnam, racism and economic inequality do their country a disservice?

Do you believe that young men who refuse to participate in the armed forces because of their opposition to the war in Vietnam are cowards, slackers, or unpatriotic?

Do you believe that George Washington, Patrick Henry, or Benjamin Franklin were revolutionaries?

Do you believe that Black people are free and equal in the United States?

Do you feel any hostility to people who, like George Washington, Thomas Jefferson, and Abraham Lincoln, have beards or wear their hair long?

If your children are male, do they have long hair or beards, or wear what you consider to be unorthodox clothing?

If your children are female, do they wear brassieres all the time, or wear what you consider to be unorthodox clothing?

Which if any of the following drugs do you use: Marijuana? Tobacco? Alcohol? LSD? Coca-Cola? Diet pills? Would you object if your child smoked marijuana?

Would you let your son or daughter marry a Yippie?

Ten women and two men were chosen for the jury. At the start of the trial, just as he had done the previous month, Seale formally requested that the trial be postponed until his attorney, Charles R. Garry, recovered from gall bladder surgery. Judge Hoffman refused, telling Seale he would be adequately represented by his lawyer of record, Kunstler. Seale disagreed, saying that Kunstler had signed appearance records simply to help him before the trial. Seale protested the start of the trial without his chosen attorney.

The defendants often displayed outrageous behavior; they refused to follow courtroom decorum. They wore purple pants, orange shirts, and Indian headbands. Abbie Hoffman donned a Chicago Police Department shirt at his arraignment. One day, the defendants draped the defense table with the Viet Cong flag. On another day, Hoffman and Rubin showed up wearing judicial robes. Strange issues were debated in the courtroom: when and how often defendants could go to the men's room, how much smiling and laughing was allowed in the court.

During the government's opening statement, Judge Hoffman cautioned Hayden not to shake his fist in the direction of the jury. "That is my customary greeting, your honor," Hayden replied.

"That may be your customary greeting, but we do not allow shaking of fists in this courtroom."

When Abbie Hoffman was introduced, Judge Hoffman announced: "The jury is directed to disregard the kiss thrown by the defendant Hoffman and the defendant is directed not to do that sort of thing again."

Judge Hoffman did not mask his hostility toward the defense. On the opening day, he issued warrants for the arrest of four defense attorneys who were not present in court. They had helped prepare the case, but had since withdrawn. Hoffman had one of the lawyers arrested and brought to jail, but rescinded the order when he realized they had notified the court of their withdrawal. A few days later, Hoffman was presented a motion by 150 lawyers from all over the nation who came to Chicago to protest the judge's conduct. Stephen G. Breyer, an assistant professor at Harvard Law School who would later be appointed to the U.S. Supreme Court, came to Chicago to participate in the protest, according to the *Chicago Tribune*. The lawyers asked that the judge declare a mistrial and drop contempt proceedings. Hoffman denied the motion. When dozens of lawyers descended on the Federal Building to demonstrate, they were greeted by Campbell—in robes with a stenographer, clerk, and marshal. The judge declared that court was in session, and threatened to hold the lawyers in contempt. They dispersed.

The government presented fifty-three witnesses and showed reels of television footage about the convention. Prosecutors called city officials to the stand to discuss applications made by the defendants to assemble and protest around the city. They also called undercover Chicago police officers,

paid informants, FBI agents, and a newspaper reporter to detail plans discussed publicly and privately by the eight. The government attempted to prove that the defendants conspired to create a riot. The defendants tried to show that the real conspiracy was by the federal and city governments, which were determined to stop legitimate protest.

The prosecution's case was punctuated by Seale, who attempted several times to speak on his own behalf and serve as his own attorney. Hoffman denied every one of his requests, saying that the complexity of the case made self-representation inappropriate. Seale persevered, making the request every time his name was mentioned and often calling Hoffman a "pig" or "fascist." On October 29, Seale asked to cross-examine a witness who had mentioned his name.

Denied again, Seale told the judge: "You have George Washington and Benjamin Franklin sitting in a picture behind you, and they were slave owners. That's what they were. They owned slaves. You are acting in the same manner, denying me my constitutional rights."

After a short discussion, Hoffman replied, "Well, I have been called a racist, a fascist—he has pointed to the picture of George Washington behind me and called him a slave owner and—"

"They were slave owners," Seale interrupted. "Look at history."

"As though I had anything to do with that."

"They were slave owners. You got them up there."

"He has been known as the father of this country, and I would think that it is a pretty good picture to have in the United States District Court."

"We all share common guilt, your honor," attorney Kunstler said.

"I didn't think I would ever live to sit on the bench or be in a courtroom where George Washington was assailed by a defendant in a criminal case and a judge was criticized for having his portrait on the wall," Hoffman said.

The judge was particularly upset over being labeled racist because he saw himself as a liberal on race matters. Hoffman was proud of the historic 1968

This page: Judge Julius J. Hoffman—"He was taken by the majesty of the judicial system and the law, and he felt he had something to live up to," said his former law clerk, William Snyder.

VERNA SADOCK

Facing page: Bobby Seale was bound and gagged in the District Court for three days, starting on October 29, 1969. "I want to say that the way that I have been treated is inhumane," Seale said.

VERNA SADOCK

order he handed down that desegregated the South Holland, Illinois, school district. He was the first judge in the North to compel school integration.

When Seale refused to stop arguing, the judge told the marshals: "Take the defendant into the room in there and deal with him as he should be dealt with in this circumstance."

This was a first in American jurisprudence.

Seale was bound and gagged, then returned to court in chains. "I didn't think I could be bound and gagged, not until he did it," recounted Seale, looking back more than three decades after the trial. "The threats were vague; I didn't think he really meant he would tie me up. I couldn't imagine it."

Hoffman told Seale he would remove the gag if he agreed not to disrupt the court, but Seale refused. He clanked his metal chains against the metal chair and started mumbling, "I want my right to defend myself." He saw that a couple of the jurors were crying.

Said Kunstler, at the trial: "I wanted to say the record should indicate that Mr. Seale is seated on a metal chair, each hand is handcuffed to the leg of the chair on both the right and left sides so he cannot raise his head, and a gag is tightly pressed into his mouth and tied at the rear, and that when he attempts to speak, a muffled sound comes out as he has done several times since he has been bound and gagged."

After Seale managed to speak through the gag, Hoffman declared: "Mr. Marshal, I don't think you have accomplished your purpose with that contrivance. We will have to take another recess."

Ten minutes later, Seale was returned with his mouth covered by tape so he could not utter a sound. He rattled his chains, and, at the end of the cross-examination of a government witness, managed to say, "Let me cross-examine the witness. I have a right to cross-examine."

With that, Hoffman excused the jury and called an end to the session.

Seale returned to court the following day, October 30, bound and gagged with tighter restraints. In an effort to keep him quiet, mar-

William Kunstler

shals tied him to a wooden chair with hospital straps and used gauze to cover his mouth.

"This is no longer a court of order, your honor," said Kunstler. "It is a disgrace."

On the third day, marshals overdid the gag, Seale recounted. "They got wider and longer bandages, tried to put gauze down my mouth, but I bit the marshal." Seale remained bound and gagged until November 4. On the following day, Seale was asked to sit down three times when he tried to cross-examine a witness.

"Look, old man," he told Hoffman, "if you keep up denying me my constitutional rights, you are being exposed to the public and the world that you do not care about people's constitutional rights to defend themselves."

Finally, Hoffman called a halt. He declared a mistrial as to Seale and severed him from the case. The judge immediately found Seale guilty of sixteen counts of contempt and sentenced him to more than four years in prison. The Conspiracy Eight became the Conspiracy Seven, or Chicago Seven.

Seale, looking back three decades later, said he was psychologically hurt by the dark days of the trial, but his largest regrets were for the twenty-nine Black Panther members and fourteen police officers killed during police-

Attorney William Kunstler was sentenced by Judge Julius J. Hoffman to four years and thirteen days for contempt because of his conduct during the Conspiracy Seven trial.
VERNA SADOCK

Panther shootouts, and for nine Panther members still in prison. "I have these people dead, other lives disrupted. These are my scars," he said.

The trial slowed after Seale was removed. Abbie Hoffman and Hayden often slept in court. Weiner read books. Dellinger organized an upcoming antiwar rally. On December 9, the defense case began, led by Kunstler and his associate, Weinglass. They presented an all-star cast of left-wing celebrities, including poet Allen Ginsberg; authors Norman Mailer, James Kunen, and William Styron; comedian Dick Gregory; LSD guru Timothy Leary; politicians Jesse Jackson, John Conyers, and Julian Bond; and folk singers Pete Seeger, Phil Ochs, Arlo Guthrie, Country Joe McDonald, and Judy Collins.

Many of the performers attempted to sing. When Collins began singing "Where Have All the Flowers Gone?" Judge Hoffman said to Kunstler, "We are not here to be entertained, sir. We are trying a very important case."

The attorney replied, "This song is not an entertainment, your honor. This is a song of peace and what happens to young men and young women during wartime."

Surprise witnesses were called by the defense, but to little avail. When Chicago Mayor Richard J. Daley took the stand in January 1970, the U.S. attorney protected him from all but softball questions.

"This was the day toward which the trial had been building for three weeks—since the defense began its presentation—and everyone went away feeling let down," wrote columnist Tom Fitzpatrick in the *Chicago Sun-Times.*

"There were too many marshals—at the time sixteen were in the court— and too many people in Ivy League business suits and not enough in colorful costumes. The defendants were not their usual combative selves.

"They seemed as fascinated by a close-up view of the mayor as everyone else," he wrote.

The only one who showed spunk was Abbie Hoffman, who wore an "Honorary Irishman" button for the occasion. After the lunch break, before the judge returned, young Hoffman strode to the center of the courtroom, put up his dukes, and said, "Why don't we just settle this right here?"

Daley laughed.

Kunstler had even less success getting former Attorney General Ramsey Clark to the stand. Following maneuvers by U.S. Attorney Thomas Foran and his assistant, Richard G. Schultz, the judge determined that Clark's testimony would be irrelevant and would delay the trial. The defense had expected Clark to say that the U.S. government did not consider the defendants to be dangerous.

Kunstler said Hoffman was the first District Court judge in history to bar a willing defense witness.

The *New York Times* editorialized: "The refusal of Federal Judge Julius J. Hoffman to let Ramsey Clark, the former United States Attorney General, testify before the jury in the trial of the 'Chicago Seven' constitutes the ultimate outrage in a trial that has become the shame of American justice."

The banter between Kunstler and the judge never lessened. At one point, Hoffman told Kunstler that he was incorrectly trying a political case. "It is a criminal case," Hoffman said. "There is an indictment here. I have the indictment right up here. I can't go into politics here in this court."

"Your honor, Jesus was accused criminally, too," said Kunstler, "and we understand really that was not truly a criminal case in the sense that it is just an ordinary—"

"I didn't live at that time," said the judge. "I don't know. Some people think I go back that far, but I really don't."

Judge Hoffman clashed with attorney Weinglass, too, and rarely got his name right, calling him Weinstein, Feinstein, Fineglass, Weinberg, and Weinrammer. At one point, the defense team held up a sign reading WEINGLASS when the judge mispronounced his name.

Only two of the defendants, Abbie Hoffman and Rennie Davis, took the witness stand.

After Abbie Hoffman was sworn in, he was asked his name.

"Just Abbie. I don't have a last name, judge. I lost it," he replied.

Later, in his testimony, he said: "My name is Abbie. I am an orphan of America."

"Where do you reside?" he was asked.

"I live in Woodstock Nation."

"Will you tell the court and jury where it is?"

"Yes. It is a nation of alienated young people. We carry it around with us as a state of mind in the same way the Sioux Indians carried the Sioux Nation around with them."

Hoffman was asked if he had entered into an agreement with the other six defendants to come to Chicago to promote violence.

"An agreement?" Hoffman asked.

"Yes," said Weinglass.

"We couldn't agree on lunch."

Rennie Davis testified that he was surprised when the city refused to waive a curfew for demonstrators in Lincoln Park. The city had done just that for the Boy Scouts, he said.

"Well, you didn't consider the Yippies Boy Scouts, did you?" prosecutor Foran asked.

"Well, I considered that under the civil rights act that American citizens have equal protection of the law, whether Boy Scouts or people with long hair, Mr. Foran. That is part of this country," Davis replied.

"You think that the Yippies with what they were advertising they were going to do in Lincoln Park are the same as the Boy Scouts?" Foran asked. "Is that what you are saying?"

"Well, as someone who has been very active in the Boy Scouts during all of his young life, I considered—"

"Did you ever see the Boy Scouts advertise public fornication, for heavens sake?" the prosecutor asked.

"The Yippies talked about a Festival of Life and love and—"

"They also talked about public fornication and about drug use and about nude-ins on the beach. They also talked about that, didn't they?"

"They talked about love, yes, sir."

"You and I have a little different feeling about love, I guess, Mr. Davis."

After twenty weeks, the defense rested on February 3, 1970. The following day, during rebuttal, Judge Hoffman revoked Dellinger's bail and sent him to Cook County Jail after Dellinger responded to the testimony of Deputy Chief of Police James Riordan by saying, "Oh, bullshit. That's an absolute lie."

The incident threw the court into pandemonium, with Abbie Hoffman telling the judge, who was Jewish, "You are a disgrace to the Jews. You would have served Hitler better."

In his closing speech, Foran criticized the defendants for associating their names with great leaders. "These men have named St. Matthew and Jesus and they have named Lincoln and Martin Luther King," said Foran. "Can you imagine these men supporting these men?"

"Yes I can!" shouted Dellinger's twenty-year-old daughter, Natasha, from the spectator section. "I can imagine it because it's true."

"Remove those people, Mr. Marshal," the judge ordered.

"That's my daughter," Dellinger roared.

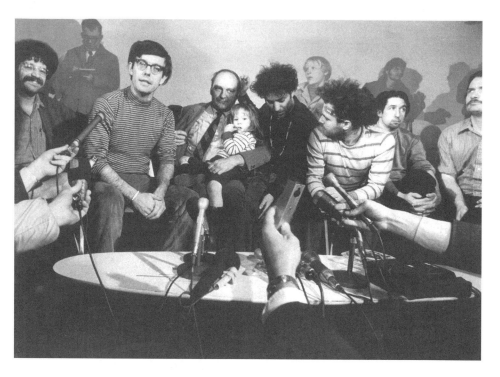

"I won't listen to any more of these disgusting lies," shouted Dellinger's thirteen-year-old daughter, Michele.

She, too, was removed.

"It's hard for me to write this twenty-two years later without crying," Dellinger said in his autobiography. "And at the time, I had to go right back to jail and couldn't even comfort them. Not even during a prison visit, since I wasn't allowed any. I couldn't even find out how badly Michele and Tasha were hurt. Once again, the sins of the parents, my sins, were being visited on their children, my children."

AFTER THE JURY HAD retired for its deliberation, Hoffman immediately began contempt proceedings against all seven defendants and their two attorneys. "From the outset of the trial the court admonished and warned the defendants and their counsel to refrain from such conduct, particularly when committed in the presence of the jury," Hoffman said. "They chose deliberately to disregard such admonition, right down through yesterday afternoon's hearing, and have openly challenged and flaunted their contempt for both this court and for the system of law it represents."

Each of the men was allowed to speak before his sentence was announced. After Dellinger and Davis were led out of court, Hayden told the judge: "So, your honor, before your eyes you see the most vital ingredient of your system collapsing because the system does not hold together."

"Oh, don't be so pessimistic," Hoffman replied. "Our system isn't collapsing. Fellows as smart as you could do awfully well under this system."

Rubin gave Hoffman a book and inscribed it: "Julius. You radicalized more people than we ever could. You're the country's top Yippie."

As he was led to jail, Abbie Hoffman kissed his wife, Anita, and said: "Water the plant."

The contempt count was quite specific. Abbie Hoffman, for instance, was sentenced to one day in jail for blowing a kiss to the jury, four days for baring his body to the jury, five days for insulting the judge, six days for insulting the judge in Yiddish, and seven days for entering the court in judicial robes. In total, he received an eight-month sentence for twenty-four counts. Dellinger was sentenced for more than twenty-nine months, Davis and Rubin more than twenty-five months, Hayden more than fourteen months, Froines more than five months, and Weiner more than two months. The at-

torneys fared no better: Kunstler was sentenced to more than forty-eight months and Weinglass more than twenty months for their conduct in court.

The jury, out four days, found all seven not guilty of conspiracy charges and found Froines and Weiner not guilty of teaching and demonstrating the use of incendiary devices. Five defendants—Hoffman, Dellinger, Davis, Rubin, and Hayden—were found guilty of crossing state lines to incite a riot.

Hoffman denied the defendants bail and sent them directly to jail. He gave them each the maximum five-year sentence and fined them each $5,000. They were released from jail a week later when the Court of Appeals ruled against Hoffman's denial of bail.

In 1972, the appeals court reversed the riot convictions, writing, "The demeanor of the judge and the prosecutors would require reversal even if errors did not." The government decided not to retry the riot case, but did retry the contempt charges in 1973. A federal District Court judge from Maine, Edward Gignoux, came to Chicago to consider the two hundred contempt citations. He dismissed all but thirteen, and determined that no further jail sentences were warranted. The Chicago Seven case was finally over.

THE TEN OTHER DISTRICT COURT JUDGES generally supported Hoffman. The day before the jury returned its verdict, the judges met in Campbell's chambers to discuss the case.

The minutes state: "At the suggestion of Chief Judge Campbell, by a standing vote of thanks, all of the judges expressed their affection for and appreciation to Judge Julius J. Hoffman for the excellent manner in which he presided over the lengthy and difficult conspiracy trial just concluded."

The judges also decided that attorneys Kunstler and Weinglass be barred from practicing law in the district. The decision, the judges agreed, would not be released until after the case was completed.

Following the trial, Parsons referred to the defendants as "a bunch of brats." Campbell later said: "I used to beg Julius every morning, 'Hold them in contempt, give them six months for contempt committed in the presence of the court.' I said it's not appealable. At the end of six months, let it go to another judge for retrial and let them get ready again. But he wouldn't do it. He loved the publicity, bad as it was. I remember him once answering me, 'Bill, don't you realize that the editor of the *London Times* himself called me yesterday?'"

In November 1969, the court's executive committee—composed of Campbell, Perry, and Napoli—dismissed a petition from thirty-five attorneys asking the court to stop hearing all criminal cases while the Chicago Seven trial was in progress. The attorneys, led by Frank W. Oliver, argued that the "extraordinary events" surrounding the trial, such as increased security and demonstrations, made it impossible to get fair trials. The judges wrote that the petition was "inartfully drafted," and concluded that it was "frivolous and impertinent."

The judges justified Hoffman's actions against Seale.

"While a defendant in a criminal case has an absolute right to be present during his trial, he does not have a right to brazenly make a shambles of the criminal judicial process and attempt to force a mistrial," the three judges wrote. "The Seventh Circuit has recently ruled that a trial judge may restrain disruptive and disrespectful conduct by whatever means necessary, even if those means include physical restraints and gagging."

Oliver was later reprimanded by the executive committee for holding a press conference on the matter, because he violated the local rule of speaking out on a pending case. The attorney was barred from practicing law for one year in the District Court.

In December, the court voted unanimously—but without Hoffman—to send a letter scolding the Chicago Bar Association for a scene in the 1969 Christmas Spirits show called "Heir." It portrayed a judge shouting, "Off with his head." The letter, signed by Campbell, said the skit was in bad taste.

"The members of the Court, of course, recognize and respect the right of members of the bar singly or collectively to comment seriously or humorously on the manner in which we discharge our judicial responsibilities," he wrote. "Our concern with the present episode, however, is that it represents editorial comment on a pending case."

Following the verdict, all the district judges except Hoffman petitioned the Court of Appeals to serve as "friends of the court" during the appeal of contempt convictions. The judges wrote that the power to punish by contempt "is essential to the fulfillment of our oath of office and to the administration of justice in the U.S. District Court." The appeals court denied consideration of the request. "It would be inappropriate for the judges of the District Court to take a position that would advocate or even appear to advocate the interest of any party in the appeals," the appeals judges wrote.

Judge Hoffman was a hero to many, a household name in Chicago and in much of the nation. He appeared on the cover of *Newsweek* magazine, was invited to the White House by President Nixon, and was honored by many organizations. To many, however, he became synonymous with the arrogance of the criminal justice system. Here was—right or wrong—the Establishment. Yet another Hoffman—actor Dustin, who watched part of the trial—contemplated bringing the story of the trial to the Broadway stage.

In 1978, the judge looked back with *Chicago Tribune* columnist Bob Greene. Hoffman told Greene that he couldn't act on his philosophy like the defendants could. "Jerry [Rubin] was against the war in Vietnam, and it turned out that the war was a disaster for the country," Hoffman said. "We lost the war, and it turned out that we shouldn't have been there in the first place. But I had to send boys to prison for evading the draft. And it turned out that many, many good boys went to jail."

The judge had mellowed. Away from court, he showed his other personality, looking back at the Vietnam years. He, too, perhaps was a victim.

"I sometimes lie awake at night," he said, "half-dreaming and I think about all those nice-looking boys saying, 'I'm guilty. I'm not going to war.'

"But I had no alternative. I had to send them to jail. I had to. Didn't I?"

THE NEXT TRIAL to test the will of the court was the "Conspiracy Fifteen" case. Fifteen men and women were charged with breaking into and vandalizing the Selective Service office at 2355 West Sixty-third Street in 1969 and burning draft records. Stung by the way the Chicago Seven defendants promoted themselves and their case, Judge Edwin A. Robson announced that he would allow no out-of-court comments by anyone connected with the Conspiracy Fifteen. "It is fundamental to our system of constitutional democracy that issues of law and fact in a criminal proceeding be resolved in the courts and not in the news media or the streets," he declared. But the Court of Appeals reversed Robson's order, ruling it unconstitutional. "We believe equally fundamental to our system is the right of all citizens, even if they be criminal defendants, to exercise their First Amendment Rights," the appeals judges wrote.

Robson was determined to maintain decorum in his court. He charged two spectators with contempt for refusing to stand as he entered and departed the court during the arraignment of the Conspiracy Fifteen defendants. And he charged one of the defendants, Fred J. Chase, with contempt during the trial for not rising promptly. Another defendant, Edward Hoff-

mans, was dragged from the courtroom by marshals. "Each time that Hoff-
mans refused to rise Monday, Robson ordered federal marshals to 'assist'
him to his feet," the *Chicago Daily News* reported. Fifteen people were originally indicted. Four never showed up for trial. Three others jumped bond
and fled after the trial began. One was declared mentally incompetent. The
others were found guilty.

After the trial, attorney Frank W. Oliver, who had defended three of the
defendants for free, was slapped with two $500 fines on contempt charges by
Robson. Before being sentenced, Robson asked Oliver if he had anything to
say.

"I am singularly unmoved by the court's order," the attorney said. "I am
singularly unrepentant, and if I had to do it over again I believe I'd do exactly what I did."

IN 1972, JUDGE NAPOLI sentenced each member of a group known as the
Four of Us to one year in prison. The four defendants—Mary Lubbers,
John Baranski, Thomas Clark, and Eileen Kreutz—entered an Evanston,
Illinois, draft board office in 1972, poured beef blood on five hundred draft
records, and called police to report their actions. After the police arrived, the
group asked for a moment to pray before they were taken into custody.
Their trial was in stark contrast to the Chicago Seven, wrote *Sun-Times*
columnist Tom Fitzpatrick.

"Here we have a courtroom packed with their relatives and friends," Fitzpatrick wrote. "Every one of them is well-dressed. Every one is deliberately
restrained and polite. So are the four defendants.

"There is no theater.

"No dialectics.

"They are four attractive young people and they are going at the jury and
Judge Napoli with love."

Three of the defendants represented themselves in court, so there was
little legal haranguing. Napoli gave the defendants a great deal of leeway;
they were allowed to make political points, deliver moral invectives, and discuss their religious, philosophical, and ethical beliefs in a legal context. But
Napoli moved the trial along quickly. Testimony was complete in four days.

"Judge Napoli seems a kind and patient man," Fitzpatrick wrote. "The
U.S. attorneys who are in charge of the prosecution have no rancor, no sense
of outraged indignation to convey to the jury."

William Bauer, who was U.S. attorney at the time, agreed three decades later. "Alex Napoli was probably the most even-tempered man I ever met," said Bauer. "He was high class. He knew exactly what he was doing. Had the Conspiracy Seven been tried before him, it would have been blunted early on. At the first sign of ridiculousness, everything would have stopped. The jury would have been withdrawn. The defendants would have been made to sit in jail until they behaved themselves and were ready to start again."

The Four of Us defendants argued that their decision to damage draft records was based on morals, which superseded the law. They saw the trial as a chance to question the legality of the war and the government. They put government witnesses—Selective Service employees, police, and FBI agents—on the defensive.

"Mr. Mandich, you said you were an agent for the federal government; is that right?" defendant Lubbers asked special agent George Mandich.

A. No, I said I was an agent for the FBI.
Q. And the FBI is an agency of the federal government?
A. That's right.
Q. So, therefore, you really are an agent of the federal government, in a sense.
A. In a sense, yes.
Q. Are you responsible for enforcing the laws of the United States, and for investigating violations of federal laws?
A. Within the jurisdiction of the Federal Bureau of Investigation, yes.
Q. Is enforcing laws which come under the Constitution of the United States within the jurisdiction of the Federal Bureau of Investigation?
A. Those designated by the Constitution.
Q. Which are?
A. Well, there are approximately a hundred and some violations which are investigated by the FBI.
Q. Do violations of branches of the government, violations of perhaps a misuse of power, come under one of those things that the FBI is responsible for investigating?
A. Not that I know of, no.
Q. Not at all? Is there any agency of government that is responsible for investigating misuses of power by any branches of government?
A. Not that I know of.
LUBBERS. Thank you. I didn't think so, either.

The defense called priests, religious educators, a uniformed Marine, a history professor, and a law professor to discuss whether the Vietnam War was legal. Assistant U.S. Attorney Steven Kadison objected to most of the testimony, and his objections were sustained, but the defendants made their points. For example, when they called Philip Rubin, a veteran who served one year in Vietnam, to the stand, Kadison objected to every question. But Lubbers persevered.

"Phil, when you were in Vietnam, did you witness the slaughter of civilians?" Objection. Sustained. "Did you in fact use white phosphorous grenades?" Objection. Sustained.

The questions kept coming:

"Aren't those grenades only useful against human beings?"

"Did you feel that the civilians who were being slaughtered by white phosphorous were in imminent danger in Vietnam?"

"Do you recall times where you violated the Geneva Convention of 1949 relative to the protection of civilian persons in time of war?"

Perhaps most poignant was the interplay between the defendants and their parents, who were called to testify about the lessons they taught their children. Baranski's father, John, before an objection, told the court that he was very proud of his son. Lubbers asked her father, William, about the most important principles he tried to pass down.

A. The essence of that belief is that we should live in harmony with our friends and with the rest of the people in the world; that we should do what we can to help them.

Q. And did you instill in us a respect for the commandment 'Thou shall not kill'?

A. I did.

Q. And is one of the precepts of the Catholic religion and the Christian religion that we are our brother's keeper?

A. It is.

Q. Could you explain what you taught us to believe—who you taught us to believe our brother was?

A. Everyone.

Q. And if we saw our brother in need, or dying, or starving, you instilled in us a desire to do something about it?

A. I tried to.

Q. How then, Dad, did you teach us that we were to resolve the differences?

KADISON. Objection, your honor.

A. I will sustain the objection.

Q. Dad, on the basis of your religion, and as you taught us, do you believe that life is sacred?

A. I do.

Napoli, in his instructions, told the jury that the Vietnam War was not on trial. "You are not to concern yourselves with political or moral questions, such as the legality of the war in Vietnam, or the morality of any war or the quality or virtues of the draft law," he said. After a lengthy deliberation, the jury returned a guilty verdict on one of the charges. The jurors said they were not swayed by the moral arguments. Their verdict was overturned because the indictment was incorrectly worded, according to the Court of Appeals.

AS THE VIETNAM WAR dragged on, Selective Service cases piled up. By the early 1970s, all Selective Service cases were routed to Campbell. He made defendants a deal: They could sign up now, plead guilty to draft violations, and accept a three-year term of community service, or ask for a trial with another judge. A large majority of the defendants signed up or pleaded guilty. "He wasn't soft, but he was predictable and fair," said Joe Beeler, an attorney who represented many draft defendants. If defendants pleaded not guilty, Campbell would rule on pretrial motions and the case would be assigned by lot for trial with another district judge.

Campbell wanted to provide parity.

"I could see some judges in the court giving them five years in prison and other judges practically a slap on the wrist all for this," said Campbell. "And the government was waging war at the time and we needed conscription and I think it's the duty of the court to go along, so I worked this out and talked practically all of the judges into sending their Selective Service cases that landed on their calendars—sending them all to me. And then I took care of them."

In 1971, Campbell took an unusual stand against the government. He decided, in *United States v. Thomas Leichtfuss,* to order Selective Service files opened to draft defendants, so they could determine if the induction order was valid. Up until that time, defendants were routinely given only their individual files in preparing their cases. Campbell ruled that prosecutors must hand over any information that might help the defendants. He also ruled that defendants were entitled to inspect and review all Selective Service administrative rules and most any record they needed to defend themselves, such as the names, addresses, and even criminal records of government witnesses.

Once again, Campbell was harking back to his idea that all parties in a suit—even in criminal cases—should, in his words, "Exchange files!" before a trial begins.

Selective Service officials were upset with Campbell's decision because it opened the powerful agency to scrutiny.

"The Justice Department called me and said, 'Do you get along with Judge Campbell?'" recalled Bauer, the U.S. attorney at the time. "I said, 'Certainly, I get along with everyone, particularly Judge Campbell.'

"'Does he realize what he is doing is going to destroy Selective Service?' I said, 'I don't know whether he does or not.'

"'Tell you what I'll do, I'll find out,'" Bauer said, and went to visit Campbell's chambers.

"'Judge Campbell, I've been asked by the Justice Department to find out if you know whether you realize that you are destroying the Selective Service.'

"He said, 'You bet I know.' I said, 'Thank you.' I went down and said, 'Yeah, he knows.'"

This was not out of character, Bauer said. "He stood up for what he thought was right. He thought the Selective Service was cranking up the war effort when they should be cranking it down. He put the burden on the government."

DEMOCRAT THOMAS FORAN continued to serve as U.S. attorney in 1969, after Republican Richard M. Nixon was elected president, so that he could finish prosecution of the Chicago Seven case. At the conclusion of the trial, Nixon appointed Bauer as U.S. attorney. Bauer, the former DuPage County state's attorney, had already been considered as a possible District Court judge, and he took the job with the understanding that he would be nominated later for a judgeship.

Bauer figured that he would serve as U.S. attorney for about two years, so he wanted to build the office rapidly. When he took over, he said the office was undermanned and overworked with its staff of twenty-two attorneys. He doubled the size of the attorney staff, and then nearly tripled it, hiring such people as future U.S. Attorney and Illinois Governor James R. Thompson as his first assistant; future U.S. Attorneys Samuel K. Skinner, Dan Webb, and Anton R. Valukas; future Illinois Attorney General Tyrone Fahner; and future U.S. District Court Judges Charles P. Kocoras and James H. Alesia. Bauer doubled the number of indictments, and directed the staff toward new targets: polluters, white-collar criminals, and politicians.

He also reassessed all the cases. He read the first six thousand pages of the Chicago Seven trial transcript and decided to drop charges against Bobby Seale. "He should not have been indicted, but that's neither here nor there," Bauer said recently. "He was a bad man, but he didn't commit the crime he was charged with. He didn't cross the state line to incite rioting. He came here to make a speech to the Black Panthers, and they lured him to the park."

What most distinguished the office of Bauer and his Republican successors, Thompson and Skinner, was its fearless prosecution of public corruption—from city aldermen to state legislators. After a jury found Alderman Tom Keane, the second most powerful man in Chicago government, guilty of mail fraud and conspiracy in 1974, Judge Bernard Decker announced: "The spectacle of public officials standing before a bar of justice after convictions is becoming all too common."

In pursuit of public corruption, Bauer and his attorneys started right at the top, when he announced the indictment of Otto Kerner Jr. Nobody in the state's history had better political credentials. His father, Otto Kerner Sr., had served as the state attorney general and as a Seventh Circuit Court of Appeals judge from 1939 to 1952. The younger Kerner's father-in-law, Chicago Mayor Anton Cermak, took a bullet for President-elect Franklin D. Roosevelt in 1933. (Some believe that the bullet was meant for Cermak.) Kerner Jr. served as a major general in the Illinois National Guard, as the U.S. attorney from 1947 to 1954, and was elected to two terms as the Illinois governor. In 1967, he was appointed by President Johnson to lead the National Advisory Commission on Civil Disorders, known as the Kerner Commission, and the following year he was appointed as a judge on the Seventh Circuit.

Kerner, his longtime political colleague Theodore Isaacs, and others were named in a nineteen-count indictment in late 1971 for illegally profiting from horse racing track stock. The governor had allegedly made about $150,000 from buying the stock at deflated prices and selling it back at a profit. In return, he gave privileges to a racetrack operator.

"When I first heard the story, I didn't believe it because I didn't believe

Facing page: Former Illinois governor Otto Kerner and his daughter, Helena, leave the Dirksen Federal Building on July 9, 1974, after a federal judge refused to reduce his three-year prison sentence. Kerner had a long career in the Federal Building.
PERRY C. RIDDLE/
CHICAGO DAILY NEWS

Otto Kerner . . . was even that kind of guy," said Bauer in a 1988 interview with the *Chicago Daily Law Bulletin.* "So I said, 'You don't have to convince a jury. You have to get by me, and I'm tougher than any jury you ever saw because I don't believe it.'"

Bauer became convinced of Kerner's guilt, however, and worked to obtain an indictment on charges of conspiracy, bribery, mail fraud, and income tax evasion. It was returned one month after Bauer left the U.S. attorney's office for the District Court. New U.S. Attorney James R. Thompson, along with first assistant Samuel K. Skinner, rode the elevator up to Kerner's chambers on the twenty-seventh floor of the Federal Building and handed him the sixty-four-page document on December 15. Kerner replied: "A fine Christmas present this is, gentlemen."

Following the January 1972 arraignment of Kerner and Isaacs, their attorneys asked that Richard Austin be disqualified as acting chief judge. He had stepped up to serve in Robson's stead after Robson took sick in 1971. The attorneys, stung by a decision of Austin to send the case to the executive committee for assignment, argued that Austin be disqualified as acting chief judge because he had turned seventy the previous year. Federal law required that chief judges be under seventy. The committee decided to call a judge outside the district to hear the case.

The following day, January 21, Judge Parsons held a press conference to declare that he, not Austin, was the acting chief judge. "This district is famous for having very famous and notable cases tried and reversed . . . because of judicial error," Parsons said. He was worried that the decision to seek an outside judge before all the district judges recused themselves might jeopardize the case.

"Dutifully and yet at the same time reluctantly, I am compelled by law to acknowledge that as of January 23, 1971, on which my beloved brother [Austin] reached his seventieth birthday, I lawfully became and continue to be now lawfully chief judge."

Then, according to news accounts, Parsons

said: "I should have done something about this long ago, but I'm colored—I don't want to be pushy. This matter puts it in my lap. A lesser case wouldn't do it, but these lawyers have the ability to go direct to the U.S. Supreme Court and it frightens everybody, and I'm frightened, too."

The issues in the six-week jury trial held before District Court Judge Robert L. Taylor, called in from Knoxville, Tennessee, were so complicated that Thompson, who tried the case, said there were "portions of the case I still don't understand." To offset the financial dealings presented by prosecutors, Kerner called fifteen character witnesses, including civil rights activist Roy Wilkins and General William C. Westmoreland, who had served as Kerner's commander during World War II. A jury found him guilty in 1973. Kerner, the first federal judge ever convicted of a criminal offense while in office, was sentenced to a federal penitentiary for three years and fined $20,000. He resigned from the Seventh Circuit and served eight months in prison. He was released in 1975 after doctors confirmed he had terminal cancer. He died the following year. Ironically, Bauer was named to fill his seat on the bench.

Kerner was not the first former governor to appear as a defendant in the Federal Building. Republican William G. Stratton, who served as governor from 1953 to 1957, was charged with converting political contributions to personal use and not reporting them as taxable income. Specifically, he was indicted for evading $46,000 in taxes. Stratton, in a 1965 jury trial before Judge Will, denied the charges, saying that his role as governor and state party leader all mixed with his life as a private citizen.

The trial started out badly for Stratton, who was reprimanded by Will for grimacing and laughing in court. "I don't see what's so funny about this, governor," he said. "These are not frivolous points we are trying to decide."

The government called eighty-five witnesses, but it couldn't outweigh Stratton's star witness, Senator Everett M. Dirksen, the "silver-tongued" orator and an old friend of Stratton. Dirksen told the jury that he thought it was OK for Stratton to use campaign money for clothes that his family used for political events and for his house, which was a political center of the party. He was asked by Will if he had ever used contributions on clothing.

Dirksen, who had a story for every occasion, told about his first trip to Washington in 1933 as a freshman legislator. He was described by the newspapers as "the man who attended the inauguration in a rented suit," he told the jury.

"It was a frightful embarrassment," he said, "and it resulted promptly in the raising of a fund of $2,700 to buy me a white tie and a long-tailed coat." Dirksen said he would have felt justified to use campaign funds for that purchase.

Dirksen was the last witness called by Stratton. In an unprecedented gesture, Dirksen bowed to the jurors as they left the courtroom, smiled, and shook every juror's hand as they passed.

He saved Stratton. The jury found the former governor not guilty. They later told Will that Dirksen's testimony had been decisive.

THE EARLY 1970s may have been a low point for the court. It was embroiled in two conspiracy trials and appeals court decisions that circumscribed its power to discipline attorneys and outside criticism. The Chicago Council of Lawyers, created to seek reform in the city's legal profession, was particularly critical of some District Court judges. The council sponsored and published lawyer surveys of District Court judges, which became known by court officials as "beauty contests."

"For many years, with only a few saving exceptions, the Chicago federal bench was the most wretched in the nation," wrote Joseph Goulden in *The Benchwarmers.* "Avarice, stupidity, politics, mule-headed pettiness, pathological behavior on the bench, favoritism towards business interests: such were the sorts of evils that could be found in Chicago justice."

Goulden's primary targets were Judges William Campbell, who "found time to amass a multi-million-dollar real estate fortune"; James Parsons, who at least once "presided over court while stone-eyed drunk"; Abe Marovitz, who as a young lawyer "enjoyed sharing the night life with Mob figures"; and William Lynch, who as an attorney was identified as a "chief intermediary in moving racetrack stock" between track owners and Governor Otto Kerner. Goulden laid much of the blame for the state of the court on Senator Paul Douglas for allowing the Chicago political Democratic machine to dictate many court appointments.

Decades later, some court insiders dismiss Goulden's charges as the excesses of a muckraking journalist. Others, however, consider his portrait as an authoritative look at the era.

To the court's rescue during the 1970s came U.S. Senator Charles Percy, who had a special interest in the law. Percy had attended night law school at Chicago-Kent while serving as president of Bell & Howell Company, but

Senator Charles H. Percy
speaks to a crowd of
eight hundred people
on July 17, 1970, at the
rededication of Chi-
cago's Federal Building
as the Everett McKinley
Dirksen Federal Building
in honor of the late Re-
publican senator. Mayor
Richard J. Daley and
Louella Dirksen, the sen-
ator's widow, sit directly
behind Percy. Chief
Judge Edwin A. Robson
temporarily lifted a ban
on photographers to
permit coverage of the
event in the courtyard
east of the building.
**BILL MARES/*CHICAGO
SUN-TIMES***

the board of directors had asked him to quit. They thought night school was unbecoming.

The law school dropout became a senator in 1966, and he depended on a small, informal group of former judges and top lawyers to help him pick federal judges. Republican Dirksen, the state's senior senator, approached Percy after taking office and showed him the forms needed by senators to recommend federal judges. "I know you went to law school, but you are not a lawyer," Dirksen told Percy. "Two signatures have to be on this. Why don't I just pick the people, and you just sign it."

Percy sent Dirksen's first choice to his advisers for review, and they rejected him. Dirksen's second choice was a lawyer that Percy himself had fired during his Bell & Howell days. He was rejected, too.

"Dirksen said, 'You seem to know a lot about this system,'" Percy recalled. "You appoint them and I will sign the forms."

During his eighteen years in office, Percy recommended twenty-two federal judges, including John Paul Stevens, whom he supported for a seat on the Seventh Circuit Court of Appeals. Stevens, a classmate of Percy's at the University of Chicago, was later promoted to the U.S. Supreme Court. Said Judge Bauer, "Percy had a genuine feeling for the law, a genuine desire to put the best on the court. [Prentice H.] Marshall, [George] Leighton, Stevens.

He wound up creating one of best District Courts in the history of the country."

A tougher critic, commentator Don Rose, agreed. "A quiet revolution has transformed the federal bench here . . . to one of the best—and in the process has begun the permanent dismembering of the entrenched Democratic political machine," he wrote in the *Chicago Sun-Times*.

Party affiliation and political connections were not important to Percy in most of his selections. He announced early on that he was doing away with "ethnic seats" on the courts. Almost every judge whom he appointed tells stories about Percy's inattention to politics. Prentice H. Marshall, in his oral history, recalled being called by Percy's aide, Joe Farrell, in 1973, and being asked about a federal judgeship.

"'Before we go any further, I'm a Democrat,'" Marshall told Farrell. "He said, 'We know that.' I said, 'I ran for public office as a Democrat.' 'We know that.' 'My wife and I were chairmen of the Citizens for Kennedy in DuPage County in 1960.' 'We know that.' I think I went on to say I've never voted in the Republican primary and I have never contributed to a Republican candidate. He said those things are unimportant. 'The question is whether you are interested.'"

Journalist Tom Littlewood pointed out in 1976 that Percy's first sixteen official judicial recommendations included no women. Percy did consider Soia Mentschikoff, a law professor at the University of Chicago, for a District Court seat in 1972, but she withdrew after an American Bar Association Committee called her qualified for the appellate court but not for the District Court because she did not have trial experience.

"Having committed himself to an uncompromising policy of naming the best available person, Percy insists that he will not deviate to please either racial minorities or women," Littlewood wrote for the magazine *Illinois Issues*. "He could have scored public relations points by yielding to pressure and picking Jewel Stradford Lafontant, a black woman from Chicago who is a deputy solicitor general in the Justice Department. She is an attractive Republican, but Percy's consultants gave her low grades on legal ability. Until a woman who is better qualified than any available man is proposed, Percy says there will be no women federal judges nominated by him."

PERCY SET THE TONE for his Northern District of Illinois appointments with Frank J. McGarr, an attorney chosen in 1970 to fill the court's twelfth judgeship. McGarr was a Chicago product, born and raised in the city and educated at Loyola University Chicago and its School of Law. He served as first assistant U.S. attorney during the 1950s and as first assistant Illinois attorney general from 1969 to 1970 and maintained a private practice during the 1950s and 1960s. He served as chief judge from 1981 to 1986 and left the court in 1988 to return to private practice.

McGarr took on the "admiralty case of the century" and ruled in 1988 that the Chicago-based Amoco Corporation pay $85.2 million in damages for the 1978 oil spill from the supertanker *Amoco Cadiz* off France's Brittany coast. The ship ran aground, spilling more than 68 million gallons of oil on one hundred miles of French coastline. It was the worst oil spill to reach land, and McGarr's award was the largest ever assessed at the time in an environmental case. The *Amoco Cadiz* case was complex, involving a U.S. company, Spanish shipbuilder, Liberian tanker, Italian crew, German tugboat, and French coastline. Ninety French communities and fifty businesses filed for damages. McGarr ruled that Amoco and subsidiaries were liable for damages because of the company's negligence in the design, repair, and maintenance of the supertanker. In his 459-page ruling, he said the French claims were "greatly exaggerated, but nonetheless real."

He said: "We are making new ground in admiralty law. It's always been tradition, going back to the ancient Phoenician traders, that the loss of cargo is limited to the value of the ship. But here we have a company that sent a ship to sea carrying cargo that didn't belong to it and did damage of tremendous magnitude."

His decision was appealed until 1990, when Amoco agreed to pay its full amount, plus interest.

In 1971, Percy recommended Thomas McMillen for the seat held by William Campbell. Born in downstate Decatur, McMillen graduated from Princeton University and Harvard University Law School and served as a Cook County Circuit Court judge for five years. McMillen's most memorable case was filed by Walter Polovchak, a Ukrainian boy who wanted to stay in the United States after his parents returned to their homeland. McMillen ruled in 1985 that the U.S. Immigration and Naturalization Service violated the due process rights of Polovchak's parents in 1982 when it stopped them from taking their son back to Ukraine. McMillen's ruling had little effect, since Walter was allowed to stay in the United States during his

appeal. By the time the appeals court acted, the case was moot—Polovchak
had turned eighteen.

William Bauer, who replaced Joseph Sam Perry, sat on the District Court bench from 1971 until 1975, when he was elevated to the Court of Appeals. His most publicized case was the 1972 trial of Chicago Police Captain Clarence Braasch and twenty-two former and present East Chicago Police District cops charged with extorting monthly payments from fifty-three Near North Side Chicago tavern owners.

The prosecution, led by Assistant U.S. Attorney Dan K. Webb, turned out to be a blueprint for large-scale police corruption cases. Immunity was offered straight up the line so the prosecution could have cooperative witnesses. First bar owners were offered immunity if they talked, then key cops were immunized. Nineteen of the twenty-three officers were convicted in the nine-week trial. Braasch was the highest-ranking Chicago police officer to ever be convicted of a felony. Days after the convictions, Chicago Police Superintendent James Conlisk resigned.

"The impact was enormous on police," said Bauer. Or so he thought. Two years later, he sentenced three former Austin District policemen to prison for shaking down twenty-eight West Side tavern owners.

Bauer also conducted the Purolator trial. Six men were charged with stealing $4.3 million, half a ton of cash, from a vault owned by Purolator Security Company at 127 West Huron in 1974. It was the largest cash haul in the nation's history at the time. Bauer tried the alleged masterminds, Pasquale Marzano and Luigi DiFonzo, who were both arrested in possession of much of the cash. Surprisingly, a jury found Marzano guilty and DiFonzo not guilty.

Richard McLaren was appointed to the bench in 1972, replacing Julius Hoffman, perhaps to get McLaren out of Washington. McLaren, a graduate of Yale University and Yale Law School, was chief of the Justice Department's antitrust division. He led the government's fight against the International Telegraph & Telephone Company, which contributed substantial money to the Republican National Convention. Nixon, in a 1971 taped conversation that was later revealed, said: "I want something clearly understood, and if it is not understood, McLaren's ass is to be out of there within one hour. The ITT thing—stay the hell out of it. Is that clear? That's an order. I do not want McLaren running around prosecuting people, raising hell about conglomerates, stirring things up."

Soon after the conversation, McLaren was nominated as a federal judge.

Richard G. Kleindienst, deputy U.S. attorney general, lauded McLaren when he was sworn in as district judge. "We had a situation of a rush toward conglomerates, and if continued, 85 percent of the production capacity would have wound up in a hundred corporations," Kleindienst said. "It didn't seem an optimistic forecast. The fact that the conglomerates once again are back to a normal basis is due primarily, if not solely, to Dick McLaren." Judge McLaren died four years after his appointment, at age fifty-seven. He was sick for about two years before his death.

Philip Tone joined McLaren on the District Court bench in 1972 to fill the court's thirteenth seat. Born in Chicago, Tone attended Iowa State University and its College of Law, and served as a law clerk for U.S. Supreme Court Justice Wiley Rutledge. Tone was on the District Court for only two years before being elevated to the Seventh Circuit Court of Appeals. Tone was considered, along with John Paul Stevens, for the U.S. Supreme Court appointment that Stevens won. To Charles Kocoras, an assistant U.S. attorney who would later become a District Court judge, Tone was a model.

"I always thought that was the kind of judge I'd like to be," Kocoras said recently. "You always want to adopt every bit of their mannerisms. I realized early on I had my own personality, and I can't carry myself like Phil Tone. So I had to learn from him the best of his qualities and filter it in my own way. Fairness, integrity, hard work. I liked his work product."

Percy's first Democratic nominee for the court, replacing Alexander Napoli, was Prentice H. Marshall, who was born and raised in Oak Park. Percy's choice of a Democrat created enmity among Republican politicians; forty-six state Republican legislators publicly "deplored" the nomination. Marshall, who was considered one of the court's top intellectuals, struggled through high school but bloomed at the University of Illinois at Urbana-Champaign and its College of Law, where he graduated first in his class. "You know, I'm absolutely hooked," he told his wife six weeks into his first semester. "I'm absolutely in love with this, with the law." Marshall clerked for Judge Walter Lindley of the Court of Appeals, and then worked in private practice from 1953 to 1967. Marshall was defeated by William Bauer for DuPage County state's attorney in 1959, before Bauer's rise in the Republican ranks. "Bill and I became very fast friends and I know, although Bill has never said it to me directly, but I know that Bill Bauer was very instrumental in my being appointed to the District Court," Marshall said.

Marshall, in an oral history, stated the most important issue he dealt with was charges of discrimination against the City of Chicago and its police department. The cases grew out of three lawsuits that charged the Chicago Police Department with racial, ethnic, and gender discrimination. One of the suits, filed by Renault Robinson, head of the Afro-American Patrolmen's League, charged that police officials had unfairly disciplined him for speaking out on civil rights issues.

"I thought the evidence was very compelling that the city had discriminated against African-American patrolmen," Marshall said in an oral history. "Discrimination against women was virtually conceded by Jim Rochford, who was then the superintendent of the police and a very able guy. He made it very clear that he did not want female line officers. Title VII says that you cannot discriminate on the basis of gender."

In 1974, Marshall ruled that the department's hiring examination discriminated against minority applicants. He ordered a new test. He ruled in 1976 that the city should pay minority police officers for lost earnings because of discriminatory acts. Marshall, in effect, reviewed all the hiring and promotion of officers during the 1970s. He stopped the flow of federal revenue sharing money to the city department until police officials figured out more equitable hiring and promotion practices. In 1988, the City of Chicago agreed to pay more than $9 million to settle claims that the police department discriminated against minorities and women. It was the first major class-action suit the city had settled. Marshall also approved the payment of $600,000 to Robinson and his organization. Following his ruling, Marshall considered similar discrimination cases against the city.

In 1976, Marshall issued a permanent injunction to stop Immigration and Naturalization Service agents from sweeping into factories and homes in the Northern District of Illinois to question Hispanics about their citizenship status. "The Immigration and Naturalization Service was really being pretty oppressive out in the truck farming area northwest of the city," Marshall recounted. "They would go up there and break into the dormitory and line people up, demand their green cards. Their pattern was really quite discriminatory against Latinos."

Marshall's most publicized case was the 1982 trial of Roy L. Williams, president of the International Brotherhood of Teamsters, for conspiring with four others to bribe a Nevada senator to vote against a bill the Teamsters opposed. Williams was found guilty and sentenced to ten years in prison.

Coconspirator Allen M. Dorfman, who was also sentenced to prison, was shot to death in 1983 soon after the verdict. Marshall, who freed Dorfman pending sentencing on a $5 million bond, said, "I really think that the so-called Outfit guys figured that Allen would try to talk his way out of prison. . . . I suppose that case attracted more media attention nationally than any of the others because Roy Williams was the president of the Teamsters and followed the pattern of Teamster presidents who got indicted and convicted."

President Gerald Ford's first two choices to the District Court were Joel Flaum and Alfred Kirkland Sr. in 1974. At the time of his appointment, Flaum, thirty-eight, who became known as the "boy judge," was the youngest federal judge in the country. He replaced Philip Tone after Tone was elevated to the Seventh Circuit Court of Appeals. As an assistant Cook County state's attorney, Flaum helped prosecute mass murderer Richard Speck. Subsequently, he served as first assistant Illinois attorney general and as first assistant U.S. attorney for the Northern Illinois District. He was elevated to the Seventh Circuit Court in 1983.

In 1979, as a District Court judge, Flaum ruled that minors did not need parental consent before obtaining an abortion. But he upheld the provision of the Illinois Abortion Act that required a twenty-four-hour waiting period before an abortion could be performed. Notably, both sides of the abortion issue found agreement with parts of the decision. It came a few years after a three-judge District Court panel—District Court Judges William Campbell and Edwin Robson and Court of Appeals Judge Luther M. Swygert—struck down the state's ninety-seven-year-old antiabortion laws as unconstitutional, paving the way for the state's first modern legal abortions. Later, the U.S. Supreme Court made abortion legal all over the country.

Kirkland, born and raised in Elgin, attended the University of Illinois and its College of Law. He spent most of his years as an attorney in Elgin. Kirkland did not last long on the court. He took a permanent leave because of a medical disability in 1979. After replacing William Bauer as a District Court judge, Kirkland ordered the Chicago Board of Education to provide free daily breakfasts to about 140,000 eligible students who were not receiving the meals. Kirkland found that the majority of district school principals had not signed up for the federal nutrition program. He ordered that federal funds be withheld until the entire district complied. "It was the intent of Congress that every needy child should be entitled to a free breakfast without regard to whether he attended a needy school," he said.

Robson stepped down as chief judge, as per law, on his seventieth birthday, April 16, 1975. No ceremony was held, but Parsons's staff honored him
with cake and coffee in his chambers and gave him a pen etched with the
date and words "Chief Judge." Parsons thus quietly became chief judge, the
first African American in the nation to hold the position. Many in the court
family worried whether Parsons could take the reins. Commentator Don
Rose wrote that "severe personal problems proved to be a disaster" for the
judge. His wife, Amy, had died in 1967. His son had been severely beaten by
police, and Parsons had spent years under the eye of U.S. marshals after numerous threats had been made against his life. "Parsons carried with him the
burden of history," said Court Clerk H. Stuart Cunningham.

Parsons was tentative at first as chief judge, but became more comfortable
during his six-year term. He brought pomp and grace to the court; he loved
and encouraged ceremony and formality—from investitures to the velvet
curtains of the Freeport courthouse. Barrel-voiced and eloquent, Parsons
was the model of the dignified federal chief judge.

PRESIDENT FORD'S FINAL THREE NOMINATIONS for the court were
picked by Senator Percy.

John F. Grady, born in Chicago, attended Northwestern University and
its School of Law. He served in the criminal division of the U.S. attorney's
office from 1956 to 1961, including one year as chief of the division, and then
moved to Waukegan to start a private practice. He worked as a solo practitioner for fifteen years, specializing in trial work. Grady was surprised in
1975 when told that he was being considered for the court, because Grady
did not know the senator and was not active in politics. "The idea of becoming a federal judge never crossed my mind," he said. His nomination was
proposed by the Chicago Council of Lawyers.

Grady presided over the 1980 MCI Communications antitrust lawsuit
against AT&T. A jury awarded the upstart MCI $600 million, but that
amount was reduced during the appeals. Grady allowed jurors to keep notes
at the long trial. Later in his career, he allowed jurors to ask questions in civil
cases.

During his years on the bench, Grady has developed a reputation as a particularly tough judge in political corruption and police misconduct cases. In
1977, after a jury found five defendants guilty of a $1.3 million political
bribery scheme to get a sludge-hauling contract, Grady sentenced one of the

leaders to ten years in prison, unheard of at the time for white-collar crimes. After ten police officers from the Marquette District were convicted of drug trafficking, he sentenced them to long terms in prison. "I was naive enough to think that the sentences I imposed in the case would teach police a lesson," said Grady, who served as the chief judge of the court from 1986 to 1990. "There have been half a dozen similar cases since then. It's as if the Marquette Ten never happened."

Percy's next choice, George Leighton for the seat held by Abraham Lincoln Marovitz, was another surprise.

"I suppose I had three strikes against me on the judicial nomination," Leighton told a reporter when his appointment was confirmed. "First, there was already a black U.S. judge in the district and no great outcry for another. Second, I am a lifelong Democrat, and we have a Republican national administration. And third, I'm 63 years old, and usually such appointments do not go to men or women over the age of 60."

But Leighton had always been a late bloomer. His parents had come from the Cape Verde Islands, off the coast of Africa, and settled in Massachusetts. Son George had little time for school; he was taken from class every March to tend and harvest the strawberry and cranberry crops on Cape Cod. Leighton never finished high school, but he won a college scholarship in an essay-writing contest. He persuaded Howard University to accept him as an unclassified student. He soon made the dean's list, graduated magna cum laude, and was admitted to Harvard Law School, from which he graduated after three years in the U.S. Army.

Leighton moved to Chicago in 1946. The city was very different then for African Americans. The Chicago Bar Association did not admit black lawyers at the time, nor did the American Bar Association. In the Loop, blacks could not eat in most restaurants or stay at hotels. "A black man couldn't even drive a cab in the Loop during the 1940s and '50s," he said. "Jitneys on South Park would drop people on Roosevelt Road."

Leighton, who worked with Attorney Thurgood Marshall as attorney for the National Association for the Advancement of Colored People, said he knew that segregation was wrong, but he did not remember being outraged. He was radicalized in 1951, however, when he served as attorney for Harvey E. Clark Jr., the African American man who was barred from moving his family into Cicero. Because Clark had a signed rental lease, Leighton filed a lawsuit in federal court to open the door for the Clark family. Following the ensuing riot in Cicero, Leighton was indicted by a Cook County grand jury for conspiring to cause the riot. He worried and couldn't sleep, thinking of the possibility of ending up in prison. Thurgood Marshall came to Chicago to defend Leighton in Cook County Circuit Court, and the indictment was dismissed.

"The people who returned that indictment against me didn't realize what a great favor they were doing me," Leighton said recently. "See, nobody has to tell me how it feels to be accused of a crime that he didn't commit." He served as a Cook County Circuit Court judge from 1964 to 1969 and as a state appellate court judge from 1969 until his appointment to the district bench in 1976.

Leighton's most historic case was the trial of Puerto Rican nationalist members of FALN, an acronym for Fuerzas Armadas de Liberación Nacional, or Armed Forces of National Liberation. The group, based primarily in New York City and Chicago, claimed responsibility for more than one hundred bombings beginning in the early 1970s in its struggle to free Puerto Rico from United States rule. Ten FALN members had been convicted and sentenced earlier by Judge McMillen.

District Court Judge George Leighton (left) poses with Chief Judge James Benton Parsons after Leighton was sworn in on February 27, 1976. **CARMEN REPORTO/CHICAGO SUN-TIMES**

The trial in 1985 before Leighton was tinged with political overtones. Three of the defendants—Alejandrina Torres, Edwin Cortes, and Alberto Rodriguez—refused to be represented by an attorney or put on a defense. They called themselves prisoners of war, fighting for Puerto Rico's independence in a colonial conflict. They believed that violence was morally justifiable. The defendants were charged with conspiring to bomb two military installations in 1983. Before the bombings, however, the FBI infiltrated a series of FALN safe houses in East Rogers Park, Uptown, and the South Side, where the group manufactured bombs. Judge McGarr granted the government permission to wiretap the apartments, but investigators went a step further by secretly using a video camera. Leighton ruled the videotape was inadmissible, but was overruled by the Court of Appeals. The black-and-white video, played during the trial, showed Torres and Cortes assembling a bomb while at a kitchen table in Uptown. It proved to be the key to the government's case.

After a four-week trial, the defendants were convicted of seditious conspiracy and sentenced to thirty-five years in prison. A fourth defendant, Jose Luis Rodriguez, age twenty-four, was placed on probation by Leighton. Following the verdict, about thirty backers raised their clenched fists and sang "La Borinqueña," a song of the Puerto Rican independence movement. The three convicts were released by President Bill Clinton in 1999 after they accepted a deal for clemency.

President Ford's final choice for the court was John Powers Crowley, a graduate of DePaul University College of Law and New York University School of Law. As an assistant U.S. attorney in the 1960s, Crowley had prosecuted former Governor Stratton. Then he went into private practice, establishing himself as one of the premier attorneys in the city. He was asked by Percy in 1976 to sit on the District Court, replacing Richard Austin.

Crowley became the first district judge in the court's long history to leave the bench in midcareer and return to private practice when he stepped down in 1981. His reasons were varied. He felt that judges were underpaid and he was unsettled by the increased workload since his appointment. He was also troubled by the public nature of a judge's life caused by such things as financial disclosure statements. "Being a judge means complete exposure of your life, and I have always tried to be a private person," he wrote in *Chicago Lawyer* magazine after he stepped down.

"A federal judge is the last generalist left in the profession," he wrote. "We're called upon daily to deal with the Constitution, securities, antitrust, tort, breach of contract and criminal cases." Crowley was challenged as a judge but left, he said, because he missed the camaraderie of the bar. "We lawyers oppose one another. We learn the good and the bad about each other, and we develop some strong friendships. I miss those friendships."

Eight years later, at age fifty-two, Crowley died of cancer.

CHAPTER SIX

1977–2002:
"You Can't Touch
a Federal Court"

THE VILLAGE OF SKOKIE, ILLINOIS, just north of the Chicago city limits, had a unique distinction in the decades after World War II. Several thousand of its seventy thousand residents were Holocaust survivors or the sons and daughters of survivors. That is why Frank Collin, leader of the Chicago-based National Socialist Party of America, applied in 1977 to the Skokie Park District for a permit to march with his neo-Nazi sympathizers through the village.

Skokie responded quickly to try to stop the march. The park district and the village passed ordinances directed against Collin and his few followers. The village approved an ordinance banning marchers from wearing military-style uniforms, an ordinance banning marchers from distributing racist literature, and an ordinance requiring that marchers obtain $350,000 in insurance coverage.

Skokie succeeded in getting an injunction in state court to stop Collin, but the Illinois Supreme Court eventually reversed the decision. Collin, with the assistance of the American Civil Liberties Union, began working his case through the federal courts, arguing that his First Amendment right of speech was being denied by Skokie.

The Northern District of Illinois had dealt with a similar case. In 1966, Judge Joseph Sam Perry issued both a temporary and permanent injunction against the American Nazi Party to stop it from demonstrating near Jewish synagogues or in Jewish neighborhoods during the Jewish High Holidays. Perry stated that the planned marches were designed to "incite riot and for the purpose of revenge," and said he was protecting the constitutional right to worship. "This court would enjoin a Salvation Army band from blaring outside of a Catholic Church during mass," he wrote. "This court would enjoin a troop of nudists, who sought to parade in native attire on Easter in front of a church."

Collin challenged the three Skokie ordinances in the courtroom of Judge Bernard Decker, who took the case on December 2, 1977. Collin was forthright about himself and his purpose. Asked by his attorney, David Goldberger of the ACLU, what his plans were for Skokie when he applied for a permit in early 1977, Collin explained: "My intentions at that time were to conduct a public demonstration on the first of May in front of the Village Hall with approximately thirty to forty uniformed members of our organization in paramilitary uniforms, with the swastika, as part of our uniform and on our placards, and the signs were to read 'For White Free Speech,' 'Free Speech for White People.'"

Questioned by Skokie attorney Harvey Schwartz about his party's views regarding black Americans, Collin replied: "We believe that the negro race is biologically inferior to the white Aryan race."

Moments later, he said: "We believe, with the first five presidents of the

Neo-Nazi organizer Frank Collin announces in July 1978 that his group will not march in the Chicago suburb of Skokie. *CHICAGO SUN-TIMES*

United States, that the negroes should be repatriated to their African homeland, as quickly as possible."

When asked what the party's policy was with regard to Jews, he replied:
"Basically, we believe that the Jews are in the forefront of the international
communist revolution and that they have inordinate political and financial
power in the United States and throughout the world."

"And, do you believe that American Jews should be exterminated?"

"No."

"What do you believe should be done with them?"

"I think that Jewish involvement in communism and in the Federal Reserve conspiracy should be exposed and documented and presented to the
American public for their own conclusions," he said.

When asked to describe the uniform of his party, Collin replied: "We
wear brown shirts with a dark brown tie, a swastika pin on the tie, a leather
shoulder strap, a black belt with buckle, dark brown trousers, black engineer
boots, and either a steel helmet or a cloth cap, depending upon the situation,
plus a swastika arm band on the left arm and an American flag patch on the
right arm."

Asked if the uniform intentionally resembled the uniform of the German
Nazi Party, he replied: "To some degree."

Skokie, to defend itself, called village officials to the stand to discuss how
it attempted to foster harmony among residents and avoid confrontation by
creating commissions and passing laws over the preceding twenty years.
Schwartz argued that the three ordinances in question continued that tradition.

The most poignant witness was Sol Goldstein, a village resident and Holocaust survivor who had led Skokie's opposition to a prior pro-Nazi demonstration. Goldstein told about his experiences in the Jewish ghetto in Kovno,
Lithuania, during World War II. He described the uniform of the S.A., the
feared "brown shirts" of the Nazi Party—"From the bottom, tall boots,
brown uniform in the form of a red band on the left arm, a swastika on the
hat and a swastika here in front on the chest, on the chest side, on the left
side of the shirt"—and described October 28, 1941, "the most tragic day in
my life." All of Kovno's Jews were ordered to a main square and made to
form two groups. "Thirteen thousand went to the right and . . . fifteen thousand went to the left." He went with the fifteen thousand, "without knowing
whether this was better or worse." The thirteen thousand were transported

about four miles from the city. People escaping from that group later told him that "all of these thirteen thousand were told to undress themselves, to give away all of their belongings, and they were shot to death."

He was later asked, "Are you familiar with the uniform of the National Socialist Party of America?"

"Yes, sir."

"Can you describe it?"

"Very briefly, it is the same uniform as the S.A. in Nazi Germany."

"What does that uniform and swastika mean to you?"

"Death in a most terrible form."

DECKER RULED FOR THE NAZIS on February 23, 1978. He said the ordinances violated Collin's right to free speech. "The Supreme Court has held that 'above all else, the First Amendment means that government has no power to restrict expression because of its message, its ideas, its subject matter, or its content.'"

Decker struck down the insurance requirement as well. Because the village had the power to waive the fee requirement, he called it "covert censorship." He ruled against the military-style uniform ordinance, writing that it would prohibit, among other things, American Legion members in parades. And he declared the racist literature ordinance unconstitutional.

"It is better to allow those who preach racial hate to expend their venom in rhetoric rather than to be panicked into embarking on the dangerous course of permitting the government to decide what its citizens may say and hear," Decker wrote.

The decision was appealed to the Seventh Circuit Court of Appeals, which agreed with Decker. The U.S. Supreme Court refused to hear the case.

Collin got a permit to demonstrate at Village Hall on June 25, 1978. Just prior to that date, however, he announced he had decided against the march, saying he would be satisfied to march at the Federal Plaza in Chicago and in his Marquette Park neighborhood. The Skokie case was over.

The issues of the Holocaust returned to the court that year when Judge Julius Hoffman presided over the prosecution of Chicagoan Frank Walus, the first of many U.S. residents accused of being a Nazi collaborator during World War II. Walus, originally from Poland, was charged with hiding his Nazi past on his citizenship application. The Justice Department flew witnesses in from all over the world to identify Walus as a heartless Gestapo

sympathizer who was responsible for the deaths of many Holocaust victims.
Walus's neighbors also testified about references he had made regarding his
Nazi connection. Walus denied the charges. He said he was forced by the
Germans to work on farms during the war. He was convicted of hiding his
Nazi past and ordered to surrender his U.S. citizenship.

After the trial, Walus produced affidavits from eight people confirming
his story and discussing his years on the farms. Documentary records that
were found after the trial also bolstered his argument. The government concluded that it could find no evidence linking him to the German war machine. "We regret that these newly discovered facts were not known before
this point, and we join in expressing that regret to Mr. Walus," said U.S. Attorney Thomas P. Sullivan when he announced the government's decision
not to retry the case. Walus was vindicated.

PRESIDENT JIMMY CARTER nominated seven people to the court in the
Northern District of Illinois during his term in office. Six were white males;
one was the court's first woman in its 162-year history. Six were Democrats;
Charles P. Kocoras labels himself an independent. All were recommended by
Democratic Senator Adlai E. Stevenson III, who served in the Senate from
1970 to 1981.

Stevenson, who had worked closely with Percy, said he continued the Percy
process of seeking recommendations from bar groups, attorneys, and judges.
"The best qualified candidates need to be coaxed," Stevenson recently said.
"They need to be persuaded to give up lucrative practices. They don't answer
want ads, are not willing to go through the public process of applying."
Stevenson never chose a Republican for the District Court, but he said,
"Honest to God, politics never entered my mind."

He did choose the first woman, Susan Getzendanner. "I wouldn't have
chosen a woman just for the sake of choosing a woman," he said. "I was ea-
ger for diversity on the bench. By that time there were many qualified
women."

Getzendanner was a trailblazer. Born in Chicago, she took a job as a secretary for lawyers after high school and said she realized: "Hey, I'm as smart as
they are, but they're making all the money. There's no reason why I can't be a
lawyer, too." One of two women in her Loyola University Chicago School of
Law class, she graduated first among eighty. After law school, she worked as
a clerk for Judge Hoffman, who had a reputation for hiring women as law

clerks. She was then hired by the law firm of Mayer, Brown & Platt and became the firm's first female partner. Getzendanner convinced herself she could make it past the tough bar association screening process and the Senate nomination hearings in Washington, D.C., for the federal judgeship. Much of her practice had been in federal court, both as a civil litigator and as a volunteer in the Federal Defender Program. "I certainly didn't strive for the job, but once it was offered to me, it was an incredible opportunity and I took it. I think my self-confidence carried me through."

She made headlines the day she was installed in 1980. "Once I got to the bench, the big issue was whether the judges would shake my hand or kiss me as I walked down the row of the judges," she recalled years later. "I think they ended up giving me a kiss on the cheek." Actually, she received handshakes, instead of the traditional bear hug. One week later, she refused her honorary membership in the all-male Union League Club. "It's an awful thing to be discriminated against," she said. "I don't think these white males understand what it's like."

Getzendanner was lively and irreverent. When she stepped down from her federal judgeship in 1987, she said the thing she would miss most was her wonderful audience. "Everybody laughs at the jokes of federal judges. They have to." Years later, when a sculptor honored her as one of the city's one hundred most important women in history by installing a huge boulder in her name in the Loop, Getzendanner said: "I don't see myself as the marble statue type. I don't ride a horse. I don't carry a sword. A rock is fine. My children are mildly embarrassed, but the heck with them."

NICHOLAS BUA, CARTER'S FIRST CHOICE to the court, succeeded William Lynch. He became legendary for his clean desk. He was considered the most efficient judge in the district because of his uncanny ability to settle cases. "He had a reputation that he could value a potential settlement to the nearest nickel," said court clerk H. Stuart Cunningham. Born in Chicago, Bua served on the court from 1977 to 1991, when he left to go into private practice. Bua said he had wanted to be a federal judge since he was twelve, when he watched his Italian-born mother become a citizen in the old courthouse. "I walked into a regal building, with marble pillars and thick carpeting, and I thought, I would love to sit in a court like that." Bua dropped out of high school during his first semester to work full-time to support his family following the death of his father. "As far as I know, I'm the only judge in the country who didn't graduate high school." He got his high school equivalency degree, graduated from the DePaul University College of Law, practiced privately for ten years, and spent fourteen years as a village court judge, Cook County Circuit Court judge, and Illinois Appellate Court judge.

Stanley Roszkowski, a Southern Illinois native, graduated from the University of Illinois and its College of Law. He was in private practice in Rockford for twenty-two years before his appointment to the Northern District of Illinois, replacing Richard McLaren. After being appointed to the court in 1977, Roszkowski at first worked in the Loop and took cases from the Western Division of the District Court, but he maintained his house in Rockford. During the mid-1980s, Roszkowski became the first district judge to work full-time in Rockford. Roszkowski ruled that then Bulls part-owner Arthur Wirtz and partners were guilty of antitrust violations when they stopped a Milwaukee businessman, Marvin Fishman, from gaining control of the team in 1972. Fishman told the court that Wirtz, owner of the Chicago Stadium, refused to meet with him to negotiate a lease while Fishman worked out final details of the team purchase. Meanwhile, Wirtz and other investors bought the Bulls. Roszkowski awarded Fishman $17 million but denied his request to take over ownership of the team.

James Moran was nominated to fill the court's fourteenth seat in 1979. Moran, born in Evanston, served as the court's chief judge from 1990 to 1995. He graduated from the University of Michigan and Harvard Law School and worked in private practice for almost twenty years. A Democrat, he served one term in the Evanston City Council and one term in the Illinois House. His most important political connection was his friendship with Adlai Stevenson III from law school days. Stevenson, as U.S. senator, pushed for Moran's nomination. Moran oversaw one of the earliest major sex-discrimination cases in the nation's history. It began in the District

Facing page: Susan Getzendanner, the District Court's first woman judge, takes a telephone call after announcing in 1987 that she will leave the bench. **BOB BLACK/ CHICAGO SUN-TIMES**

Court in 1968 after flight attendant Mary Sprogis was required to resign from United Airlines because of the company's no-marriage rule. She filed a federal discrimination suit against the airline and was ordered rehired two years later by Judge Joseph Sam Perry, who determined that the no-marriage rule was illegal. In 1986, Moran approved a settlement in which United agreed to pay $33 million in back pay and to reinstate about eight hundred flight attendants who were affected by the United policy. Each attendant who was forced to quit received up to $22,000.

Marvin E. Aspen was another city kid; he grew up in Albany Park, attended public grammar and high school, and used a CTA map to determine where he was going to go to college and later law school. Loyola University Chicago offered him a full scholarship, so he took the Lunt Avenue bus and an el train to school every day. By the time he reached Northwestern University School of Law, he drove to school in a car pool. Aspen worked in private practice, as an assistant Cook County state's attorney, and as an assistant corporation counsel for the City of Chicago, heading the office's appeals and federal litigation section, before being elected as a Cook County Circuit Court judge. He was nominated to fill the Northern District of Illinois's fifteenth seat in 1979 and served as the court's chief judge from 1995 to 2002. Aspen oversaw the 1984 plagiarism trial of Michael Jackson, who was charged with stealing the hit song "The Girl Is Mine" for his epic *Thriller* album. "For the better part of the day, both on direct and cross-examination, he testified in the form of a one-man concert; singing, tapping his fingers, stomping his feet, simulating the sounds of musical instruments and completely charming the spectators as only a polished show business performer could," Aspen wrote. "Small wonder the jury was reluctant to find him guilty of any wrong-doing." Six years later, Aspen ruled against his alma mater, Loyola University, when it sought to construct a twenty-acre landfill in Lake Michigan to expand its North Side campus. "What we have here is a transparent giveaway of public property to a private entity," the judge wrote. "The lake bed of Lake Michigan is held in trust for and belongs to the citizenry of the state." The decision, he later joked, likely drowned his chances of ever being appointed to Loyola's board of trustees.

Milton I. Shadur, like Judge Hubert L. Will before him, graduated from Washington High School in Milwaukee, the University of Chicago, and the University of Chicago Law School. He was named to fill Will's seat. Will quipped: "This guy has been following me all my life." Shadur was in private practice for thirty-one years with the small Chicago firm founded by Chicagoan Arthur Goldberg, who would later be appointed to the U.S. Supreme Court. Shadur considers himself as initially a Percy recommendation, because the senator first submitted his name to President Ford. The nomination came too late in a presidential election year, but Shadur was later recommended by Stevenson and nominated by President Carter. Many of Shadur's cases have turned on issues that affect the lives of Illinois's most vulnerable people. He forced Stateville prison to grant inmates in protective custody the same rights and privileges available to other inmates. He pushed the state child welfare system into improving its services for abused and neglected children, shortening the time they languished in foster care. He forced the Cook County Board to nearly double the size of the county jail in order to relieve overcrowding. Shadur views such judicial actions as the forced result of the failures of the other branches of government to carry out their own responsibilities. "We are the least democratic segment of public officials in our society," he said. "We get lifetime appointments. We are not responsible to the electorate, and yet we are the ones who end up having to resolve these things."

For Susan Getzendanner, the first woman judge, life on the bench held its disappointments. She was surprised at the routine nature of her court calendar. She said she was swamped in deciding mortgage foreclosures, turn-back-the-odometer cases, and individual employment discrimination suits. "I felt like I was running an employment agency," she said, deciding whether employees who fell asleep on the job were being disciplined properly. Getzendanner, who filled the court's sixteenth seat, had expected to be deciding class-action, civil rights, and antitrust cases that would affect society, but they were few and far between. In 1982, however, she did rule that the Chicago Police Department's Red Squad had illegally spied on political dissidents and awarded $300,000 in damages to twenty plaintiffs. Getzendanner didn't dwell on decisions; few of her trials lasted more than three weeks. Getzendanner left the bench at age forty-eight, in 1987, because she was restless and bored and couldn't imagine working under such conditions for another seventeen years until retirement. Getzendanner believes she will be remembered for her 1987 decision to bar the American Medical Association permanently from keeping its members and hospitals from associating with chiropractors. It brought chiropractors closer to mainstream medicine. And, she said wistfully, "I think I will be remembered for being the first female judge and a damn good one."

Charles P. Kocoras was President Carter's choice for the final appointment he would make to the District Court. Kocoras took the seat of Alfred Kirkland Sr. Born in Chicago, Kocoras graduated from DePaul University with an accounting degree and then went to DePaul University College of Law. "Three days into law school I knew it was for me," he said. "I loved the law from the beginning. It had a certain sense to it, a certain structure, a certain approach to problem solving and life." Kocoras served as an assistant U.S. attorney from 1971 to 1977, then as chairman of the Illinois Commerce Commission before his appointment in 1980 to the District Court. He took over as the court's chief judge in mid-2002. Kocoras kept the Chicago schools open during the fall of 1993 despite state law that required the School Board to have a balanced budget before it could open. "I was probably on somewhat shaky legal ground," he said years later. "It wasn't a secret to me. To let these kids suffer because some adults couldn't come together on a decision was wrong. And if there was a way in the law that I could make sure those kids didn't get hurt, I was going to do that." The decision was reversed by the Court of Appeals, but by then the financial crisis had been averted.

IN 1978, THE WESTERN DIVISION moved into the Rockford Federal Building, ending a decades-old battle by Rockford attorneys to move the court from the historic city of Freeport to Rockford. Like many small-town courts, the second-floor Freeport court above the post office was dominated by characters—from bankruptcy referee Sherwood Dixon, who had once served as the state's lieutenant governor, to Edith Hannah. "She was the deputy clerk in charge for several decades, and boy she was," said P. Michael Mahoney, the division's magistrate judge. The rural outpost was a favorite spot for a few of the District Court judges. In 1917, Judge Kenesaw Mountain Landis came to Freeport to sentence 117 men who resisted the World War I draft. The men, called "slackers" by the *Chicago Tribune,* pleaded guilty to not signing up for the draft and said they were conscientious objectors. Many were Swedish immigrants who had come to the United States to avoid war. They held an antiwar parade in Rockford, which caught the attention, and ire, of federal authorities. Landis, when he arrived in Freeport, called the men "whining and bellyaching puppies."

money and federal poverty money, including funds for the Model Cities program, until a plan was worked out to build new units in white neighborhoods.

Chicago Mayor Richard J. Daley took Austin's ruling against the CHA personally. Daley, who was behind Austin's appointment to the District Court bench, thought that Austin had embarrassed the mayor and made him vulnerable before an election. Daley was critical of Austin, which touched off a public feud. "I haven't taken on anybody," Austin responded when asked by a reporter why he had taken on Daley. "The mayor isn't a party to the lawsuit. The law is what I'm interested in."

Soon after, the feud escalated. Austin accused Daley of ordering a police raid on his beloved Olympia Fields Country Club. The judge demanded that sheriff officials take a lie detector test to determine who was behind the raid. "If they pass," Austin offered, "I'll donate $200 to the Model Cities program because I understand the city is short on dough."

Meanwhile, the tenants' lawsuit against HUD moved up the judicial ladder. In 1976, the U.S. Supreme Court ruled that HUD should become a over in remedying public housing discrimination throughout the entire opolitan area, including the suburbs. Five years later, District Court John Powers Crowley, who inherited the Gautreaux case after Austin's oversaw a consent decree signed by the CHA, HUD, and Gautreaux stipulating that HUD would provide federal rent subsidies to -one hundred low-income families in nonminority neighborhoods.

and federal politics, however, once again conspired to continue e aims of the consent decree. In 1987, Judge Marvin Aspen, who the case after Crowley's retirement, appointed private developer evin to oversee and construct all new Chicago public housing, e Chicago Housing Authority as a builder. Since that decision, tat Company has built or rehabilitated two thousand units in mmunities in Chicago.

CHA is the longest ongoing case in the Northern Illinois been in the courts of three District Court judges over a period irty-six years. Between 1976 and 1998, the housing program eral subsidies for twenty-five thousand residents to move to grated communities throughout Chicago and the suburbs. eaux litigation began in 1966, few believed that the courts eemingly intractable racial discrimination plaguing Chi-

"The moment the court opened it was evident from the questioning by the judge that this was going to be a typical 'Landis' day for the court fans," the *Tribune* reported. He asked each defendant his name, country of birth, how long he had been in the United States, and whether he would register.

When the first defendant said he was not willing to kill or hurt anyone, Landis asked, "Well, do you want me to believe that if a man came up to you with a hickory club you would let him beat you into pulp without trying to defend yourself? Wouldn't you fight back?"

"No. I guess I would run away," the man replied.

Following Landis's tenure, Judge Charles Edgar Woodward spent a considerable amount of time hearing cases in Freeport during the 1930s, and Elwyn Shaw, who lived in Freeport, preferred hearing cases there into the 1940s. Joseph Sam Perry took the Freeport call from the 1950s to the mid-1960s, when the District Court decided that nonsenior judges would rotate serving in the Western Division.

Judges used to stack the few cases on Freeport's dockets together so they could get done in a week or so. The arrival of the District Court judge in the town was a big event, often noted with a reception. "Judge Parsons liked coming out here," said Mahoney. "He remodeled the courthouse, took part in ceremonies, was toasted at receptions. He had a spot in his heart for the

The newly constructed United States Post Office and Courthouse in Freeport during the early 1900s. The District Court's Western Division was based in Freeport from 1905 until it moved to Rockford in 1978.
STEPHENSON COUNTY HISTORICAL SOCIETY

Western Division; he loved the history of the area, the connection with Lincoln and Grant." For decades, Rockford attorneys tried to move the court to their growing community of about a hundred thousand. Freeport, which had a population of about twenty-five thousand, was centrally located in the Western Division. Attempts to move the court were resisted by residents of both Galena and Freeport. However, in 1978, under U.S. Representative John B. Anderson's influence, the United States Courthouse at 211 South Court Street was opened in Rockford. In 1985, Judge Stanley Roszkowski was given the Western Division as his permanent assignment. The number of cases there increased significantly, especially after the transfer of DeKalb and McHenry Counties to the division. The Western Division now also includes Jo Daviess, Stephenson, Winnebago, Boone, Carroll, Ogle, Whiteside, and Lee for a total of ten of the district's eighteen counties.

The Federal Bureau of Investigation, Drug Enforcement Administration, and U.S. attorney each has an office in Rockford. Seven assistant U.S. attorneys work there full-time. In 2001, about seventy criminal cases and 550 civil cases were filed, including many from prisoners at a state facility in Dixon. The division holds an average of ten criminal trials and fifteen civil trials annually. Funding for a new federal courthouse in Rockford has been appropriated by Congress. Construction is expected to be completed by 2005.

Since 1989, one case has dominated the court in Rockford—a lawsuit filed by a parents group named People Who Care charging the Rockford school district with intentionally discriminating against African Americans and Hispanics. In 1993, Mahoney, in a 537-page report, wrote that the district had "committed such open acts of discrimination as to be cruel and committed others with such subtlety as to raise discrimination to an art form." An order entered in 1996 included racial quotas for such things as cheerleaders and remedial classes. The Court of Appeals, which eventually dissolved the order and returned the school to local control, warned that students "should not be made subjects of utopian projects." The appeals court decided that enough time and money had been spent under the terms of the order.

The Rockford case is one example of the way the court changes the way we live. Since the 1960s, many of the nation's federal courts have been called upon when civic institutions are seen as violating basic constitutional rights. The two major cases that wound their way through the courts during the 1970s both involved alleged rights violations.

Gautreaux v. CHA actually began in 1966, when acti[treaux] and five other Chicago Housing Authority reside[nts] class-action lawsuits charging that the CHA and U.S. De[partment of Hous]ing and Urban Development violated their rights by con[struction of public housing developments in African A[merican neighbor]hoods. Lawyers from the American Civil Liberties Union, tenants' attorneys, accused the public agencies of an inte[ntional plan of] racial discrimination outlawed by the Civil Rights Act. [In] 1967, the Chicago Housing Authority constructed only six[ty-three] thousand public housing units in white neighborhoods, a[t Gau]treaux's lead attorney, Alexander Polikoff. "The pattern o[f segregation has] been nearly perfect," the lawyers charged in their brief.

In February 1969, Judge Richard Austin agreed with th[e lawyers] that the CHA had "deliberately chosen sites for such proje[cts to] avoid the placement of Negro families in white neighborh[oods ...] that evidence showed that the CHA and the City Council practiced segregationist policy in determining public housin[g ... au]thority was guilty of racial discrimination in selecting build[ing sites, in as]signing tenants, and in submitting sites to selected alderme[n who reflected] their constituents' racial sentiments," the judge wrote. Fiv[e months later] Austin ordered that the next seven hundred public housing [units be built on] scattered sites in predominantly white neighborhoods. A[fter those were] ordered, 75 percent of public housing units must be buil[t in white neighbor]hoods.

The rulings came less than a year after Gautreau[x ...] one. Gautreaux, who moved into public housing i[n ...] organizer who had brought Martin Luther King [... Altgeld] Homes on the Far South Side for a rally. "Dorot[hy ... thou]sands of black women and men like her aroun[d ... made the Gau]treaux suit possible," wrote historian Harol[d ... Her] determination, and their challenges made [... will] not stand."

But what followed was years of proc[eedings ...] ings, the CHA and the Chicago City C[ouncil ...] refusing to approve the constructio[n ... To] counter the inaction, Austin fro[ze ...]

"The moment the court opened it was evident from the questioning by the judge that this was going to be a typical 'Landis' day for the court fans," the *Tribune* reported. He asked each defendant his name, country of birth, how long he had been in the United States, and whether he would register.

When the first defendant said he was not willing to kill or hurt anyone, Landis asked, "Well, do you want me to believe that if a man came up to you with a hickory club you would let him beat you into pulp without trying to defend yourself? Wouldn't you fight back?"

"No. I guess I would run away," the man replied.

Following Landis's tenure, Judge Charles Edgar Woodward spent a considerable amount of time hearing cases in Freeport during the 1930s, and Elwyn Shaw, who lived in Freeport, preferred hearing cases there into the 1940s. Joseph Sam Perry took the Freeport call from the 1950s to the mid-1960s, when the District Court decided that nonsenior judges would rotate serving in the Western Division.

Judges used to stack the few cases on Freeport's dockets together so they could get done in a week or so. The arrival of the District Court judge in the town was a big event, often noted with a reception. "Judge Parsons liked coming out here," said Mahoney. "He remodeled the courthouse, took part in ceremonies, was toasted at receptions. He had a spot in his heart for the

The newly constructed United States Post Office and Courthouse in Freeport during the early 1900s. The District Court's Western Division was based in Freeport from 1905 until it moved to Rockford in 1978.
STEPHENSON COUNTY HISTORICAL SOCIETY

Western Division; he loved the history of the area, the connection with Lincoln and Grant." For decades, Rockford attorneys tried to move the court to their growing community of about a hundred thousand. Freeport, which had a population of about twenty-five thousand, was centrally located in the Western Division. Attempts to move the court were resisted by residents of both Galena and Freeport. However, in 1978, under U.S. Representative John B. Anderson's influence, the United States Courthouse at 211 South Court Street was opened in Rockford. In 1985, Judge Stanley Roszkowski was given the Western Division as his permanent assignment. The number of cases there increased significantly, especially after the transfer of DeKalb and McHenry Counties to the division. The Western Division now also includes Jo Daviess, Stephenson, Winnebago, Boone, Carroll, Ogle, Whiteside, and Lee for a total of ten of the district's eighteen counties.

The Federal Bureau of Investigation, Drug Enforcement Administration, and U.S. attorney each has an office in Rockford. Seven assistant U.S. attorneys work there full-time. In 2001, about seventy criminal cases and 550 civil cases were filed, including many from prisoners at a state facility in Dixon. The division holds an average of ten criminal trials and fifteen civil trials annually. Funding for a new federal courthouse in Rockford has been appropriated by Congress. Construction is expected to be completed by 2005.

Since 1989, one case has dominated the court in Rockford—a lawsuit filed by a parents group named People Who Care charging the Rockford school district with intentionally discriminating against African Americans and Hispanics. In 1993, Mahoney, in a 537-page report, wrote that the district had "committed such open acts of discrimination as to be cruel and committed others with such subtlety as to raise discrimination to an art form." An order entered in 1996 included racial quotas for such things as cheerleaders and remedial classes. The Court of Appeals, which eventually dissolved the order and returned the school to local control, warned that students "should not be made subjects of utopian projects." The appeals court decided that enough time and money had been spent under the terms of the order.

The Rockford case is one example of the way the court changes the way we live. Since the 1960s, many of the nation's federal courts have been called upon when civic institutions are seen as violating basic constitutional rights. The two major cases that wound their way through the courts during the 1970s both involved alleged rights violations.

Gautreaux v. CHA actually began in 1966, when activist Dorothy Gautreaux and five other Chicago Housing Authority residents filed landmark class-action lawsuits charging that the CHA and U.S. Department of Housing and Urban Development violated their rights by concentrating the construction of public housing developments in African American neighborhoods. Lawyers from the American Civil Liberties Union, who served as the tenants' attorneys, accused the public agencies of an intentional pattern of racial discrimination outlawed by the Civil Rights Act. Between 1954 and 1967, the Chicago Housing Authority constructed only sixty-three of its ten thousand public housing units in white neighborhoods, according to Gautreaux's lead attorney, Alexander Polikoff. "The pattern of segregation has been nearly perfect," the lawyers charged in their brief.

In February 1969, Judge Richard Austin agreed with the tenants, ruling that the CHA had "deliberately chosen sites for such projects which would avoid the placement of Negro families in white neighborhoods." He wrote that evidence showed that the CHA and the City Council had deliberately practiced segregationist policy in determining public housing sites. "The authority was guilty of racial discrimination in selecting building sites and assigning tenants, and in submitting sites to selected aldermen who reflected their constituents' racial sentiments," the judge wrote. Five months later, Austin ordered that the next seven hundred public housing units be built on scattered sites in predominantly white neighborhoods. After that, the judge ordered, 75 percent of public housing units must be built in white neighborhoods.

The rulings came less than a year after Gautreaux's death, at age forty-one. Gautreaux, who moved into public housing in 1953, was a community organizer who had brought Martin Luther King Jr. to her Altgeld-Murray Homes on the Far South Side for a rally. "Dorothy Gautreaux, and the thousands of black women and men like her around the country, made the Gautreaux suit possible," wrote historian Harold Baron. "Their dreams, their determination, and their challenges made it clear that the old order could not stand."

But what followed was years of procrastination. Following the 1969 rulings, the CHA and the Chicago City Council balked at Austin's mandate by refusing to approve the construction of any new public housing units. To counter the inaction, Austin froze $26 million in federal public housing money and federal poverty money, including funds for the Model Cities program, until a plan was worked out to build new units in white neighborhoods.

Chicago Mayor Richard J. Daley took Austin's ruling against the CHA personally. Daley, who was behind Austin's appointment to the District Court bench, thought that Austin had embarrassed the mayor and made him vulnerable before an election. Daley was critical of Austin, which touched off a public feud. "I haven't taken on anybody," Austin responded when asked by a reporter why he had taken on Daley. "The mayor isn't a party to the lawsuit. The law is what I'm interested in."

Soon after, the feud escalated. Austin accused Daley of ordering a police raid on his beloved Olympia Fields Country Club. The judge demanded that sheriff officials take a lie detector test to determine who was behind the raid. "If they pass," Austin offered, "I'll donate $200 to the Model Cities program because I understand the city is short on dough."

Meanwhile, the tenants' lawsuit against HUD moved up the judicial ladder. In 1976, the U.S. Supreme Court ruled that HUD should become a player in remedying public housing discrimination throughout the entire metropolitan area, including the suburbs. Five years later, District Court Judge John Powers Crowley, who inherited the Gautreaux case after Austin's death, oversaw a consent decree signed by the CHA, HUD, and Gautreaux lawyers stipulating that HUD would provide federal rent subsidies to seventy-one hundred low-income families in nonminority neighborhoods.

Local and federal politics, however, once again conspired to continue stalling the aims of the consent decree. In 1987, Judge Marvin Aspen, who inherited the case after Crowley's retirement, appointed private developer Daniel E. Levin to oversee and construct all new Chicago public housing, removing the Chicago Housing Authority as a builder. Since that decision, Levin's Habitat Company has built or rehabilitated two thousand units in fifty-seven communities in Chicago.

Gautreaux v. CHA is the longest ongoing case in the Northern Illinois District. It has been in the courts of three District Court judges over a period of more than thirty-six years. Between 1976 and 1998, the housing program has provided federal subsidies for twenty-five thousand residents to move to one hundred integrated communities throughout Chicago and the suburbs. "When the Gautreaux litigation began in 1966, few believed that the courts could remedy the seemingly intractable racial discrimination plaguing Chicago's public housing system," wrote Janet Koven-Levitt in the *John Marshall Law Review*. "As remedial efforts faltered throughout the 1970s, critics began to prey upon Gautreaux as a prototypical example of the legal problems inherent in court-ordered structural reform. Today, in contrast, the policies Gautreaux ultimately embraced are lauded nationally."

The district's second-oldest ongoing case was filed by Michael Shakman, an attorney seeking election as a delegate to the 1970 Illinois Constitutional Convention, and by lawyer Paul M. Lurie. Shakman and Lurie argued that the political patronage system deprived candidates and voters of a free and fair electoral process. More than forty thousand patronage jobs in and around Chicago had created a giant army of political workers and a huge treasury for the Democratic Party Central Committee of Cook County, which, they said, put any candidate not supported by the Central Committee at a distinct disadvantage. Shakman sought to ban the firing or disciplining of patronage workers who refused to contribute or work for the sponsoring organization, as well as politically based hiring.

The case was first assigned to Judge Abraham Lincoln Marovitz, who had been active in the Chicago regular Democratic organization and was one of Daley's closest friends. Marovitz dismissed the suit, but his decision was reversed by the Court of Appeals. After the case was returned, he disqualified himself. As the lawsuit worked its way to trial, Shakman's attorneys reached partial settlements with local and state officials and agencies and signed consent decrees that prohibited firings or demotions for political reasons. In 1979, Judge Bua extended what has become known as the Shakman Decree by prohibiting government hiring for political considerations. Several defendants—including the City of Chicago, Cook County state's attorney and treasurer, and state attorney general—signed consent decrees agreeing to abolish patronage hiring. Other defendants appealed, and Bua's decision was later overturned by the appeals court, but without affecting the validity of the consent decrees previously entered.

The Shakman Decree has largely been a success, but, as the *Chicago Tribune* editorialized in 2002, patronage has taken different forms through the decades. The *Tribune* wrote: "The city workforce is, over all, more professional, though political mopes that somebody sent still have a mysterious way of landing on the payroll. . . . The power of Democratic ward organizations has weakened, but the Democratic Party and the [Richard M.] Daley administration are still virtually unchallenged in the city. Hiring patronage has largely been supplanted by pinstripe patronage—that is, the political favors come in the form of lucrative contracts rather than jobs at the Department of Streets and Sanitation."

THE BLACK PANTHER CASE, a civil rights lawsuit filed in connection with the 1969 police raid that killed two Panthers, was the longest case ever tried in the Northern District of Illinois. About thirty-seven thousand pages of testimony were taken in a trial that lasted eighteen months. It was finally resolved in 1982, twelve years after it was filed.

Police carry the body of slain Black Panther leader Fred Hampton from 2337 West Monroe after a gun battle on December 4, 1969. The civil case surrounding the shooting was the longest in District Court history. JOSEPH MARINO/ *CHICAGO DAILY NEWS*

The suit grew out of a December 4, 1969, predawn raid by fourteen state's attorney police on an apartment at 2337 West Monroe occupied by members of the militant Black Panther Party. Seven survivors of the raid and two relatives of the slain Panthers, Fred Hampton and Mark Clark, filed a $47.7 million lawsuit against law enforcement officers in 1970. Cook County State's Attorney Edward Hanrahan, who had formerly served as U.S. attorney, said the raids were ordered to search for "sawed-off shotguns and other illegal weapons" in the apartment. Hanrahan reported that the police officers were fired upon as they tried to enter the apartment. He said occupants shouted "Shoot it out" and continued firing as police attempted to take the apartment in a vicious gun battle. Nineteen weapons and a large cache of ammunition were seized. Four members of the party were seriously wounded and taken to Cook County Hospital. Three other party members were arrested and taken to Cook County Jail. Later that day, Panther member Bobby Rush—currently a U.S. representative—disputed the police account, saying: "Hampton was murdered in his sleep." He argued that the Panthers had not fired a shot.

All seven surviving Panthers were indicted in Cook County Circuit Court, but their indictments were dropped.

A federal grand jury, impaneled in January 1970, heard testimony by several of the police officers. The Panthers refused to cooperate fully with the grand jury because they did not want to reveal how they might testify if they filed a civil lawsuit against the government. The grand jury, despite this one-sided testimony, issued a detailed report critical of Hanrahan and all the law enforcement officials. The twenty-three jurors were dubious of the police account, especially after the FBI determined that raiders fired more than eighty shots and the Panthers fired only one. But the jury was also critical of the seven Panther survivors who refused to testify, concluding, "It is impossible to determine if there is probable cause to believe an individual's civil rights have been violated without the testimony and cooperation of that person."

The Panthers' 1970 lawsuit was filed against twenty-eight officials who planned or participated in the raid. Judge Joseph Sam Perry and the Panthers' two attorneys were at odds almost from the beginning, when Jeffrey Haas and G. Flint Taylor asked the judge to recuse himself. The attorneys, in their appellate brief, wrote that when Perry questioned potential jurors, he unthinkingly asked everyone the same questions, inquiring whether blacks belonged to the Ku Klux Klan and whether whites belonged to the Black

Panther Party. He referred to blacks as "colored people." During the trial, Perry often fell asleep. He held both attorneys in contempt, for reasons that were never clear to the attorneys, and did not give them a chance to speak before he passed sentences. Both contempt charges were reversed by the Court of Appeals.

The discord reached its peak toward the end of testimony during an exchange between Haas and Perry.

"Well, you don't like anything, as far as you are concerned, except your way," Perry said.

"Well, Judge, there hasn't been anything that has happened—"

"—and you are not going to have your way."

"I know," said Haas. "My way is a fair trial, and I know I'm not going to get it, judge. That is totally clear in this courtroom."

"You bet your life you are not going to get it," said Perry.

After a year and a half of testimony, Perry dismissed Hanrahan and twenty defendants in 1977 without letting the case go to the jury. Seven other defendants—Chicago police officers who fired their guns during the raid—continued to stand trial on charges they used excessive force and violated the civil rights of the Panthers. The jury deadlocked after three days of deliberations, and Perry dismissed the case against them in a highly unusual move. He ordered the plaintiffs to pay trial costs, estimated up to $1 million.

Two years later, the Court of Appeals reinstated the case against twenty-four of the defendants and punished federal officials for failing to produce documents requested by the Panthers' attorneys. When the Supreme Court refused to consider the government's appeal, the case was sent back to the District Court for a retrial. In 1982, the parties agreed to a $1.8 million out-of-court settlement. Chicago, Cook County, and the FBI agreed to split the costs.

"The criticism didn't bother me at all," Perry said after the trial. "I know that a judge who does what he thinks is right may be criticized."

RONALD REAGAN NOMINATED thirteen Northern District of Illinois judges during his two terms in office. Ten men and three woman were chosen, including the court's first African American woman, Ann Claire Williams. Reagan's first eight choices were recommended by Republican Senator Charles Percy, who was defeated in his reelection bid in 1984. From 1985 to 1993, the state was represented by Democratic senators under Republican

presidents, so the task of recommending federal judges was taken over by ranking Republican U.S. Representative Robert Michel, the House minority leader. Michel, of Peoria, was criticized for making selections for a district in which he did not live, but he relied on recommendations from representatives who did live in the district—in particular U.S. Representative Henry J. Hyde, who served on the House Judiciary Committee. Twelve of Michel's choices were Republicans; Williams labeled herself as an independent.

Reagan's first appointments were William T. Hart and John Nordberg. Hart, born in Joliet and raised in Aurora, was the son of William Hart, editor and publisher of the *Aurora Beacon News.* Judge Hart graduated from Loyola University Chicago and its School of Law and served as an assistant to the U.S. attorney for two years and as a special assistant Illinois attorney general. He worked in private practice from 1956 until his appointment to the Northern Illinois District bench in 1982, replacing John Powers Crowley. Hart oversaw the 1985 jury trial of TV commentator Walter Jacobson, who was charged with libeling tobacco company Brown & Williamson. Jacobson, in a commentary, implied that the company linked "pot, wine, beer, sex, and wearing a bra" to Viceroy cigarettes in order to induce teenagers to smoke. He ended by saying of cigarette makers: "They're not slicksters. They're liars." Tobacco officials testified that they talked to Jacobson's assistant before the broadcast and told him that the proposed Viceroy cigarette

The contemporary court, pictured in 1999. Front row (from left): Judges Duff, Hart, Marovitz, Kocoras, Aspen, Moran, Alesia, Nordberg. Second row (from left): Judges Marovich, Manning, Leinenweber, Conlon, Zagel, Gottschall, Hibbler, Bucklo, Norgle Sr., Gettleman. Back row (from left): Judges Lindberg, Holderman, Pallmeyer, Coar, Kennelly, Williams, Castillo, Andersen, Reinhard.

campaign had been scrapped before any commercial was broadcast. The jury found that Jacobson had libeled the tobacco company and awarded it $3 million in general damages and $2 million in punitive damages.

John Nordberg was appointed to the District Court the same day as Hart in 1982, filling the seat of Bernard Decker. Born in Evanston, Nordberg attended Carleton College and the University of Michigan Law School. He was in private practice for twenty-six years and served as a Cook County Circuit Court judge. On August 3, 1983, a man broke into Nordberg's twenty-first-floor courthouse office, announced "This is a coup d'etat," and took two of his law clerks—including current Bankruptcy Judge Carol A. Doyle —and a visitor hostage. The man, who said he was carrying explosives, barricaded the door of the office law library with a chair. Nordberg was presiding over a trial in his nearby courtroom until he was informed of the incident. He offered to be substituted as a hostage, but the FBI refused his request. Agents talked to the man for hours until he released the hostages one by one during the eight-hour standoff. FBI agents and Chicago police then subdued and arrested the man. "They told me being a judge was a lifetime appointment, but they never mentioned anything like this," Nordberg told reporters.

Paul Plunkett served as an assistant U.S. attorney during the early 1960s, helping to prosecute Teamsters President James Hoffa. Plunkett, whose father was an FBI agent and an assistant U.S. attorney, graduated from Harvard University and Harvard Law School. He worked in private practice until his appointment to the bench in 1983, replacing James Parsons. "It took me about ten years, but I now regard myself as a judge," he told the *Chicago Daily Law Bulletin* in 1997. Plunkett presided over the 1996 jury trial of the Gangster Disciples, the Midwest's largest and most violent street gang and one of four "super gangs" that dominated the city following the dismantling of the El Rukns. Jurors convicted four of the highest-ranking Gangster Disciples leaders of engaging in a continuing criminal enterprise. Seven gang members and a former Chicago gang crimes police officer were also convicted of conspiring to distribute narcotics in Chicago and the suburbs. The key to the government's case was a collection of taped prison conversations by gang chairman Larry Hoover made with the help of transmitters worn on visitor badges. After the verdict, Plunkett told gang members to "pack their toothbrushes" when they showed up for posttrial motions.

Ilana Diamond Rovner, born in Riga, Latvia, narrowly escaped the Holocaust with her parents. As a girl of seven, she wanted to be a lawyer. "I thought lawyers really did good. They made sure horrible things didn't happen. They redressed injustice," she said. After graduating from Bryn Mawr College and the Chicago-Kent School of Law, she worked as a law clerk for Judge Parsons and as an assistant U.S. attorney. She served as deputy governor and legal counsel for Governor James Thompson from 1977 until her appointment to the Northern Illinois District bench in 1984, taking the seat of Joel Flaum. "When I was appointed to the District Court, I decided that I had to have a sterner, more serious demeanor when I came out on the bench," she said. "My first day, I was very serious, very businesslike. I tried to keep my voice lower, modulated. I did it about twenty minutes and then I said I will faint if I have to keep this nonsense up, and I just became me." During her eight years on the bench, Rovner heard almost every case from Operation Incubator, an undercover investigation into bribery of public officials that netted four Chicago aldermen and fifteen other officials. In 1992, she was appointed to the Seventh Circuit Court of Appeals.

Charles Norgle Sr. was nominated to fill the court's new seventeenth judgeship in 1984. Born in Chicago, he graduated from Northwestern University and the John Marshall Law School. His early legal career was based in DuPage County, where he served as an assistant state's attorney and deputy public defender and as a circuit judge for twelve years. Norgle has drawn, by the court's random assignment system, far more than his share of tough cases. As a rookie, he presided over the 1985 trial of Richard LeFevour, former chief judge of Cook County Traffic Court and a kingpin in the Operation Greylord investigation of judicial corruption. LeFevour, the highest-ranking judge charged in the probe, was sentenced to twelve years in prison after a jury found him guilty of taking hundreds of thousands of dollars in bribes to dismiss drunken driving cases and fix parking tickets over more than a decade. That same year, Norgle ordered special aldermanic elections that paved the way for Chicago Mayor Harold Washington's aldermanic majority and the end of the deadlock known as Council Wars. In 1987, Norgle presided over the first major trial against the El Rukn gang. Gang members, including leader Jeff Fort, were convicted of conspiring to commit terrorists acts in exchange for money from the Libyan government. During the 1990s, Norgle helped create the state's first so-called Hispanic Congressional District, ordered former U.S. Representative Mel Reynolds to be force-fed in prison after going on a pretrial hunger strike, and ruled that actor Leslie

Nielsen could appear in a TV commercial dressed as the Eveready Energizer bunny.

James F. Holderman, born in Joliet, filled the court's eighteenth seat in 1985. He was raised on his family's farm in Grundy County, the district's least-populous county. Holderman became a lawyer because he relished knowing the rules. He remembers playing baseball one night as a ten-year-old in downstate Verona. "There was a foul ball. I was on third base. The catcher ran back to the screen behind home plate to catch the ball. While the ball was in the air, I went back and tagged third base. When the catcher caught the ball, I raced in and scored. None of my teammates knew you could score a run on a foul ball. I knew that because, even at age 10, I liked studying and following the rules," he said. Holderman graduated from the University of Illinois at Champaign-Urbana with a degree in agricultural science and received his law degree from the University of Illinois College of Law. He worked as an assistant U.S. attorney from 1972 to 1978. Then he went into private practice prior to his appointment to the District Court. Five weeks after the September 11, 2001, terrorist attacks on the United States, Holderman refused to issue a temporary restraining order against a federal ban on demonstrations and events in the Federal Plaza. "We are in troubled times at this point," he said. "That doesn't mean the Constitution can be obliterated by the government. But I believe the government has taken reasonable steps." The ruling came during the height of the anthrax scares.

Ann Claire Williams initiated the court's nineteenth judgeship. She received an undergraduate degree from Wayne State University and a graduate degree from the University of Michigan while teaching three years in a Detroit elementary school. "I actually went to law school on a dare," she recently said. "A friend of mine was getting his master's in social work. We were kind of competitive. He came by one day and said, 'What are you going to do?' I said, 'I don't know. I'm not sure.' He said, 'I'm going to law school,' and I said, 'So am I.'" Williams scored high on her Law School Admission Test and was accepted at Notre Dame Law School. After graduation, she worked as an assistant U.S. attorney from 1976 until her nomination at age thirty-five to the Northern District of Illinois in 1985. Williams sentenced former Illinois Governor Dan Walker to prison after he pleaded guilty to bank fraud, misapplication of bank funds, and perjury. Walker had hoped to avoid prison, but Williams sentenced him to seven years in prison, five years probation, and a substantial fine. Walker, the third former Illinois governor to stand in the criminal dock of the District Court, served the longest sentence. In 1999, Williams was appointed the first African American judge on the Seventh Circuit Court of Appeals.

Brian Barnett Duff was nominated in 1985 to fill the court's twentieth judgeship. He was recommended by Charles Percy, a friend with whom Duff had campaigned for two decades. He graduated from the University of Notre Dame and DePaul University College of Law and was elected to the Illinois General Assembly three times, becoming the House minority whip. He served as executive vice president for a small insurance company and worked in private practice before being elected in 1976 as a Cook County Circuit Court judge. Duff was a maverick who relished his independence on the bench. He became the first federal judge in the country to determine that Hispanics could use the federal voting rights act to challenge voter registration procedures. He oversaw an agreement that allowed the appointment of nine Spanish-speaking deputy registrars to go door-to-door in Will County to sign up voters before the 1988 general election. In 1992, Duff presided over a complex case that ended in one of the largest prisoner rights jury awards in the history of the district. Inmate Tommy Ortiz was awarded $758,800 for allegedly being beaten by a guard and for being kept unfairly in solitary confinement. Duff later overturned the verdict as excessive but ordered Ortiz released from solitary confinement. Duff's individualistic style has earned him criticism over the years, including four highly publicized opinions against him from the Court of Appeals in 1996. In October, Duff sent a letter requesting that he be removed from active duty because of a medical problem. Chief Judge Marvin Aspen entered an order directing that Duff's cases, except for those pending a ruling, be redistributed to other district judges. Duff underwent scheduled heart surgery within weeks of the letter and has never been assigned new cases. He has steadfastly continued to go to his court office on a regular basis.

Harry Leinenweber was the first judge chosen solely by U.S. Representative Robert Michel, who recommended the appointments of several judges during the period when the state had two Democratic senators and the nation had a Republican president. Leinenweber was appointed to fill the court's twenty-first seat in 1985. Born in Joliet, he graduated from the University of Notre Dame and University of Chicago Law School. He was in private practice in Joliet for twenty-three years and served as a member of the Illinois General Assembly for ten years. In 1987, he married U.S. Representative Lynn Martin, who went on to serve as labor secretary for President George H. W. Bush. Leinenweber took on Gangster Disciples leader Larry Hoover in 1998 when Hoover confronted the judge at his sentencing hearing. "This trial has been a politically motivated farce," Hoover told the judge as he spoke for the first time since his 1995 drug indictment. The judge told Hoover that he could have used his talents for good. "You were able to do what you did in jail for twenty-five years—you're amazing," Leinenweber said. "You must be a very charismatic person. . . . You misused a gift you got from God." Then he gave Hoover the maximum—six life sentences.

James Zagel was born in Chicago and graduated from the University of Chicago and Harvard Law School. He worked as an assistant Cook County state's attorney, assistant Illinois attorney general, executive director of the Illinois Law Enforcement Commission, director of the Illinois Department of Revenue, and director of the Illinois State Police before his appointment—recommended by Governor James Thompson—in 1987 to the District Court. He filled the post held by Frank McGarr. After portraying a judge in the Jessica Lange film *Music Box,* Zagel was cast by director David Mamet as a physician in the *Homicide* film. "He thought I was a professional actor," said Zagel, who took the stage name J. S. Block. (His middle name is Block.) Zagel, who had edited popular law school textbooks since 1972,

District Court Judge Kenesaw Mountain Landis plays a judge in the 1917 film *The Immigrant*. The film, directed by Edwin L. Hollywood, was produced by the federal government. The actor is Warren Cook. CHICAGO HISTORICAL SOCIETY

turned to writing a novel in 2002. *Money to Burn,* based on a fictitious District Court judge who robbed the Federal Reserve Bank of $100 million in cash that was destined to be incinerated, was based on characters in fiction and insights picked up during his years on the bench. "Judges will tell you that being a judge is a lonely place in life, that you lose all your old friends because you are afraid of influence on your decisions," Zagel wrote. "This is false; you don't lose many friends except in the normal way. . . . The truth is that you can't make any new friends because the people you meet now are usually people who might want something from a person who wears a black dress every day at work and you never know why they want to be your friends."

James H. Alesia rose from traffic cop to federal judge, replacing George Leighton. Born in Chicago, Alesia worked as a Chicago police officer for four years while attending Chicago-Kent School of Law. "If I was working the night shift, I would go to school during the day. If I was working days, I would go to night school." He was in private practice for eleven years before serving as an assistant U.S. attorney from 1971 to 1973. He also served as an administrative law judge and then returned to private practice prior to his appointment to the Northern District of Illinois in 1987. Alesia presided over one of the court's most remarkable mob trials. A jury in 1992 convicted mobster Gus Alex of racketeering and extortion. But it was Lenny Patrick,

District Court Judge James Zagel plays a judge in the 1989 film *Music Box.* He is shown with the film's stars Jessica Lange and Frederic Forrest.

his main accuser, who transfixed Alesia's packed courtroom. Patrick, a seventy-eight-year-old described as a "geriatric gangster," was the highest-ranking mobster ever to turn government witness. "I don't want to die in prison," he told the jury, explaining why he was so candid about his former partner, Alex, and his fifty years in organized crime. "I'm the dirtiest thing living on the Earth," he admitted. Patrick said he had killed six people during his career. "Everybody's so afraid of me they shiver when they see me," Patrick told the jury. But, he said, "I don't get a kick out of killing people. I done it to protect myself."

Suzanne B. Conlon graduated from Mundelein College and Loyola University Chicago School of Law. She worked as a law clerk for Judge Edwin Robson before entering private practice early in her career. She served as an assistant U.S. attorney for ten years, including five years in the Central District of California, and served as executive director of the U.S. Sentencing Commission. She also was special counsel to the associate attorney general of the United States. She was appointed to the Northern District of Illinois in 1988, replacing Thomas McMillen. Conlon kept the Chicago Cubs in the Eastern Division of the National League after she granted a preliminary injunction in 1992 blocking the plans of Major League Baseball Commissioner Fay Vincent to move the team to the Western Division. Conlon vacated the order after the Cubs and baseball agreed to halt realignment plans. Conlon's initial decision that Vincent had overstepped his authority was ironic since she sat in the district's judgeship established by Kenesaw Mountain Landis, the man who became baseball's ultimate authority as its first commissioner. Conlon's decision may have been a contributing factor in Vincent's dismissal as commissioner.

George Marovich, Reagan's final nomination, was born in East Hazel Crest and graduated from the University of Illinois and its College of Law. He worked in private practice and served as a Cook County Circuit Court judge from 1976 until his 1988 appointment to replace Getzendanner. Marovich sent ten soybean traders to prison in 1991 after they were convicted of scheming to cheat Chicago Board of Trade customers out of more than $200,000. "This case is about pervasive fraud," Marovich said. The traders had maintained during their trial that their actions in the pit were not criminal. In a courtroom filled with friends and relatives of the traders, Marovich told them: "What you did was wrong, it was very wrong. The sooner you come to grips with that fact, the sooner you will be able to get on with your lives." Then he announced: "I sure hope everyone at the CBOT is paying attention." The sentencing ended a long investigation of the futures industry at the Board of Trade and Chicago Mercantile Exchange, the two largest commodity exchanges in the world. Three trials were held in the District Court, but the soybean traders trial was the only clear-cut victory for the U.S. attorney's office. Ten Board of Trade soybean traders were convicted in early 1991 of illicit trading. The investigation and results forced both exchanges to overhaul their policies.

OPERATION GREYLORD, A MASSIVE INVESTIGATION of the Cook County Circuit Court, dominated the criminal calendar of the Northern District of Illinois during the 1980s. Fifteen judges, fifty lawyers, thirteen police officers, and more than a dozen other court officials were convicted in the undercover sting.

Greylord began in the 1970s, when reports of judicial corruption began reaching the offices of U.S. Attorney Thomas Sullivan and Cook County State's Attorney Bernard Carey. The stories centered around "miracle workers"—lawyers who were able to win impossible cases by passing money to crooked judges through court workers who served as bagmen. Following the acquittal of mob assassin Harry Aleman, the U.S. attorney's office and FBI started investigating the Cook County Circuit Court, largest unified court system in the nation. Law enforcement officials staged fake robberies and other crimes so that agents could enter the system and test judges. Perhaps the miracle of Greylord was that the secret investigation was not leaked before it became public. The court's involvement began in 1980, when Chief Judge Parsons approved an FBI request to plant recording devices in the chambers of a suspect, Circuit Judge Wayne Olson. It was the first time a bug had been authorized for use in a judge's chambers anywhere in the United States, according to James Tuohy and Rob Warden in *Greylord: Justice, Chicago Style.*

Three years later, the first Greylord indictments were handed down. "In my judgment, when the project is over and all the cases have been tried, I believe this will be viewed as one of the most comprehensive, intricate, and difficult undercover projects ever undertaken by a law enforcement agency," said U.S. Attorney Dan Webb, who inherited the investigation from Sullivan.

The first Greylord trial began on March 5, 1984, before Judge John Nordberg. The U.S. attorney's office, which spearheaded the investigation, called

Harold Conn, a deputy clerk in Traffic Court, to trial. Conn did not have the high visibility of the judges who were to follow, but the U.S. attorney's office wanted to test its procedure before taking on judges. Conn was charged with taking small bribes from government mole Terrence Hake, who posed as a corrupt defense attorney for two years. Hake had worn a concealed microphone, and was the major witness against many of the Greylord defendants. He testified at this first trial that Conn passed the money to fix seven traffic cases. Conn admitted that he handled the money but denied the charge that he committed extortion or racketeering, the official charges against him. His attorney asked for a mistrial because he said the

Cook County Circuit Judge Richard LeFevour appears shaken as he leaves the Dirksen Federal Building on November 21, 1984, after pleading not guilty to Operation Greylord charges. LeFevour, one of the top judges brought to trial as part of the Greylord corruption investigation, was later convicted and sentenced to prison, where he died. **TOM CRUZE/ CHICAGO SUN-TIMES**

government's investigation was illegal and its techniques—creating fake cases and wiring moles—was improper.

The motion, if approved, could have doomed the investigation.

"If Nordberg ruled against the government, and if he were affirmed on appeal, Greylord would fall apart," Tuohy and Warden wrote. "Further prosecutions would not proceed." Nordberg delayed in making a decision. "This is one of the first cases of its kind in the federal courts," he said. "We are sailing in uncharted water." Finally, he denied the motion. The jury found Conn guilty. He was sentenced to six years in prison—and Greylord proceeded full speed ahead. Nordberg's decision was affirmed by the Court of Appeals, which stated that the judge had given the jury "appropriate cautionary instructions."

Next up was the first Greylord judge, Associate Circuit Court Judge John Murphy, who appeared before Judge Kocoras in 1984. Murphy, charged with racketeering, extortion, and mail fraud, was prosecuted by Webb himself. Once again, Hake and FBI agents testified that they had passed bribe money to Murphy. The star witness, though, was Jimmy LeFevour, a bagman for his cousin, Judge Richard LeFevour, who ran Traffic Court and presided over the bribery schemes as well. Jimmy LeFevour, who agreed to testify in order to save his government pension, told jurors he delivered bribes from defense attorneys to Murphy about a dozen times. Jimmy LeFevour said he directed Murphy to fix many other cases at the direction of Judge LeFevour. Kocoras, taking his cue from Nordberg's ruling on the legitimacy of Greylord, instructed jurors that the investigation and its techniques were proper. Murphy was convicted and sentenced to ten years in prison.

Associate Circuit Court Judge John Laurie was the next to be called to trial, before Judge Prentice H. Marshall. Laurie was charged with accepting $3,000 in bribe money from Hake. During his testimony, Hake told the jury that when he asked Laurie for an "NG," not guilty verdict, the circuit judge said, "Sure." During Conn's trial, however, Hake had referred to the same conversation with Laurie. At that trial, Hake had said the judge said "We'll see" when asked for a not guilty verdict.

Laurie's attorney, Patrick Tuite, jumped on the discrepancy. "I'm going to use Hake to go with me to a singles bars so that when I ask a lady if she'll go out with me and she says, 'We'll see,' Hake will tell me she said, 'Sure.'"

Hake's varying accounts of the conversation led to a not guilty verdict for Laurie on all counts, and the Greylord investigation stalled.

The next trial, of Associate Circuit Court Judge John Devine before Judge Susan Getzendanner, was pivotal. A loss would stall the Greylord momentum—perhaps forever. Devine was the only judge whom Hake could say he actually paid, and he had a tape to prove it. Devine was charged with extortion, mail fraud, and racketeering—and was found guilty on most charges. He was given fifteen years by Getzendanner, who simply told him at the sentencing hearing: "I'm not going to make any speech. Your crime is despicable."

Other judges, including LeFevour, Olson, Judge John F. Reynolds, Judge Raymond Sodini, and Judge John H. McCollom, marched into the District Court accused and marched out convicted. Two judges—Laurie and Francis Maher—were acquitted. When Judge Reginald Holzer appeared, charged with taking loans from lawyers in return for favoritism, Assistant U.S. Attorney Scott Turow told the jury, "He turned his official position into a cash station." Holzer was found guilty and originally sentenced to eighteen years in prison by Marshall. It was the longest sentence to be issued in the prosecution.

Greylord was a double-edged sword for the district. The revelations of corruption cast a stain on the entire judiciary. "What distinguished the federal judges, and this has always been true, is the level of integrity," said Getzendanner. "In the state court, you could be touched. There are judges who are active takers." But the federal court was different. "That is a wonderful thing about the court, and that is still true today: You can't touch a federal court."

PRESIDENT GEORGE H. W. BUSH appointed three judges to the Northern District of Illinois. Each came by way of recommendation from Robert Michel. They were all Republicans.

George Lindberg, who was born in Crystal Lake and graduated from Northwestern University and its School of Law, was Bush's first appointment. Lindberg worked for a Chicago polygraph company and conducted about five thousand lie-detector investigations. He served three terms as a member of the Illinois House, where he won the nickname "Mr. Ethics" for his lead in pushing the Illinois Governmental Ethics Act. In 1973, Lindberg was elected Illinois's first state comptroller and later served as deputy Illinois attorney general. He was elected to the Illinois Appellate Court in Elgin from 1978 until his appointment to the District Court bench in 1989, replacing Prentice H. Marshall. Lindberg ruled in 1992 that three Chicago aldermen violated the constitutional rights of an art student after they seized his painting at a private Art Institute of Chicago exhibition. The painting, which portrayed the late Chicago Mayor Harold Washington wearing women's underwear, was considered insulting to Washington and to the African American community. Said former Alderman Bobby Rush: "We went there to quell an imminent riot and possible disorder. We did what we did for the noblest of reasons." Lindberg disagreed, as did the Seventh Circuit Court of Appeals, which ruled that his decision was correct. The city agreed to pay artist David Nelson $95,000 for his legal fees. In another case involving the Art Institute, Lindberg oversaw a settlement between the Searle and Gutmann families over ownership of Edgar Degas's *Landscape with Smokestacks,* seized by the Nazis during World War II. Lindberg ordered the families to meet personally to discuss a solution, and they did, reaching a financial settlement and agreeing to donate the artwork jointly to the Art Institute.

Wayne Andersen's appointment to the federal bench appears astounding, since he made a steep climb from Cook County Traffic Court directly to U.S. District Court. But Andersen had credentials to back up his application for the job. Born in Chicago, he graduated from Harvard University and the University of Illinois College of Law. He worked in private practice, served as an administrative assistant to Illinois House Majority Leader Henry Hyde and was named deputy Illinois secretary of state. Andersen started work as a Cook County Circuit Court judge in 1984 and helped reform the court's traffic division as its supervising judge. He was appointed in 1991 to the district bench, taking the seat of Stanley Roszkowski. Andersen banned wholesale gun sweeps of Chicago Housing Authority buildings in 1994. The judge sided with the American Civil Liberties Union, which protested apartment searches without tenant consent following gang shootouts. Andersen said the police could conduct sweeps with approved search warrants or conduct searches of individual tenant apartments if they received approval. He ruled that the blanket CHA sweeps violated the Fourth Amendment, which prohibits "unreasonable searches and seizures." The *New York Times* called it a "courageous ruling," writing: "One of the things that made this case fascinating and even poignant was that many tenants had intervened on the side of the Housing Authority."

Philip G. Reinhard was nominated to fill the court's twenty-second seat. Born in LaSalle, he graduated from the University of Illinois and University of Illinois College of Law. He practiced law in Rockford and then served as

the Winnebago County state's attorney for two terms. He was elected as a Winnebago County Circuit Court judge and Illinois Appellate Court judge and served from 1976 until his appointment as a District Court judge in 1992. Reinhard, who is assigned to the Western Division in Rockford replacing Judge Roszkowski, gave severe sentences to five Rockford gang members found guilty of conspiring to violate drug laws involving powdered cocaine and crack. Jurors, in making their decision, were not asked to specify which of the drugs was considered in the verdict. Reinhard used sentencing guidelines for crack cocaine, which involve much tougher penalties than the guidelines for powdered cocaine. Defense attorneys protested, arguing that the judge's sentence should be based on the drug that carried the lesser penalty if not specified, but the Court of Appeals and the U.S. Supreme Court upheld Reinhard's decision.

ON JULY 20, 1992, the Northern District of Illinois suffered its worst tragedy when prisoner Jeffrey Erickson escaped momentarily in the basement of the Dirksen Federal Building and shot two security officers. Deputy U.S.

Marshal Roy "Bill" Frakes, thirty, and Court Security Officer Harry Belluomini, fifty-eight, were killed in the escape attempt.

Erickson was on trial for a series of bank robberies. His wife, Jill, had fatally shot herself during a chase and shootout in their final robbery, which resulted in Erickson's arrest. Erickson escaped on the fifth day of his trial before Judge Alesia. The prisoner was apparently given a handcuff key, which he used to release his cuffs while riding with other prisoners down an elevator to the basement. Erickson wrestled a gun from another security officer, shot Frakes and exchanged fire with Belluomini. Wounded in the back by Belluomini, Erickson started up the garage ramp that led into rush-hour traffic on Jackson Boulevard. Witnesses heard Erickson say "I'm going to jail. I'm going to jail. I'm going to die anyway, I'm going to take everybody with me" moments before he turned the gun and shot himself in the head. A handcuff key was found near his body.

Authorities now believe that a prisoner at the Metropolitan Correctional Center smuggled the key into the prison for Erickson. The two officers were honored with a plaque in the lobby of the Dirksen Federal Building.

U.S. Marshal's Office Deputy U.S. Marshal Roy "Bill" Frakes (top) and Court Security Officer Harry Belluomini were killed during Jeffrey Erickson's failed escape.

PRESIDENT BILL CLINTON appointed twelve judges to the Northern Illinois District, including five women, three African Americans, and the court's first two Hispanic judges. Each of the first six judges was the joint recommendation of Democratic Senators Paul Simon and Carol Moseley-Braun. Senator Dick Durbin recommended the next five choices, and Republican Senator Peter Fitzgerald recommended the only Republican, John Darrah, appointed during the Clinton years.

The Democratic senators revived the Percy process and formalized committees that made recommendations to them. In 1999, when Fitzgerald joined the Senate, he made a deal with Durbin that specified that the senator whose president leads the country would make three out of every four choices to the federal bench. Fitzgerald solicits applicants, and his office has a policy of interviewing every prospective judge, but he does not seek recommendations from bar groups.

Ruben Castillo, Clinton's first choice, saw the play *Inherit the Wind* as a junior in high school, read about Clarence Darrow, and was hooked. He determined he would be a lawyer. Born in Chicago, Castillo graduated from Loyola University Chicago and Northwestern University School of Law, supporting himself by working as a clerk in night bond court. He served as an assistant U.S. attorney from 1984 to 1988 and as regional counsel for the Mexican American Legal Defense and Educational Fund. Castillo led the court fight to redraw Illinois's congressional districts after the 1990 census, which paved the way for the 1992 election of Luis Gutierrez as the state's first Latino congressman. After a short stint in private practice, Castillo himself broke a barrier when he was named to the District Court in 1994, filling the seat of Nicholas Bua. "I wanted to avoid always being seen as the first Hispanic-American judge," Castillo said. "I was hoping that at some point somebody would just relegate it to footnote status." He oversaw the settlement of a long copyright dispute between Oprah Winfrey and two photographers who sought ownership and control of sixty thousand photos they took of Winfrey's early talk shows. Winfrey argued that she was coauthor of the photos because she had paid for them. The photographers charged that Winfrey had unlawfully used their photographs in a book she authored. A compromise was reached. "This courthouse has been seen as a place where somebody can come in and seek justice against the richest and most powerful and come out feeling good," Castillo later said. "Maybe not win, but feeling that they had their fair shake."

Blanche Manning, born in Chicago, graduated from Chicago Teachers College, Roosevelt University, the John Marshall Law School, and the University of Virginia School of Law. She served as an assistant Cook County state's attorney from 1968 to 1973 and as an assistant U.S. attorney from 1978 to 1979. She has been a judge since 1979, serving on the Cook County Circuit Court and Illinois Appellate Court. She was appointed to the District Court bench in 1994 to the seat held by Milton Shadur. What sets Manning and her courtroom apart is what happens there most every Monday evening. That's when her twenty-first-floor venue fills with swing-era music of her Barristers Big Band, composed of two dozen or so law professionals. Manning, a former music major in college, helped found the group in 1999. She dusted off her bass clarinet during the late 1980s to play in the Chicago Bar Association Symphony Orchestra and her tenor sax to play in three or four jazz groups. The Barristers start rehearsal at 5:30 P.M. and fill her side of the courthouse with music. Only once has it interfered with an ongoing trial. "Judge Conlon told me that all of a sudden people in the courtroom started swaying to the music. It surprised me because her courtroom is two floors above mine."

David Coar, who also was appointed in 1994, graduated from Syracuse

University, Loyola University Chicago School of Law, and Harvard Law School. He worked as an associate professor and associate dean for the De-Paul University College of Law and served for three years as U.S. trustee, administering Chapter 11 cases in Bankruptcy Court. He was appointed to a fourteen-year term as a bankruptcy judge in the Northern District of Illinois in 1986 and become the first bankruptcy judge ever appointed to the District Court bench. He replaced Ilana Rovner. Coar ordered antiabortion leaders to stop blocking abortion clinics across the country and pay $257,000 in damages they had caused to two abortion clinics. A jury found the antiabortion leaders had violated the federal Racketeer Influenced and Corrupt Organizations (RICO) Act of 1970, a law originally aimed at organized crime. The verdict, based on a lawsuit filed by the National Organization for Women, found that Operation Rescue and antiabortion activists were practicing a form of extortion against clinic owners.

Robert Gettleman graduated from Boston University and Northwestern University School of Law. After serving as a law clerk to two chief judges in the Seventh Circuit Court of Appeals, he worked in private practice from 1970 to 1994, when he was named to replace John Grady. Gettleman's work, he said, was shaped by disability. "You are a product of your experiences and having had polio when I was young—I got polio when I was seven," he told the *Chicago Daily Law Bulletin.* "Until I was seventeen, I had a brace on my leg. Obviously that's a big influence on your life, and I think it makes you look at the world a little differently." In 1988, Gettleman was part of a team of lawyers who won a case that resulted in the Chicago Transit Authority being ordered to buy buses with wheelchair lifts. "Every time someone with a wheelchair gets onto a CTA bus, I'd say, 'I guess it's not so bad being a lawyer after all,'" he told a reporter. In 1999, Gettleman sentenced the man who built the Dirksen Federal Building to jail for evading $1 million in income tax. Henry Paschen Jr., seventy-two, was given a two-year prison term, fined, and ordered to do community service. Gettleman told Paschen: "Two well-known quotes come to mind when one thinks about taxes. Oliver Wendell Holmes and Leona Helmsley. Holmes said, 'Taxes are what we pay for civilized society.' Helmsley said, 'We don't pay taxes. Only the little people pay taxes.' You had a choice of which philosophy to follow. You chose Helmsley.'"

Elaine Bucklo graduated from St. Louis University and Northwestern University School of Law. She practiced law in Chicago and served as a visiting law professor at the University of California at Davis School of Law. She was appointed as a magistrate in the Northern District of Illinois in 1985 and became the first magistrate judge appointed to the District Court in 1994, taking the seat of John Nordberg. During the late 1990s, Bucklo took on many of the major trials surrounding Operation Silver Shovel, one of the U.S. attorney office's most successful undercover operations against political corruption. Eighteen defendants, including six aldermen, were found guilty of bribery-related crimes. Seven of the defendants were convicted, or pleaded guilty, in Bucklo's court. Bucklo imposed one of her stiffest sentences on John Christopher, who worked for the government for more than three years paying off politicians and recording the transactions on audiotapes. The term, thirty-nine months, was near the maximum because Christopher had continued his life of crime even while being paid by the government.

Joan Gottschall graduated from Smith College and Stanford Law School. She worked in private practice for eleven years and also served as a staff attorney for the Federal Defender Program. She was appointed as a Northern District of Illinois magistrate judge in 1994, where she served until her appointment to the District Court in 1996, replacing James Moran. Gottschall has been in the center of two major political issues. In 1996, she made it possible for Chicago Mayor Richard M. Daley to close Meigs Field in order to build a lakefront park. She ruled against the State of Illinois's attempt to stop the city and the Chicago Park District from closing the ninety-one-acre lakefront airport. Her decision, however, did not put an end to the airport. Daley agreed to put his plans on hold. In another case, Gottschall in 2000 sentenced the former manager of the state driver's licensing facility in McCook to eighteen months in prison for participating in a scheme to give licenses to unqualified truck drivers in exchange for campaign donations. Marion Seibel said she had sold at least $82,000 in political fund-raising tickets to raise money for George Ryan, who was then secretary of state and later was elected governor. Gottschall has sentenced at least eight of the defendants, including two facility managers. By early 2002, forty-five people had been charged in the Operation Safe Road probe.

Rebecca Pallmeyer was born in Tokyo, where her parents worked as Lutheran missionaries. Her parents moved back to the United States when she was young, and she grew up in St. Louis. Pallmeyer graduated from Valparaiso University and the University of Chicago Law School. She was in private practice for five years, served as an administrative law judge for the Illinois Human Rights Commission, and was appointed a Northern District of Illinois magistrate judge in 1991. She was named to the District Court in 1998, filling the seat of William Hart. Pallmeyer oversaw two significant cases concerning Hispanics in 2000. In March, she and Judge Castillo approved a $900,000 settlement between Mount Prospect and three Hispanic police officers who accused the village of employment discrimination and racial profiling. The officers charged that commanders told or permitted them to target Hispanic drivers to boost arrest totals. Village officials denied the charges but voluntarily agreed to do away with arrest quotas. In December, Pallmeyer approved a settlement valued at $375 million that benefited between two and five million Mexican immigrants in the United States who wire money back to their families in Mexico. Their attorneys argued that money-transfer companies used false and misleading advertisements and unfairly profited from exchange rates. The settlement, which provided coupons to reduce service charges, was believed to be one of the largest class-action cases made up mostly of Mexicans and Mexican Americans.

William Hibbler, who grew up in Chicago, graduated from the University of Illinois at Chicago and DePaul University College of Law. He supported himself through law school working for United Parcel Service. Following graduation, he worked in private practice and served as an assistant Cook County state's attorney and as an associate judge in the Cook County Circuit Court from 1986 to 1999. As presiding judge of the court's juvenile justice division, Hibbler helped reduce overcrowding at the Cook County Juvenile Corrections Center, once known as the Audy Home. Hibbler was named District Court judge in 1999, replacing James Alesia. In the tradition of the District Court, Hibbler stepped into the middle of a major labor dispute when he ordered thirteen thousand United Airlines mechanics to end a work slowdown that was plaguing the national air carrier. Hibbler granted United a temporary restraining order against the airline mechanics union in November 2000 and directed the mechanics not to hamper travel during the busy Thanksgiving holiday season. He lifted the order in December, however, and refused requests by United attorneys to hold the union responsible for $49.9 million in damages. The dispute simmered through 2001 but was eventually resolved the following year when mechanics approved a new contract.

Matthew Kennelly graduated from the University of Notre Dame and Harvard Law School. He served as a law clerk for Judge Prentice Marshall for two years before working fifteen years in private practice. He was appointed in 1999 to the district bench, filling the seat of Paul Plunkett. Kennelly dismissed a lawsuit filed by the Environmental Protection Agency seeking to enter a Wauconda man's property to test for environmental hazards. Neighbors of John Tarkowski had complained for years about the junk on his property. EPA officials determined during the 1990s that the property contained no legally significant contamination. When Tarkowski refused further EPA requests, the agency filed a lawsuit against him. Kennelly concluded that the EPA's demand for access was an abuse of discretion. In a case that garnered national publicity, Kennelly sentenced Elizabeth Roach to probation after she pleaded guilty to stealing $250,000 from her employer. Roach's attorneys successfully argued that she stole to pay for shopping sprees that helped lessen psychological difficulties. "Ms. Roach suffered from a serious medical condition," Kennelly wrote. "In order to ameliorate her depression—put another way, in an effort to self-medicate—she engaged in compulsive behavior, namely shopping binges. She was not in any real way able to control that behavior."

Ronald Guzman, born in Rio Piedras, Puerto Rico, graduated from Lehigh University and New York University School of Law. He worked in private practice and as an assistant Cook County state's attorney prior to his appointment as a Northern District of Illinois magistrate in 1990. Guzman was the first Hispanic to hold a federal judicial post in the district and was the second Hispanic on the District Court bench when he was elevated in 1999, replacing Brian Duff. As a magistrate, Guzman presided over a trial at which a jury awarded $572,000 to an Oak Lawn man fired from his company because he suffered a terminal brain tumor. It was the first case against a private employer by the Equal Employment Opportunity Commission under the Americans with Disabilities Act. As a District Court judge, Guzman gave the final OK that doomed five of the last buildings on Maxwell Street on the Near South Side. He ruled that the area had a "less than negligible" chance of making the National Register of Historic Places and rejected the final pleas of preservationists. The decision was particularly difficult for Guzman because he admired the historic nature of Maxwell Street and had even shopped at the market many times. Guzman, however, believed that the street had already been severely altered by the time the issue reached his court. Hours after his decision, four buildings of the once-great market were knocked down by bulldozers.

Joan Humphrey Lefkow graduated from Wheaton College and Northwestern University School of Law. She worked as a staff attorney for the Legal Assistance Foundation of Chicago and as an administrative law judge for the Illinois Fair Employment Practices Commission. She was executive director of the Cook County Legal Assistance Foundation before being named a Northern District of Illinois magistrate in 1982. She was appointed as a district bankruptcy judge in 1997, a position she held until her 2000 appointment to the District Court bench, succeeding Ann Williams. Lefkow attended a one-room schoolhouse growing up in rural Kansas. From kindergarten through fifth grade, she was taught along with fewer than a dozen children from nearby farms by one teacher. She recalled how her teacher would bring students to the front of the class by grades. "If you were interested and bright, you could listen to what was going on and you would learn," she told a reporter. In sixth grade, she started attending a two-room schoolhouse. "All I can say is I learned my grammar and arithmetic pretty well," she said.

John Darrah, born in Chicago, graduated from Loyola University Chicago and its School of Law. He served as deputy DuPage County public defender and as assistant DuPage County state's attorney during the 1970s and was in private practice for ten years. He served as a DuPage County Circuit Court judge from 1986 until 2000, when he was named a District Court judge to fill the seat vacated by George Marovich. In 2002, Darrah stopped Habitat for Humanity from constructing nine homes for low-income residents in west suburban Glendale Heights. DuPage Habitat for Humanity had sued the village after officials took steps to curtail its plans to build houses for the poor. Habitat purchased twenty lots in a village subdivision in 1996. After residents spoke out against Habitat's plans, village officials passed several resolutions to block the project. Under an agreement with Habitat, the village granted four building permits but later refused additional requests. Darrah ruled the village was within its rights.

THE STREET CRIME TRIALS of the El Rukns and Gangster Disciples. Political corruption cases surrounding Operations Incubator and Silver Shovel. And the Operation Safe Road drivers'-licenses-for-bribes investigation. These were the most highly publicized trials of the 1990s. But perhaps no investigation or trial better characterized the greed and economic boom times of the 1990s than that of the Decatur, Illinois–based Archer Daniels Midland Company.

In 1996, Judge Ruben Castillo oversaw the settlement of the largest antitrust fine in history when Archer Daniels Midland officials agreed to pay $100 million for attempting to fix the worldwide prices of two of their products. "The simple message of today's proceedings is that no American company is above the law," Castillo said.

The fine did not end the government's case against the global agribusiness company, however. Later that year, Michael D. Andreas, executive vice president of the company, and two other top executives were indicted for conspiring to fix the prices of lysine, an additive to animal feed. Their indictment opened a window into the international intrigue, political manipulations, and corporate culture that had dominated the "supermarket to the world." ADM had been under investigation by the government since the early 1990s.

Andreas, heir apparent to his father, political powerhouse Dwayne O. Andreas, along with colleague Terrance Wilson were convicted by a jury. They were both sentenced to two years in jail and fined $350,000 by District Court Judge Blanche Manning in 1999. ADM's Mark Whitacre, who had cooperated with the FBI as a mole in the investigation, was sentenced to thirty months in prison. Manning determined that Whitacre, former head of the company's bioproducts division, was a "manager" of the conspiracy and that Andreas and Wilson had "controlling" jobs. Her determination surprised government prosecutors because it was Whitacre who had helped document deals between Archer Daniels Midland and Japanese and Korean companies on video- and audiotapes. Manning had allowed the tapes to be used at trial despite objections by defense attorneys. "They [the federal government] would have no case without me," Whitacre said at his sentencing hearing.

Whitacre, the government's star cooperating witness, was at first portrayed as a "whistle-blower." But he had lost his credibility and his immunity when he pled guilty in 1997 to embezzling millions of dollars from Archer Daniels Midland. Manning sentenced Whitacre to nine years in prison, then tacked on an additional twenty months to that sentence. She was later ordered by the Court of Appeals to increase the sentences of Andreas and Wilson to three years.

The court had come full circle with the Archer Daniels Midland case. In 1907, Judge Kenesaw Mountain Landis fined Standard Oil $29 million for violating government antitrust laws after a long trial but could collect nothing. Almost nine decades later, the court collected $100 million on a plea-bargain agreement in a broad-reaching antitrust case and sent company officials to prison.

THE 1990S APPOINTMENTS of magistrate judges Elaine Bucklo, Joan Gottschall, Rebecca Pallmeyer, Ronald Guzman, and Joan Humphrey Lefkow as well as bankruptcy judges David Coar and Lefkow reflect the growing prestige of the District Court's adjunct judges.

The position of magistrate was created in 1968 when the office of U.S. commissioner was abolished by Congress. Commissioners were paid per case. Beginning in 1971, magistrates held salaried jobs. Their duties and responsibilities are determined by the District Court judges. In December 1990, the official title of magistrate was changed to magistrate judge, also reflecting the increased importance of the job. Magistrate judges hold preliminary hearings, set bonds, name lawyers for indigent defendants, issue search warrants, and make recommendations to judges on certain aspects of cases. They also hold complete hearings—including bench or jury trials—for civil cases if a defendant and plaintiff agree. As of 2002, the court has ten magistrate judges. They are Presiding Magistrate Judge Arlander Keys and Judges Martin C. Ashman, Edward A. Bobrick, Geraldine Soat Brown, Morton Denlow, Ian H. Levin, Michael T. Mason, Nan R. Nolan, Sidney I. Schenkier, all in Chicago, and P. Michael Mahoney, in Rockford. Magistrate judges, who serve eight-year terms, are screened by a merit selection committee and are appointed by the District Court judges.

The position of bankruptcy judge was created in 1978 when the position of bankruptcy referee was abolished by Congress and a separate Bankruptcy Court was established as an adjunct to the District Court. The old system of referees was called the "legal backwater" of the Northern District of Illinois by the Chicago Council of Lawyers. "Much of the bankruptcy bar functioned as an insiders' club," the council reported.

Between 1984 and 1987, as the Northern District of Illinois Bankruptcy Court was reorganized, the entire bench resigned, retired, or failed to gain reappointment. The former chief bankruptcy judge, Charles B. McCormick, was censured for allowing attorneys to write opinions for him without the knowledge of opposing attorneys. Since then, the nature of the court and the quality of the judges has improved dramatically, according to the lawyers' council, which called the Bankruptcy Court one of the best benches in

Chicago. Caseloads are up to date, rules of evidence and procedure are followed, and charges of judicial bias are "relatively rare," the council reported in 1991.

Bankruptcy judges are appointed to fourteen-year terms by the Seventh Circuit Court of Appeals. The Bankruptcy Court, housed in the lower levels of the Federal Building, hears virtually all voluntary and involuntary bankruptcy matters in an attempt to work out agreements between debtors and creditors. One of the court's major aims is also to figure out reorganization plans so that faltering businesses can delay paying debt to keep operating. The District Court serves as the appeals court for bankruptcy cases.

The court now has twelve judges. They are Chief Judge Eugene R. Wedoff, William V. Altenberger, Manuel Barbosa, Ronald Barliant, Bruce W. Black, Carol A. Doyle, Robert E. Ginsberg, Erwin I. Katz, Jack B. Schmetterer, John D. Schwartz, John H. Squires, and Susan Pierson Sonderby.

THE APPOINTMENT OF NEW MAGISTRATE, Bankruptcy, and District Court judges has increased the need for more courtrooms. Ten major courtrooms, plus the Ceremonial Courtroom on the twenty-fifth floor and Court of Appeals Courtroom on the twenty-seventh floor, were built in the original building. Four district courtrooms were added during the 1970s and four

The Ceremonial Courtroom of the District Court, renamed the Parsons Courtroom, is where investitures and major proceedings are held. **GENERAL SERVICES ADMINISTRATION**

more during the 1980s. All were replicas of the original courtrooms designed by architect Ludwig Mies van der Rohe.

During the early 1990s, the federal government carved out two-story courtrooms in the mid and lower levels of the building. It was a huge technological challenge. Horizontal transfer beams had to be built as structural trusses on the sixteenth floor to make it possible to remove vertical columns in order to accommodate construction of the two-story courtrooms below. About $25 million was spent to reinforce the four remaining major vertical columns that extended from the foundation to the sixteenth floor and to create the sixteenth-floor bridge that redistributed the weight of upper floors.

In 1994, four new two-story courtrooms were added on the fourteenth floor and in 1999 four new courtrooms were added to the twelfth floor. Single-story magistrate courtrooms were also built on the thirteenth floor. The eight new major courtrooms are not replicas but updates of Mies's design. Like Mies, the designers of the new courts—Lohan & Associates for the 1994 courtrooms and Urban Design Group for the 1999 courtrooms— have attempted to use material to express the purpose of the courtrooms. Munin Choudrey, who designed the 1999 rooms, explained that he separated the gallery area from the rest of the courtroom by using slightly different lighting, ceiling, wall, and carpeting details. "In the well area, we have a higher ceiling, a greater level of illumination, and large and more elaborate

The new courtrooms built during the 1990s reflect but do not mimic the original courtrooms designed by Mies van der Rohe. **GENERAL SERVICES ADMINISTRATION**

details to visually increase its importance. Finer materials are used as one moves toward the front of the room on the furniture, decorative wall sconces, etc., to reenforce the hierarchy that culminates at the judge's bench. Behind the judge's bench, stone is used to suggest the strength of the court and to focus attention on the front of the courtroom."

The old courtrooms were refinished and refurbished during the 1990s. In 1996, the Hubert L. Will Memorial Courtroom and James Benton Parsons Memorial Courtroom were dedicated. On February 5, 1997, the name of the Dirksen Federal Building was changed to the Dirksen U.S. Courthouse, marking how the District and Appeals Courts now dominate the building. The courthouse has also been remodeled technologically. In 1996, a court-wide computer network was completed, connecting the courts in Chicago and Rockford. New phone and computer systems were installed, providing judges and court employees with everyday conveniences such as e-mail, faxes, and Internet access. In 1998, the court's web site for the public went on-line.

THE NEW TECHNOLOGY, of course, does not replace the humanity that directs each and every case filed in the federal courthouse. Perhaps that was brought home in 2001, when the court held a service in memory of Abraham Lincoln Marovitz, who died at age ninety-five earlier that year. Marovitz was the last surviving judge from the 1960s. He had long ago stopped hearing cases, but he continued being a fixture in the court, swearing in new citizens. Marovitz was an enigma. His legal opinions did not change the course of legal history, but his style and personality changed the austere Federal Building into a friendly outpost for those who crossed his life.

The ceremony was typically Abe. The Parsons Courtroom was packed with judges, friends, and celebrities as familiar stories were recounted about Marovitz. One of his former clerks, Richard J. O'Brien, recalled Marovitz as a first-rate charmer in a brocaded smoking jacket, able to cajole any lawyer into a settlement. Andrew Marovitz described his uncle as a short, skinny Jewish kid from Maxwell Street who never went to college and became the biggest man in town. And Judge William Bauer called Marovitz "the only judge I've ever met who was nonjudgmental." But it was Marvin J. Rosenblum, Marovitz's law clerk during the 1970s, who brought the house to tears. Rosenblum said Marovitz had a secret, a secret that didn't mesh with the rationality of Mies's Federal Building and Campbell's court. All the lawyers knew they could get to Marovitz because they all knew he was vulnerable to a plea of mercy when all else failed.

"It wasn't filed in Judge Abe's chambers, but, rather, addressed to that special chamber deep within his heart that was so sensitive to the frailties of the human condition," Rosenblum said. "We all knew he couldn't resist that motion."

SO MUCH HAS CHANGED since Abe Marovitz first swaggered around the Federal Building. So much has changed since individual judges—people such as Henry Blodgett and Kenesaw Mountain Landis—ruled the court. For decades, from the founding of the Northern District until the 1930s, the court was dominated by men who were the federal law in the Midwest. They were considered titans by some, tyrants by others. Following their years of power, the court was dominated by a small group of judges who lunched together at private clubs and maintained power as a loyal set. As late as the 1980s, many District Court judges met at least weekly to discuss current cases.

Now, with twenty-two judges and senior judges, the District Court has become more individualized. Current judges pride themselves on being "independent contractors," dispensing justice on their own—in their own chambers, with their own clerks and assistants—in an austere skyscraper at the south end of Chicago's Loop. But because there are now dozens of judges, no single judge or small group dominates. The days of the titans, for better or worse, are over.

Portraits of most of the Northern District of Illinois judges line the walls of the Ceremonial Courtroom. Thomas Drummond, the court's first judge, hangs next to John Peter Barnes, who always called himself the thirteenth juror. There's William J. Campbell, who built the current courthouse, and Richard Austin, who doesn't look half as tough as his reputation. And, of course, there is Julius J. Hoffman—looking down at all of us.

Few people know of the old-timers. And fewer still remember how hot and dirty the old courthouse became during the summer months.

But the names of the judges come up frequently. Their work and their decisions—once formally bound in law books and now also found by computer searches—are cited daily by lawyers and other judges. Their colleagues on the Court of Appeals often say that the District Court does not make precedent. But the Northern Illinois District Court does serve as the major court of first impression in America's heartland. For nearly two hundred years, the court's verdicts have drawn on the values of the Midwest to produce decisions that have had a profound impact on America.

Nathaniel Pope's ruling against extraditing Mormon leader Joseph Smith fulfilled the promise of this new country as a nation built upon religious tolerance. Abraham Lincoln's arguments in the *Effie Afton* case changed the mode of westward expansion. The power and place of labor unions were etched in the trials of Eugene V. Debs and "Big Bill" Haywood. And Al Capone's guilty verdict put an end to Chicago's most flashy gangster period.

But beyond the final verdicts, the court has provided a dramatic stage on which the most important social and historical issues of the times have played out. From slavery to economic growth to antiwar protests of the 1960s, this court has reflected and created change.

The District Court responds to the daily ebb and flow of what becomes history. District Court judges reflect the conscience of America. The cases they hear, shaped by the lawyers who practice before them and the crowds that fill their courtrooms, epitomize the passions and prejudices that make up a free society. Here in the heartland, Chicago's—and America's—story has come to life as the court struggles to resolve conflicts, impart fairness, and to take stands that contribute to the making and continual remaking of this country.

The judges of the Northern District of Illinois inherit a long tradition on the day they receive their commission and agree to uphold the Constitution. Greatness and arrogance, brilliance and bullheadedness precede them. What follows their oath is a search for justice. The Northern District of Illinois judges keep at it. Listening. Considering. Ruling. Sometimes wisely; sometimes with human error. But they keep reaching, as they have done for nearly two hundred years. Trying to perfect this most imperfect world.

The sixteen-story atrium in the old Federal Courthouse was topped by a painted sky beneath its dome. The clouds were symbolic—of an ethereal, perfect world. Heaven on earth. Justice, too, is ethereal.

Court Chronology

JULY 13, 1787   Congress creates the Northwest Territory, which includes the area now occupied by the State of Illinois.

MAY 7, 1800   The Northwest Territory is divided into two governments, creating the Indiana Territory.

FEBRUARY 3, 1809   The Indiana Territory is divided into two governments, creating the Illinois Territory.

APRIL 18, 1818   Congress enables admission of the State of Illinois into the Union.

MARCH 3, 1819   Congress organized Illinois as one judicial district and authorized one judgeship for the District Court.

MAY 9, 1848   Congress authorizes a term of the United States District and Circuit Courts at Chicago.

FEBRUARY 13, 1855   Illinois divided into two judicial districts, the Northern and the Southern, with one judgeship authorized for each district. The act assigned the judge for the District of Illinois to the Northern District.

MARCH 3, 1905   Congress establishes the Eastern District of Illinois and authorizes an additional judgeship for the Northern District.

MAY 29, 1928   Temporary judgeship authorized in 1922 made permanent for the Northern District.

FEBRUARY 25, 1931   Two additional judgeships authorized for the district.

MAY 31, 1938   One additional judgeship authorized for the district.

AUGUST 14, 1950   Two additional judgeships authorized for the district.

MAY 19, 1961   Two additional judgeships authorized for the district.

MARCH 18, 1966   One additional judgeship authorized for the district.

JUNE 2, 1970   Two additional judgeships authorized for the district.

OCTOBER 2, 1978   Illinois reorganized into the Northern, Central, and Southern Districts.

OCTOBER 20, 1978   Three additional judgeships authorized for the Northern District.

JULY 10, 1984   Four additional permanent judgeships authorized for the district.

DECEMBER 1, 1990   Two additional judgeships authorized for the district.

Source: Federal Judicial Center and Kenneth Carrick, former Seventh Circuit Court clerk

Tables

JUDGESHIPS OF THE NORTHERN DISTRICT OF ILLINOIS

JUDGE	TENURE	JUDGE	TENURE
JUDGESHIP 1		*JUDGESHIP 6*	
Thomas Drummond	1850–69	Michael Igoe	1938–67
Henry W. Blodgett	1870–92	William J. Lynch	1966–76
Peter Stenger Grosscup	1892–99	Nicholas Bua	1977–91
Christian C. Kohlsaat	1899–1905	Ruben Castillo	1994–
Solomon Hicks Bethea	1905–9		
George A. Carpenter	1910–33	*JUDGESHIP 7*	
Philip L. Sullivan	1933–60	Winfred G. Knoch	1953–58
James Benton Parsons	1961–93	Edwin A. Robson	1958–86
Paul Plunkett	1983–	John F. Grady	1975–
Matthew Kennelly	1999–	Robert Gettleman	1994–
JUDGESHIP 2		*JUDGESHIP 8*	
Kenesaw M. Landis	1905–22	Julius J. Hoffman	1953–83
James H. Wilkerson	1922–40	Richard McLaren	1972–74
William J. Campbell	1940–88	Stanley Roszkowski	1977–98
Thomas McMillen	1971–85	Wayne Andersen	1991–
Suzanne B. Conlon	1988–		
		JUDGESHIP 9	
JUDGESHIP 3		Hubert L. Will	1961–95
Adam C. Cliffe	1922–28	Milton I. Shadur	1980–
Charles E. Woodward	1929–42	Blanche Manning	1994–
Elwyn Shaw	1944–50		
Joseph Sam Perry	1951–84	*JUDGESHIP 10*	
William Bauer	1971–75	Bernard Decker	1962–93
Alfred Kirkland Sr.	1974–79	John Nordberg	1982–
Charles P. Kocoras	1980–	Elaine Bucklo	1994–
JUDGESHIP 4		*JUDGESHIP 11*	
John Peter Barnes	1931–58	Alexander J. Napoli	1966–72
Julius H. Miner	1958–63	Prentice H. Marshall	1973–96
Abraham L. Marovitz	1963–2001	George Lindberg	1989–
George Leighton	1976–87		
James H. Alesia	1987–	*JUDGESHIP 12*	
William Hibbler	1999–	Frank J. McGarr	1970–88
		James Zagel	1987–
JUDGESHIP 5			
George E. Q. Johnson	1932–33	*JUDGESHIP 13*	
William H. Holly	1933–58	Philip Tone	1972–74
Walter J. LaBuy	1944–67	Joel Flaum	1974–83
Richard Austin	1961–77	Ilana Diamond Rovner	1984–92
John Powers Crowley	1976–81	David Coar	1994–
William T. Hart	1982–		
Rebecca Pallmeyer	1998–	*JUDGESHIP 14*	
		James Moran	1979–
		Joan Gottschall	1996–

JUDGE	TENURE	JUDGE	TENURE
JUDGESHIP 15		**JUDGESHIP 19**	
Marvin E. Aspen	1979–	Ann Claire Williams	1985–99
		Joan Humphrey Lefkow	2000–
JUDGESHIP 16			
Susan Getzendanner	1980–87	**JUDGESHIP 20**	
George Marovich	1988–	Brian Barnett Duff	1985–
John Darrah	2000–	Ronald Guzman	1999–
JUDGESHIP 17		**JUDGESHIP 21**	
Charles Norgle Sr.	1984–	Harry Leinenweber	1985–
JUDGESHIP 18		**JUDGESHIP 22**	
James F. Holderman	1985–	Philip G. Reinhard	1992–

CHIEF JUDGES

The head of the District Court was called "senior judge" until 1948.

JUDGE	TENURE
Solomon Hicks Bethea	March 5, 1905, to August 3, 1909
Kenesaw M. Landis	August 3, 1909, to March 1, 1922
George A. Carpenter	March 1, 1922, to June 30, 1933
James H. Wilkerson	July 1, 1933, to December 31, 1940
Charles E. Woodward	January 1, 1941, to April 1942
John Peter Barnes	April 1942, to September 15, 1957
Philip L. Sullivan	September 16, 1957, to March 7, 1959
William J. Campbell	March 8, 1959, to March 19, 1970
Edwin A. Robson	March 20, 1970, to April 16, 1975
James Benton Parsons	April 17, 1975, to August 13, 1981
Frank J. McGarr	August 14, 1981, to June 30, 1986
John F. Grady	July 1, 1986, to June 30, 1990
James Moran	July 1, 1990, to June 30, 1995
Marvin E. Aspen	July 1, 1995, to June 30, 2002
Charles P. Kocoras	July 1, 2002, to

UNITED STATES ATTORNEYS

ATTORNEY	TENURE	ATTORNEY	TENURE
Thomas A. Hoyne	1855–57	Sherwood Dixon	1893–94
A. M. Herrington	1857–58	John C. Black	1894–99
Henry S. Fitch	1858–61	Solomon Hicks Bethea	1899–1905
Edwin C. Larned	1861–63	Charles B. Morrison	1905–6
Stephen A. Goodwin	1863–64	Edwin W. Sims	1906–11
Edwin C. Larned	1864–65	James H. Wilkerson	1911–14
Perkins Bass	1865–69	Charles F. Clyne	1914–22
Joseph O. Glover	1869	Edwin Olson	1922–27
Mark Bangs	1875–79	George E. Q. Johnson	1927–31
Joseph B. Seake	1879–84	Dwight Green	1931–35
Richard S. Tuthill	1884–86	Michael Igoe	1935–38
William G. Ewing	1886–90	William J. Campbell	1938–40
Thomas E. Milchrist	1891–93	J. Albert Woll	1940–47

ATTORNEY	TENURE		ATTORNEY	TENURE
Otto J. Kerner Jr.	1947–54		Samuel K. Skinner	1975–77
Irwin N. Cohen	1954		Thomas P. Sullivan	1977–81
Robert Tieken	1954–61		Dan K. Webb	1981–85
James P. O'Brien	1961–63		Anton R. Valukas	1985–89
Frank E. McDonald	1963–64		Fred Foreman	1990–93
Edward Hanrahan	1964–68		James Burns	1993–97
Thomas Foran	1968–70		Scott R. Lassar	1997–2001
William Bauer	1970–71		Patrick J. Fitzgerald	2001–
James R. Thompson	1971–75			

CLERKS OF THE COURT

CLERK	TENURE		CLERK	TENURE
James F. Owing	1843–44		Henry W. Freeman	1935–38
William Pope	?–1855		Hoyt King	1939–42
William H. Bradley	1855–92		Roy H. Johnson	1942–62
Sherburne W. Burnham	1892–95		Elbert A. Wagner Jr.	1962–70
Thomas C. McMillan	1895–1919		H. Stuart Cunningham	1970–97
John H. R. Jamar	1919–25		Michael W. Dobbins	1997–
Charles M. Bates	1925–35			

UNITED STATES MARSHALS

MARSHAL	YEAR APPOINTED		MARSHAL	YEAR APPOINTED
Robert Lemmon	1819		Lyman T. Hoy	1906
Henry Conner	1820		John J. Bradley	1914
Charles Slade	1829		Robert R. Levy	1921
Harry Wilton	1833		Palmer E. Anderson	1925
William Prentiss	1841		Henry Laubenheimer	1928
Thomas M. Hope	1844		William H. McDonnell	1934
Stinson H. Anderson	1845		Joseph E. Tobin	1946
Benjamin Bond	1850		Thomas P. O'Donovan	1946
Harry Wilton	1853		William W. Kipp Sr.	1953
Iram Nye	1856		Joseph N. Tierney	1961
James W. Davidson	1857		John C. Meiszner	1968
Charles U. Pine	1858		John J. Twomey	1973
Thomas Hoyne	1860		Frank J. Roddy	1976
Joseph Russell Jones	1861		Harvey N. Johnson Jr.	1977
Benjamin H. Campbell	1869		John J. Adams	1978
Jesse Hildrup	1877		Peter J. Wilkes	1979
Alfred M. Jones	1881		John J. Adams	1986
Frederick H. Marsh	1885		Marvin Lutes	1991
Frank Hitchcock	1889		Joseph DiLeonardi	1994
John W. Arnold	1894		James L. Whigham	2000
John C. Ames	1897		Kim Widup	2002

MAGISTRATE JUDGES

The Federal Magistrates Act of 1968 created the judicial post as it is known today. The title was changed from magistrate to magistrate judge in 1990. Prior to the act, commissioners held a similar, but more limited, position.

JUDGE	TENURE	JUDGE	TENURE
James T. Balog	1967–90	Edward A. Bobrick	1990–
Robert J. French	1968–76	Ronald Guzman	1990–99
Steven F. Helfer	1968–70	Rebecca Pallmeyer	1991–98
Olga Jurco	1971–85	Arlander Keys	1995–
Carl Sussman	1971–84	Martin C. Ashman	1995–
P. Michael Mahoney	1976–	Morton Denlow	1996–
John W. Cooley	1979–81	Ian H. Levin	1997–
Joan Humphrey Lefkow	1982–97	Nan R. Nolan	1998–
Joan Gottschall	1984–96	Sidney I. Schenkier	1998–
Bernard Weisberg	1985–94	Geraldine Soat Brown	2000–
W. Thomas Rosemond Jr.	1985–2001	Michael T. Mason	2001–
Elaine Bucklo	1985–94		

BANKRUPTCY COURT JUDGES

Positions of registers, referees, and conciliation commissioners preceded the post of bankruptcy judge. The title bankruptcy judge was adopted in 1973, and the Bankruptcy Reform Act of 1978 created the U.S. Bankruptcy Court in each judicial district in the nation.

JUDGE	TENURE	JUDGE	TENURE
Charles B. McCormick	1966–86	Susan Pierson Sonderby	1986–
Edward B. Toles	1969–86	David Coar	1986–94
Richard N. DeGunther	1971–98	Eugene R. Wedoff	1987–
Thomas W. James	1972–97	Erwin I. Katz	1987–2002
Lawrence Fisher	1972–84	Ronald Barliant	1988–
Richard L. Merrick	1974–84	John H. Squires	1988–
Frederick J. Hertz	1974–87	Joan Humphrey Lefkow	1997–2000
Robert L. Eisen	1975–87	Carol A. Doyle	1999–
John D. Schwartz	1984–	Manuel Barbosa	1998–
Jack B. Schmetterer	1985–	Bruce W. Black	2001–
Robert E. Ginsberg	1985–	William Altenberger	2001–

FIRST WOMEN TO HOLD MAJOR POSITIONS

OFFICEHOLDER	POSITION (YEAR APPOINTED)
Susie M. Brown	Special Assistant U.S. Attorney (1913)
Anna R. Lavin	Assistant U.S. Attorney (1950)
Gloria Cunningham	Probation Officer (1960)
Helen Viney Porter	Attorney in the Internal Revenue Service Regional Counsel's Office (1961)
Olga Jurco	U.S. Magistrate (1971)
Jean Powers Kamp	Staff Attorney in the Federal Defender Program (1971)
Patricia M. Collins	Special Agent of the Drug Enforcement Agency (1974)
Karen A. Anderson	Officer in Pretrial Services (1975)

OFFICEHOLDER	POSITION (YEAR APPOINTED)
Carol Wetterhahn	Inspector for the Postal Inspection Service (1979)
Susan Getzendanner	District Court Judge (1980)
Julia Packard Grip	Administrative Judge with the Merit Systems Protection Board (1980)
Ann Claire Williams	African American Woman on District Court and Court of Appeals (1985, 1999)
Susan Pierson Sonderby	Bankruptcy Court Judge (1986)
Ilana Diamond Rovner	Court of Appeals Judge (1992)
Christine G. Davis	District Director of the Immigration and Naturalization Service (1997)
Kathleen L. Kiernan	District Director/Special Agent in Charge of Chicago Field Division of the Bureau of Alcohol, Tobacco and Firearms (1998)
Kathleen McChesney	Special Agent in Charge of the Chicago Field Office of the Federal Bureau of Investigation (1999)

The Corinthian elegance of the old Federal Building atrium (left) and the steel-and-glass curtain wall of the Dirksen Federal Building (right).

Judges of the United States District Court
for the Northern District of Illinois

Thomas Drummond
(1809–90)

Henry W. Blodgett
(1821–1902)

Peter Stenger Grosscup
(1852–1921)

Christian C. Kohlsaat
(1844–1918)

Solomon Hicks Bethea
(1852–1909)

Kenesaw Mountain Landis
(1866–1944)

George A. Carpenter
(1867–1944)

James H. Wilkerson
(1869–1948)

Adam C. Cliffe
(1869–1928)

Charles Edgar Woodward
(1876–1942)

John Peter Barnes
(1881–1959)

George E. Q. Johnson
(1874–1949)

Phillip L. Sullivan
(1889–1960)

William H. Holly
(1869–1958)

Michael Igoe
(1885–1969)

William J. Campbell
(1905–88)

Walter J. LaBuy
(1888–1967)

Elwyn Shaw
(1888–1950)

Joseph Sam Perry
(1896–1984)

Winfred G. Knoch
(1895–1983)

Julius J. Hoffman
(1895–1983)

Julius H. Miner
(1896–1963)

Edwin A. Robson
(1905–86)

Richard Austin
(1901–77)

James Benton Parsons
(1911–93)

Hubert L. Will
(1914–95)

Bernard Decker
(1904–93)

Abraham Lincoln Marovitz
(1905–2001)

William J. Lynch
(1908–76)

Alexander J. Napoli
(1905–72)

Frank J. McGarr
(1921–)

Thomas McMillen
(1916–)

William Bauer
(1926–)

Richard McLaren
(1918–74)

Philip Tone
(1923–2001)

Prentice H. Marshall
(1926–)

Joel Flaum
(1936–)

Alfred Kirkland Sr.
(1917–)

John F. Grady
(1929–)

George Leighton
(1912–)

John Powers Crowley
(1936–89)

Nicholas Bua
(1925–)

Stanley Roszkowski
(1923–)

James Moran
(1930–)

Marvin E. Aspen
(1934–)

Milton I. Shadur
(1924–)

Susan Getzendanner
(1939–)

Charles P. Kocoras
(1938–)

William T. Hart
(1929–)

John Nordberg
(1926–)

Paul Plunkett
(1935–)

Ilana Diamond Rovner
(1935–)

Charles Norgle Sr.
(1937–)

James F. Holderman
(1946–)

Ann Claire Williams
(1949–)

Brian Barnett Duff
(1930–)

Harry Leinenweber
(1937–)

James Zagel
(1941–)

James H. Alesia
(1934–)

Suzanne B. Conlon
(1939–)

George Marovich
(1931–)

George Lindberg
(1932–)

Wayne Andersen
(1945–)

Philip G. Reinhard
(1941–)

Ruben Castillo
(1954–)

Blanche Manning
(1934–)

David Coar
(1943–)

Robert Gettleman
(1943–)

Elaine Bucklo
(1944–)

Joan Gottschall
(1947–)

Rebecca Pallmeyer
(1954–)

William Hibbler
(1946–)

Matthew Kennelly
(1956–)

Ronald Guzman
(1948–)

Joan Humphrey Lefkow
(1944–)

John Darrah
(1938–)

Many photographs of contemporary judges by Ronald Olson

Select Bibliography

THE AUTHOR DEPENDED on firsthand information whenever possible in re-creating the events and personalities in this book. The major source of information came from Records Group 21 of the National Archives and Records Administration in Chicago, the keeper of District Court papers. Archivists there directed me through hundreds of thousands of cases. The archives also contain the personal papers of District Court Judges William J. Campbell and James Benton Parsons. A major source of information about the early court came from Records Group 60 of the National Archives and Records Administration in College Park, Maryland. Those files contain appointment correspondence on all District Court judges, marshals, clerks, and U.S. attorneys dating back to the mid-1800s. The Chicago Historical Society maintains the personal papers of Judge Julius J. Hoffman as well as personal scrapbooks of Judges George A. Carpenter and Edwin A. Robson. The society also provided valuable accounts of early court life in Chicago. The author was greatly helped by the oral histories of Judges Campbell, Parsons, Hubert L. Will, and Abraham Lincoln Marovitz, all compiled by Collins T. Fitzpatrick, a Seventh Circuit executive. The author also depended on newspaper accounts of court proceedings. The *Chicago Sun-Times* opened its newspaper clipping morgue to the author, which was most helpful in guiding him to important cases. The author also conducted in-depth interviews with many former and current judges and practitioners of the District Court.

Alvord, Clarence Walworth. *The Illinois Country 1673–1818*. Chicago: A. C. McClurg and Company, 1922.

———, ed. *Kaskaskia Records: 1778–1790*. Springfield: Illinois State Historical Library, 1909.

Barnhart, Bill, and Gene Schlickman. *Kerner: The Conflict of Intangible Rights*. Urbana: University of Illinois Press, 1999.

Boggess, Arthur Clinton. *The Settlement of Illinois*. Chicago: Chicago Historical Society, 1908.

Busch, Francis X. *Guilty or Not Guilty*. Indianapolis: Bobbs-Merrill Company, 1952.

———. *They Escaped the Hangman*. Indianapolis: Bobbs-Merrill Company, 1953.

———. *Enemies of the State*. Indianapolis: Bobbs-Merrill Company, 1954.

Carp, Robert A., and Ronald Stidham. *The Federal Courts*. Washington: Congressional Quarterly, 1991.

Condit, Carl W. *Chicago 1930–70: Building, Planning, and Urban Technology*. Chicago: University of Chicago Press, 1974.

Dasch, George J. *Eight Spies against America*. New York: Robert M. McBride Company, 1959.

Davis, James E. *Frontier Illinois*. Bloomington: Indiana University Press, 1998.

Dellinger, David. *From Yale to Jail: The Life Story of a Moral Dissenter*. New York: Pantheon Books, 1993.

Dobyns, Fletcher. *The Underworld of American Politics*. New York: Fletcher Dobyns, 1932.

Duff, John J. *A. Lincoln: Prairie Lawyer*. New York: Rinehart and Company, 1960.

Dyer, Frank Lewis, and Thomas Commerford Martin. *Edison: His Life and Inventions*. New York: Harper and Brothers, 1929.

Eggert, Gerald G. *Railroad Labor Disputes: The Beginnings of Federal Strike Policy*. Ann Arbor: University of Michigan Press, 1967.

Epstein, Jason. *The Great Conspiracy Trial*. New York: Random House, 1970.

Fiedler, George. *The Illinois Law Courts in Three Centuries 1673–1973*. Chicago: Physicians' Record Company, 1973.

Gentry, Curt. *J. Edgar Hoover, the Man and the Secrets*. New York: W. W. Norton and Company, 1991.

Gertz, Elmer. *Gertz v. Robert Welch, Inc.: The Story of a Landmark Case*. Carbondale: Southern Illinois University Press, 1992.

Giddens, Paul H. *Standard Oil Company (Indiana): Oil Pioneer of the Middle West*. New York: Appleton-Century-Crofts, 1955.

Goulden, Joseph. *The Benchwarmers: The Private World of the Powerful Federal Judges*. New York: Weybright and Talley, 1974.

Grant, Robert, and Joseph Katz. *The Great Trials of the Twenties: The Watershed Decade in America's Courtrooms*. Rockville Centre: Sarpedon, 1998.

Harrison, Lowell H. *George Rogers Clark and the War in the West*. Lexington: University Press of Kentucky, 1976.

Hilton, George W. *Eastland: Legacy of the Titanic*. Stanford: Stanford University Press, 1995.

Howard, Robert P. *Illinois: A History of the Prairie State*. Grand Rapids: William B. Eerdmans Publishing Company, 1972.

Kennedy, David. *A Political Passage: The Career of Stratton of Illinois*. Carbondale: Southern Illinois University, 1990.

Kogan, Herman. *The First Century: The Chicago Bar Association 1874–1974*. Chicago: Rand McNally and Company, 1974.

Levin, Mark L., George C. McNamee, and Daniel Greenberg, eds. *The Tales of Hoffman*. New York: Bantam Books, 1970.

Luthin, Reinhard H. *The Real Abraham Lincoln: A Complete One Volume History of His Life and Times*. Englewood Cliffs: Prentice-Hall, 1960.

Masters, Edgar Lee. *Levy Mayer and the New Industrial Era.* New Haven: Rachel Mayer, 1927.

Murphy, Walter F., and C. Herman Pritchett. *Courts, Judges, and Politics: An Introduction to the Judicial Process.* New York: Random House, 1961.

Pietrusza, David. *Judge and Jury: The Life and Times of Judge Kenesaw Mountain Landis.* South Bend: Diamond Communications, 1998.

Posner, Richard A. *The Federal Courts: Crisis and Reform.* Cambridge: Harvard University Press, 1985.

Purvis, Melvin. *American Agent.* Garden City: Doubleday, Doran and Company, 1936.

Raskin, Jonah. *For the Hell of It: The Life and Times of Abbie Hoffman.* Berkeley: University of California Press, 1996.

Renshaw, Patrick. *The Wobblies: The Story of Syndicalism in the United States.* Garden City: Doubleday and Company, 1967.

Runyon, Damon. *Trials and Other Tribulations.* Philadelphia: J. B. Lippincott Company, 1947.

Schultz, John. *Motion Will Be Denied: A New Report on the Chicago Conspiracy Trial.* New York: William Morrow and Company, 1972.

Sloman, Larry. *Steal This Dream: Abbie Hoffman and the Countercultural Revolution in America.* New York: Doubleday, 1998.

Solomon, Rayman L. *History of the Seventh Circuit: 1891–1941.* Chicago: Bicentennial Committee of the Judicial Conference of the United States, n.d.

Spink, J. G. Taylor. *Judge Landis and Twenty-Five Years of Baseball.* New York: Thomas Y. Crowell Company, 1945.

Stein, Judith. *The World of Marcus Garvey: Race and Class in Modern Society.* Baton Rouge: Louisiana State University Press, 1986.

Stone, Irving. *Clarence Darrow for the Defense.* Garden City: Doubleday, Doran and Company, 1941.

Surrency, Erwin C. *History of the Federal Courts.* New York: Oceana Publications, 1987.

Tobin, James. *Great Projects: The Epic Story of the Building of America, from the Taming of the Mississippi to the Invention of the Internet.* New York: Free Press, 2001.

Touhy, Roger, with Ray Brennan. *The Stolen Years.* Cleveland: Pennington Press, 1959.

Tuohy, James, and Rob Warden. *Greylord: Justice, Chicago Style.* New York: G. P. Putnam's Sons, 1988.

Warren, Elizabeth. *The Legacy of Judicial Policy-Making: Gautreaux v. Chicago Housing Authority.* Lanham: University Press of America, 1988.

Webster, Samuel Charles, ed. *Mark Twain, Business Man.* Boston: Little, Brown, and Company, 1946.

Index

Banker William T. Kirby and U.S. Deputy Marshal Isaac A. Deff stroll across South Dearborn Street near the old Federal Building. The Marquette Building is in the background. *CHICAGO DAILY NEWS* COLLECTION/ CHICAGO HISTORICAL SOCIETY

RICHARD CAHAN is the author of *They All Fall Down,* a biography of architectural preservationist Richard Nickel, and coauthor of *The Game That Was,* a collection of historic major league baseball photographs. He has worked as a writer, an editor, and a photo director in Chicago since 1975.

JUDGE MARVIN E. ASPEN served as the chief judge of the U.S. District Court for the Northern District of Illinois from 1995 to 2002. He now serves as a senior District Court judge. He is also the Edward Avery Harriman Adjunct Professor of Law at the Northwestern University School of Law.

JACKET PHOTOGRAPHS

Front cover
Abraham Lincoln (p. 23)
Sewell Avery (p. 120)
Al Capone (p. 84)
Theodore Roosevelt (p. 51)
Marcus Garvey (p. 76)
Richard J. Daley (p. 156)
Abbie Hoffman (p. 167)

Back cover
James Benton Parsons (p. 144)
James Caesar Petrillo (p. 123)
Florence King (p. 80)
Stanley Pringle and Maria Callas (p. 131)
Charlie Chaplin (p. 74)
Kenesaw Mountain Landis and the New York Yankees (p. 77)
Richard LeFevour (p. 228)

Spine
Old Federal Building atrium (p. 254)

Front flap
Chicago River (p. 18)
Susan Getzendanner (p. 206)
National Guard in Cicero (p. 128)
George E. Q. Johnson (p. 96)

Back flap
Jimmy Durante (p. 150)
Jackson Boulevard in 1957 (p. 142)
Thomas Edison (p. 48)
Neo-Nazi organizers (p. 202)